THE COMPLETE IDIOT'S GUIDE TO

Microsoft® Windows® 8

by Paul McFedries

ALPHA

A member of Penguin Group (USA) Inc.

For Karen, who makes life fun.

ALPHA BOOKS

Published by the Penguin Group

Penguin Group (USA) Inc., 375 Hudson Street, New York, New York 10014, USA • Penguin Group (Canada), 90 Eglinton Avenue East, Suite 700, Toronto, Ontario M4P 2Y3, Canada (a division of Pearson Penguin Canada Inc.) • Penguin Books Ltd., 80 Strand, London WC2R 0RL, England • Penguin Ireland, 25 St. Stephen's Green, Dublin 2, Ireland (a division of Penguin Books Ltd.) • Penguin Group (Australia), 250 Camberwell Road, Camberwell, Victoria 3124, Australia (a division of Pearson Australia Group Pty. Ltd.) • Penguin Books India Pvt. Ltd., 11 Community Centre, Panchsheel Park, New Delhi—110 017, India • Penguin Group (NZ), 67 Apollo Drive, Rosedale, North Shore, Auckland 1311, New Zealand (a division of Pearson New Zealand Ltd.) • Penguin Books (South Africa) (Pty.) Ltd., 24 Sturdee Avenue, Rosebank, Johannesburg 2196, South Africa • Penguin Books Ltd., Registered Offices: 80 Strand, London WC2R 0RL, England

Copyright © 2012 by Paul McFedries

International Standard Book Number: 978-1-61564-236-6
Library of Congress Catalog Card Number: 2012946115

14 13 12   8 7 6 5 4 3 2 1

Interpretation of the printing code: The rightmost number of the first series of numbers is the year of the book's printing; the rightmost number of the second series of numbers is the number of the book's printing. For example, a printing code of 12-1 shows that the first printing occurred in 2012.

Printed in the United States of America

Note: This publication contains the opinions and ideas of its author. It is intended to provide helpful and informative material on the subject matter covered. It is sold with the understanding that the author and publisher are not engaged in rendering professional services in the book. If the reader requires personal assistance or advice, a competent professional should be consulted.

The author and publisher specifically disclaim any responsibility for any liability, loss, or risk, personal or otherwise, which is incurred as a consequence, directly or indirectly, of the use and application of any of the contents of this book.

Most Alpha books are available at special quantity discounts for bulk purchases for sales promotions, premiums, fund-raising, or educational use. Special books, or book excerpts, can also be created to fit specific needs. For details, write: Special Markets, Alpha Books, 375 Hudson Street, New York, NY 10014.

Publisher: *Mike Sanders*
Executive Managing Editor: *Billy Fields*
Senior Acquisitions Editor: *Brook Farling*
Development Editor: *Michael Thomas*
Senior Production Editor: *Janette Lynn*
Copy Editor: *Monica Stone*

Cover Designer: *William Thomas*
Book Designers: *William Thomas, Rebecca Batchelor*
Indexer: *Brad Herriman*
Layout: *Brian Massey*
Proofreader: *John Etchison*

ALWAYS LEARNING   PEARSON

Contents

Introduction

You've no doubt heard by now that Windows 8 is the worst thing since sliced bread, the embodiment of all that is evil and loathsome. Yes, it's true that Windows 8 has been getting some bad reviews from the pundits and the press. The computer cognoscenti are all over this thing, like stink on a monkey. However, do you want me to let you in on a secret? Here you go: All those experts and eggheads are wrong, plain and simple.

How can so many smart people have missed the boat on Windows 8? It's not complicated, but it is a good news–bad news thing. The good news is these alpha geeks and big thinkers are against Windows 8 because Microsoft had the gall to make their new operating system simple to use. That's right: In Windows 8, you no longer need a degree in electrical engineering to look at your photos or send an email. In Windows 8, you no longer have to wade through a thousand-page manual to listen to music or surf the web.

Okay, so what's the bad news?

Oh, right, thanks for reminding me. The bad news is although Windows 8 is simple and easy once you know how to use it, you do have to learn how to use it. When most people are first exposed to Windows 8, they don't have a clue how to proceed or where to begin. There are no visual hints to follow, no prompts to send you in the right direction. In short, Windows 8 is almost completely opaque and unintuitive to the new user. Windows 8 can, in other words, make any of us feel (temporarily) like a complete idiot.

That, in the end, is why I wrote *The Complete Idiot's Guide to Microsoft Windows 8*. My goal here is to help you and Windows 8 get along. If you find yourself staring incomprehensibly at the new Windows 8 screen, this book is for you; if you aren't a computer wizard (and don't even want to be one), this book is for you; if you have a job to do—a job that includes working with Windows 8—and you just want to get it done as quickly and painlessly as possible, this book is for you; if you don't want to learn about Windows 8 using absurdly serious, put-a-crease-in-your-brow-and-we'll-begin tutorials, then—yes—this book is for you.

No experience with Windows 8? No problem. In fact, this book doesn't assume you have *any* previous experience with *any* version of Windows. I begin each topic at the beginning and build your knowledge from there. So even if you've never used a computer before, this book will get you through those crucial and scary early stages.

No time? No problem. With *The Complete Idiot's Guide to Microsoft Windows 8*, you get just the facts you need—not everything there is to know. This means I avoid long-winded discussions of boring, technical details. Instead, you get all the information in short, easy-to-digest chunks that you can quickly skim through to find just the tidbits you need.

How This Book Is Organized

The Complete Idiot's Guide to Microsoft Windows 8 is organized into four reasonably sensible parts. To help you locate what you need fast, here's a summary of what you'll find in each part.

Part 1, Getting to Know Windows 8, offers seven chapters that are designed to help you get your Windows 8 travels off on the right foot. New Windows users will want to start with Chapter 1, which gives you a tour of the Windows 8 screen and offers some mouse and keyboard basics. From there, you learn about controlling programs (Chapter 2), working with windows (Chapter 3), dealing with documents (Chapter 4), working with files and folders (Chapter 5), installing and uninstalling programs and devices (Chapter 6), and getting onto the internet (Chapter 7).

Part 2, Having Fun with Windows 8, takes you on a trip toward the fun end of the computer spectrum. (Yes, there *is* a fun end.) With that in mind, I structured Part 2 to cover some of the more entertaining features that can be found in Windows 8. This includes using scanners and digital cameras (Chapter 8); managing your pictures (Chapter 9); playing music, sounds, and other digital media (Chapter 10); and creating and editing your own digital movies (Chapter 11).

Part 3, Getting Things Done with Windows 8, presents a to-do list of six chapters that cover workaday tasks such as sharing your computer with other family members (Chapter 12); surfing the World Wide Web (Chapter 13); exchanging email (Chapter 14); working with contacts, social networks, and calendars (Chapter 15); sending and receiving faxes (Chapter 16); and using Windows 8 portable-computer features (Chapter 17).

Part 4, Customizing, Maintaining, and Troubleshooting Windows 8, is for anyone who wants to personalize their computing experience by adjusting the screen colors, changing the background, and performing other individualistic tweaks. The first two chapters show you how to customize the desktop (Chapter 18) as well as the Start screen and taskbar (Chapter 19). You also get a step-by-step plan for maintaining your system (Chapter 20), instructions for keeping you and your computer safe while online (Chapter 21), and some very handy strategies for solving problems (Chapter 22).

Finally, the appendix provides you with a comprehensive list of Windows 8's all-too-numerous shortcut keys, just in case your mouse is having a bad day.

Extras

I've liberally sprinkled the book with features that I hope will make it easier for you to understand what's going on. Here's a rundown:

- Menus, commands, and dialog box controls that you have to select, as well as keys you have to press and stuff you have to type, appear in a **bold font.**

- Whenever I tell you to select a menu command, I separate the various menu and command names with a right arrow. For example, instead of saying "click the **File** menu, then click **Options,** and then click **Email,**" I just say this: "select **File>Options>Email.**"

- Many Windows 8 commands come with handy keyboard shortcuts, and most of them involve holding down one key while you press another key. For example, in most Windows programs, you save your work by holding down the **Ctrl** key, tapping the **S** key, and then releasing **Ctrl.** I'm *way* too lazy to write all that out each time, so I'll just plop a plus sign (+) in between the two keys, like so: **Ctrl+S.**

I've also populated each chapter with several different kinds of sidebars:

WINDOWS WISDOM

These asides give you extra information about the topic at hand, provide you with tips for making things easier, and generally just make you a well-rounded Windows 8 user.

DEFINITION

These notes give you definitions of Windows words suitable for use at cocktail parties and other social gatherings where a well-timed *bon mot* can make you a crowd favorite.

LOOK OUT!

These notes warn you about possible Windows 8 pitfalls and how to avoid them.

SEE ALSO

Each of these elements points you to another section of the book that contains related material.

HACKING WINDOWS

These juicier tidbits take you deeper into Windows 8 and show you useful tweaks that enable you to supercharge your system and take control over various aspects of Windows 8.

Acknowledgments (Kudos, Props, and Assorted Pats on the Back)

Substitute damn *every time you're inclined to write* very; *your editor will delete it and the writing will be just as it should be.*

—*Mark Twain*

I didn't follow Mark Twain's advice in this book (the word *very* appears throughout), but if my writing still appears "just as it should be," then it's because of the keen minds and sharp linguistic eyes of the editors at Alpha Books. Near the front of the book you'll find a long list of the hard-working professionals whose fingers made it into this particular paper pie. However, there are a few folks that I worked with directly, so I'd like to single them out for extra credit. A big, heaping helping of thanks goes out to acquisitions editor Brook Farling, development editor Mike Thomas, production editor Janette Lynn, copy editor Monica Stone, and technical editor J. Boyd Nolan.

Special Thanks to the Technical Reviewer

The Complete Idiot's Guide to Microsoft Windows 8 was reviewed by an expert who double-checked the accuracy of what you'll learn here, to help us ensure that this book gives you everything you need to know about Windows 8. Special thanks are extended to J. Boyd Nolan.

J. Boyd Nolan, P.E., is a software and engineering consultant who has been in the computing industry for over 20 years, performing system/network administration, database administration, and general development work. He has experience developing large-scale n-tier and web applications for business and engineering uses. He holds Bachelor's and Master's degrees in Mechanical Engineering from the University of Oklahoma (Boomer Sooner!). Boyd currently lives in Norman, Oklahoma, with the two loves of his life, his wife Lisa and son Justin.

Trademarks

All terms mentioned in this book that are known to be or are suspected of being trademarks or service marks have been appropriately capitalized. Alpha Books and Penguin Group (USA) Inc. cannot attest to the accuracy of this information. Use of a term in this book should not be regarded as affecting the validity of any trademark or service mark.

Getting to Know Windows 8

One of the great things about Windows 8 is what techno-types refer to as its "consistent interface." In plain English, this means that a lot of the techniques you learn in one Windows program can also be used in another Windows program. These are techniques you'll be using day in and day out: starting programs, using menus and toolbars, manipulating windows, opening and printing documents, and installing programs and devices. The seven chapters that populate Part 1 take you through all of these techniques and quite a few more, including the all-important task of getting on the internet.

Windows 8:
The 50¢ Tour

In This Chapter

- Getting Windows 8 up and at 'em
- Getting familiar with the Windows 8 Start screen
- Checking out the Windows 8 desktop
- Handy mouse, keyboard, and tablet techniques
- Shutting Windows down

Thrill-seeking types enjoy diving into the deep end of any new pool they come across. The rest of us, however, prefer to check things out by dipping a toe or two into the water and then slipping ever so gently into the shallow end. The latter is the more sensible approach when it comes to Windows 8, which can be like cold and murky water to the uninitiated. You need to ease in by learning a few basics about the layout of the screen and a few useful mouse and keyboard techniques; that's exactly what is covered in this chapter.

Note, however, that this chapter assumes your Windows 8 "pool" has been built and filled with water. That is, I assume either your computer came with Windows 8 already installed or you have—or a nearby computer guru has—upgraded your computer to Windows 8.

Starting Windows 8

After you poke your computer's power switch, Windows 8 begins pulling itself up by its own bootstraps. This *booting* process takes a few minutes on most machines, so this is an excellent time to grab a cup of coffee or tea and review your copy of *Feel the Fear and Do It Anyway*.

> **DEFINITION**
>
> The idea of Windows pulling itself up by its own bootstraps is actually a pretty good way to describe the process of Windows starting itself. In fact, it's the source of the verb **boot,** which means to start a computer.

After your machine has churned through a few behind-the-scenes and (happily) ignorable chores, you end up staring at a pretty picture that also tells you the current date and time. This is the "lock" screen, and it doesn't do very much. To get past it, press the **Enter** key on your keyboard. Now you see the sign-on screen, which will be similar to the one shown in Figure 1.1.

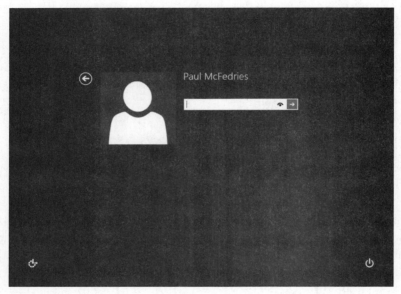

Figure 1.1: *This sign-on screen appears soon after you start your computer.*

What's happening here is Windows 8 wants to know that you're the legitimate users of the computer, so it's asking you to type your account's password. You get the full scoop on user accounts in Chapter 12, so don't sweat it too much right now.

Here's how you take care of business in the sign-on screen:

1. Type your Windows 8 password. Note that the characters you type appear as dots for security, just in case some snoop is peering over your shoulder.

2. Press your keyboard's **Enter** key.

Windows 8 will now continue its seemingly endless start-up chores, so be prepared to do a bit more thumb twiddling before the main screen finally puts in an appearance.

Getting to Know the Start Screen

The screen shown in Figure 1.2 is the Start screen, and it's the face that Windows 8 presents to the world. If you're new to Windows 8, you need to get comfortable with the lay of the Windows land. To that end, this section takes a look around the terrain you now see before you.

Figure 1.2: *The Windows 8 Start screen.*

Before getting to that, however, let me digress for just a second and talk to those who have used a previous version of Windows, such as Windows 7, Windows Vista, or Windows XP. When Windows 8 first loaded, you most likely had a what-the-heck moment. No, you do not need to get your eyes or head examined; Windows 8 is *very* different from what you're used to. The little Start orb that was tucked into the lower-left corner of the screen since time immemorial is gone, relegated to the dustbin of Windows history. In its place you now see the Start screen shown in Figure 1.2. Why the drastic renovation? Microsoft's goal here is to make it easier to launch the programs you use most often, and to provide you with up-to-date information without opening a program to get it. Did they succeed? Time will tell. The transition may be a bit rocky, but I'm here to help you through it.

Okay, we're back. The Start screen consists of a bunch of colorful rectangles, each of which shows a small picture and a word or two of text. These rectangles are called *tiles* and each one represents an *app* that you use to perform a particular task (the word *app* is short for *application*). For example, you use the Photos app to view and manage photos on your computer. Similarly, you use the Music app to manage your tunes, the Mail app for email, and the Weather app to get the latest forecast. I'll be talking about many of these apps throughout this book. For the record (and for reasons far too geeky to go into here), Microsoft refers to these as Windows 8 apps to differentiate them from Desktop apps—which I talk about in the next section.

The other major tidbit you need to know about the Start screen is that some of the tiles are clever enough to display information about what's happening. For example, the Music-app tile can tell you the name of the currently playing song, the Mail-app tile can tell you if you have unread messages, and the Weather-app tile can display the current conditions. This is called *live updating*, and it means you can get the latest info without having to start the apps.

Familiar Territory: The Desktop

The Start screen represents the main floor of the Windows house, but there's a second floor that lets you get your work (or play, or whatever) done. It's called the *desktop*, and you get there by clicking the **Desktop** tile in the Start screen. (If you haven't the foggiest idea what "clicking" is, see Basic Mouse Maneuvers, later in this chapter.)

This gets you face-to-face with the Desktop app, shown in Figure 1.3, which I divide into two sections: the desktop itself and the taskbar.

Figure 1.3: *The Windows 8 Desktop app.*

The Desktop

Ivory-tower computer types enjoy inventing metaphors for the way the rest of us use a computer. The idea is that more people will put up with a computer's shenanigans if using a computer reflects the way we do things in real life.

For Windows, the metaphor of choice is the humble desktop. You're supposed to think of the Windows screen as being comparable to the top of a real desk. Starting a program is like taking out a folder of papers and placing it on the desk. To do some work in the real world, of course, you need to pull papers out of the folder and place them on the desk. This is just like opening a file within a program (it could be a letter, a drawing, an email message, or whatever). To extend the metaphor a little, most programs also come with tools—such as a ruler, a calculator, and a calendar—that are the electronic equivalents of the tools you use at your desk.

Officially, the vast expanse that takes up the bulk of the screen in Figure 1.3 is the Windows 8 desktop, and it's where you'll likely do at least some of your work. That's because, although the apps shown in the Start screen are decent enough, the Desktop app gives you access not only to more apps, but to more powerful Windows 8 tools and features, as well.

The Taskbar

The multicolored strip along the bottom of the Windows 8 screen is called the *taskbar*. The taskbar sports three distinct features (pointed out in Figure 1.3):

- **Program icons.** This area contains a few icons. An *icon* is a small picture that represents something on your system, such as a program or a command. You use these icons to start programs and to control running programs, as I natter on about in Chapter 2.

- **Notification area.** Windows 8 uses this area to let you know when something important (or something Windows 8 *thinks* is important) is happening with your machine. These are called *notifications*, and they'll pop up from time to time to keep you "in the know." For example, Figure 1.4 shows the notification that barges onto the desktop if Windows 8 detects that your antivirus program is out of date.

- **Date and time.** This area's purpose is obvious enough: it tells you the current date and time.

Figure 1.4: *Windows 8 uses the aptly (if a bit boringly) named notification area to cough up notifications about stuff that's happening with your PC.*

WINDOWS WISDOM

We're done with the Desktop app for now, so to return to the Start screen, press the **Windows** key (it's the one shoehorned between the Ctrl key and the Alt key on the bottom-left corner of the keyboard).

A Few Mouse and Keyboard Fundamentals

Windows 8 is supposed to have all kinds of fancy-schmancy features. How do I get at 'em?

Ah, that's where your mouse and keyboard come in. You use them as input devices to give Windows 8 its marching orders. If you're new to all the personal computer malarkey, the next few sections show you the basic mouse and keyboard techniques you need.

Basic Mouse Maneuvers

If you're unfamiliar with Windows, there's a good chance that you're also unfamiliar with the mouse—the electromechanical (and, thankfully, toothless) mammal attached to your machine. If so, this section presents a quick look at a few mouse moves—which is important because much of what you do in Windows will involve the mouse in some way.

For starters, be sure the mouse is sitting on its pad or on your desk with the cord facing away from you. If you have a cordless mouse, move it so the buttons are facing away from you. Rest your hand lightly on the mouse with your index finger on—but not pressing down—the left button and your middle finger on the right button (or the rightmost button). Southpaws need to reverse the fingering.

Figure 1.3 shows you the *mouse pointer*. Find the pointer on your screen and then slowly move the mouse on its pad. As you do this, notice that the pointer moves in the same direction. Take a few minutes to practice moving the pointer to and fro using slow, easy movements.

To new users the mouse may seem an unnatural device that confounds common sense and often reduces the strongest among us to tears of frustration. The secret to mastering the mouse is twofold. First, use the same advice given to the person who wanted to get to Carnegie Hall: practice, practice, practice. Fortunately, with Windows 8 being so mouse dependent, you'll get plenty of chances to perfect your skills.

Second, understand all the basic mouse moves that are required of a modern-day mouse user. There are a half-dozen in all:

- **Point.** To move the mouse pointer so it's positioned over some specified part of the screen. For example, "point at the **Desktop** tile" means that you move the mouse pointer over the Start screen's Desktop tile.

- **Click.** To press and immediately release the left mouse button to initiate some kind of action. Need a "fer instance?" Okay, point at the **Desktop** tile and then click it. Instantly, the Windows 8 Desktop app appears, as shown in Figure 1.3. We're going to use the Desktop app for the next few techniques, so stay where you are for now.

- **Double-click.** To press and release the left mouse button *twice*, one press right after the other (there should be little or no delay between each press). To give it a whirl, point at the desktop's **Recycle Bin** icon and then double-click. If all goes well, Windows 8 will toss a box titled *Recycle Bin* onto your desktop. If nothing happens when you double-click, try again—clicking as quickly as you can—and try not to move the mouse while you're clicking. To return the Recycle Bin box from whence it came, click the **X** button in the upper-right corner of the box.

- **Right-click.** To press and immediately release the *right* mouse button. In Windows 8, right-click is used almost exclusively to display the Shortcut menu; to see one, right-click an empty part of the desktop. Windows 8 displays a menu with a few common commands related to the desktop. To remove the Shortcut menu, *left*-click an empty part of the desktop.

- **Click-and-drag.** To point at some object, press and *hold down* the left mouse button, move the mouse, and then release the button. You almost always use this technique to move an object from one place to another. For example, try dragging the **Recycle Bin** icon. (To restore apple-pie order to the desktop, right-click the desktop, click **Sort By** in the Shortcut menu, and then click **Name**.)

- **Scroll.** To turn the little wheel that's nestled between the left and right mouse buttons. In programs that support scrolling, you use this technique to move up and down within a document. If your mouse doesn't have a wheel— fear not—Windows provides other ways to navigate a document, as you'll see in Chapter 3.

Common Keyboard Conveniences

I mentioned earlier that getting comfy with your mouse is crucial if you want to make your Windows 8 life as easy as possible. That's not to say, however, that the keyboard never comes in handy as a time-saver. On the contrary, Windows 8 is chock-full of keyboard shortcuts that are sometimes quicker than the standard mouse techniques. I'll tell you about these shortcuts as we go along. For now, let's run through some of the standard keyboard parts and see how they fit into the Windows way of doing things.

WINDOWS WISDOM

Windows 8 has all kinds of keyboard combo shortcuts, so they pop up regularly throughout the book. Because I'm *way* too lazy to write out something like "Hold down the **Ctrl** key with one hand, use your other hand to tap the **Esc** key, and then release **Ctrl"** each time, I use the following shorthand notation instead: "Press **Hold+Tap**," where **Hold** is the key you hold down and **Tap** is the key you tap. In other words, instead of the previous long-winded sentence, I say this: "Press **Ctrl+Esc**." (On rare occasions, a third key joins the parade, so you might see something like "Press **Ctrl+Alt+Delete**." In this case, you hold down the first two keys and then tap the third key.)

- **Ctrl and Alt keys.** If you press Ctrl (control) or Alt (alt as in *alternate*), nothing much happens, but that's okay because nothing much is supposed to happen. You don't use these keys by themselves, but as part of a *key combination*. (The Shift key often gets into the act as well.) For example, on the Start screen, hold down the **Ctrl** key with one hand, use your other hand to tap the **Minus (-)** key, and then release Ctrl. Like magic, the Start screen tiles shrink down to tiny versions of themselves. (To return the tiles to their normal size, hold down **Ctrl**, press **Plus** (+), and then release Ctrl.)

DEFINITION

A **key combination** is a keyboard technique where you hold down one key and then press another key—or possibly two other keys.

- **Esc key.** Your keyboard's Esc key (for *escape*) is your all-purpose, get-me-the-heck-out-of-here key. In many cases, if you do something in Windows 8 that you didn't want to do, you can reverse your tracks with a quick tap (or maybe two or three) on **Esc**.

- **Windows key.** This key has the Windows logo on it, and on most keyboards it appears in the bottom row on the left side, between the Ctrl and Alt keys. (Some larger keyboards boast a second Windows key on the right side of the bottom row.) As I mentioned earlier, when you're in the Desktop app you can return to the Start screen by pressing the **Windows** key. You also use it as part of key combinations. For example, when you're in the Start screen, you can fire up the Desktop app by pressing **Windows+D**.

- **Numeric keypad.** On a standard keyboard layout, the numeric keypad is the separate collection of numbered keys on the right. The numeric keypad usually serves two functions, and you toggle between these functions by pressing the **Num Lock** key. (Most keyboards have a Num Lock indicator light that tells you when Num Lock is on.) When Num Lock is on, you can use the numeric keypad to type numbers. When Num Lock is off, the other symbols on the keys become active. For example, the up-pointing arrow on the 8 key becomes active, which means you can use it to move up within a program. Some keyboards (called *extended keyboards*) have a separate keypad for the insertion-point movement keys, and you can keep Num Lock on all the time on these.

A Touchy Subject: Using Windows 8 on a Tablet

I said earlier that Windows 8 was built with the mouse in mind, but what if you're using a computer that doesn't even have a mouse? I speak of the tablet, a device that is basically just a glass screen with no mouse or keyboard in sight. So with no input devices, how do you make your tablet do anything? The secret is that there *are* input devices: ten of them, in fact. I'm talking about your fingers, because tablets are built to respond to touch. That is, instead of using a mouse or keyboard to cajole Windows 8 into doing your bidding, you use your fingers to touch the screen in certain strategic ways. (Some tablets also come with a small penlike device called a *stylus*, and you can use the stylus instead of your finger for some actions.)

What are these strategic ways? There are tons of them, but here's just a short list to get you started (I'll talk about the rest as we go through the book):

- **Tap.** The touch equivalent of a mouse click; use your finger (or the stylus) to touch the screen and then immediately release it.

- **Double-tap.** The touch equivalent of a mouse double-click; tap and release the screen *twice*, one tap right after the other.

- **Tap and hold.** The touch equivalent of a mouse right-click; tap the screen and leave your finger (or the stylus) resting on the screen until the shortcut menu appears.

- **Slide.** The touch equivalent of a mouse click and drag; place your finger on the screen, move your finger, and then release. As with the mouse, you'll usually use this technique to move an object from one place to another.

- **Swipe.** Quickly and briefly run your finger along the screen. This usually causes the screen to scroll in the direction of the swipe; it's roughly equivalent to scrolling with the mouse wheel.

- **Touch keyboard.** An onscreen keyboard like the one shown in Figure 1.5, used to type text in the touch world. To display the keyboard in a Windows 8 app, tap and hold inside whatever box you'll be using to type the text; in a Desktop app, tap the **Keyboard** icon that appears in the taskbar.

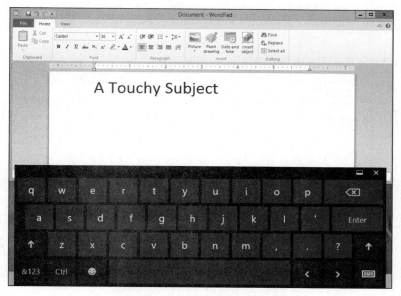

Figure 1.5: *To type on a tablet, use the touch keyboard.*

WINDOWS WISDOM

If you don't see the Keyboard icon in the taskbar, tap and hold the taskbar to unfurl the Shortcut menu, tap **Toolbars**, and then tap **Touch Keyboard**.

Shutting Down Windows for the Night

When you've stood just about all you can stand of your computer for one day, it's time to close up shop. Please tape the following to your cat's forehead so that you never forget it: *never, I repeat, never, turn off your computer's power while Windows 8 is running.* Doing so can lead to data loss, a trashed configuration, and accelerated hair loss that those new pills won't prevent.

Now that I've scared the daylights out of you, let's see the proper procedure for shutting down your computer:

1. In the Windows 8 Start screen, move the mouse pointer to the upper-right corner of the screen. If you're using a tablet, place your finger on the right edge of the screen and swipe left. The Windows 8 Charms menu appears. The Charms menu is a new Windows 8 feature that gives you quick access to a few common features, such as searching (via the Search button), the Start screen (via the Start button), and settings (via the Settings button).

2. Click **Settings**. Windows 8 displays the Settings pane.

HACKING WINDOWS

You can go directly to the Settings pane by pressing **Windows+I**.

3. Click the **Power** icon. As you can see in Figure 1.6, Windows 8 displays a few options.

4. Click the **Shut down** command. Windows 8 tucks itself in and turns off your PC.

Figure 1.6: *Click the **Power** icon in the Settings pane.*

Windows 8 also has a few other shutdown tricks that you should know about. First, you just saw that clicking the Power icon produced a menu with three commands, including Shut Down. Here's what the other two are …

- **Sleep.** Clicking this option tells Windows 8 to shut down your computer, but it also tells Windows 8 to remember which windows and programs you have running. When you restart Windows 8, it restores those programs and windows automatically. Thanks!

- **Restart.** Choose this option if you want to start Windows 8 all over again. For example, if you find that Windows is acting strangely, restarting can often put things right.

For the sake of completeness, you also get a few more options related to your Windows 8 user account. In the Start screen (press **Esc** if you still have the Settings pane open), right-click your **User Account** tile located in the upper-right corner of the screen. You see a menu that includes the following options:

- **Lock.** Choose this option to display a screen that asks you for your password. You must enter the password to get back to the Windows 8 desktop. (If you don't have a password, just press **Enter**. See Chapter 12 to learn how to protect your computer with a password.)

- **Sign out.** Choose this option to log off and then log back on using a different user account (see Chapter 12 to learn about user accounts).

- **Other users.** If your computer has multiple user accounts, click a user to remain logged on yourself, but to also log on with that user's account (again, see Chapter 12 for the details).

The Least You Need to Know

- The Windows 8 Start screen is divided into a series of rectangles called *tiles* that represent the Windows 8 apps installed on your computer.
- The Windows 8 Desktop app is carved into two main areas: the desktop—the large area that covers most of your monitor—and the taskbar—the thin strip along the bottom of the screen.
- The taskbar consists of some program icons, the notification area, and the date and time.

- The three most-used mouse movements are click (quickly pressing and releasing the left mouse button), double-click (two quick clicks), and drag (holding down the left button and moving the mouse).

- A key combination involves holding down one key, pressing a second key, and then releasing the first key. I signify such a combo with the notation **Hold+Press** (where **Hold** is the key you hold down and **Press** is the key you press); for example, **Ctrl+Esc**.

- To shut down Windows, display the Charms menu, click **Settings**, click **Power**, and then click **Shut down**.

Making Things Happen: Launching and Controlling Programs

In This Chapter

- A few ways to get a program off the ground
- Learning about pull-down menus, toolbars, and dialog boxes
- Getting the hang of these newfangled ribbons
- Techniques for switching between programs
- Shutting down a program

If you want to get your computer to do anything even remotely nonpaperweightlike, you need to launch and work with a program or three. For example, if you want to write a memo or a letter, you need to fire up a word processing program; if you want to draw pictures, you need to crank up a graphics program. If you want to use the Windows spreadsheet program, well … there isn't one. Windows 8 comes with a passel of programs, but a spreadsheet program isn't among them. If you want to crunch numbers, you need to get an additional spreadsheet program, such as Microsoft Excel.

On the other hand, Windows 8 *does* come with a decent collection of programs that enable you to perform most run-of-the-mill computing tasks. This chapter shows you how to get at those programs, as well as how to mess with them after they're up and running.

Launching a Program

If you're interested in starting a program, then you might think that the Start screen (see Figure 2.1) would be a promising place to begin. If so, give yourself a pat on the back (or have a nearby loved one do it) because that's exactly right. The next couple of sections give you the Start screen details.

Figure 2.1: *The Start screen: your Windows 8 launch pad.*

A Look Around the Start Screen

The Start screen is populated with all kinds of squares and rectangles that, you'll recall from Chapter 1, are called *tiles*. Each tile represents something that exists on your computer. (I should point out that it's possible your Start screen has already been customized, so yours may be populated with a different set of tiles.)

For example, the tile in the upper-right corner of the screen shows your Windows 8 user name and picture (see Chapter 12 to learn how to change your picture). As I described in Chapter 1, you can also use this tile to lock your computer, log off, or switch to a different user account. Similarly, you use the Mail tile to send and receive email messages, as I discuss in Chapter 14, and the Calendar tile to schedule appointments, events, and other upcoming goings-on (I explain all in Chapter 15).

The Windows 8 Start screen also has a hidden component called the Charms menu (see Figure 2.2), which you display by moving the mouse pointer to the top-right or bottom-right corner of the screen or, if you're using a tablet, by swiping left from the right edge of the screen. The Charms menu offers the following goodies:

- **Search.** Click this when you need to find something on your computer. It all sounds quite vague, I know, but you'll get the specifics in Chapter 5.

- **Share.** Click this to send a file to someone via email. See Chapter 14 for more info.

- **Start.** You can click this to return to the Start screen, even if you find your-self in some far-off and isolated section of the Windows 8 landscape.

- **Devices.** Click this to open a screen that shows you all the major devices and hardware doodads attached to your computer.

- **Settings.** Click this to display the various digital knobs and dials that enable you to configure Windows 8.

Figure 2.2: *The Start screen's Charms menu.*

HACKING WINDOWS

If you want to practice your click-and-drag skills, place the mouse pointer over the lighter part of the scrollbar, and then click and drag to the right to shift the Start screen to the left. You can click and drag the scrollbar to the left to return it.

Navigating the Start Screen

Now that you've met the denizens of the Start screen, you need to know how to make them do something useful. That's easy enough: to launch a tile, click it (or tap it if you're using a tablet).

That works well enough as long as you can see the tile you want to launch. However, it's quite possible that you have tiles off to the right that you can't see. (This will become more of an issue as you install programs on your PC, as I describe in

Chapter 6.) There are two ways to access those programs, depending on whether you're using a regular PC or a tablet:

- **Regular PC.** Move the mouse to the bottom of the Start screen to display the bar shown in Figure 2.3. This is called a *scrollbar*. Click the right-pointing arrow on the right side of the scrollbar to shift the Start screen to the left. To reverse course, click the left arrow on the left side of the scrollbar to shift things back to the right.

DEFINITION

The **scrollbar** is the narrow strip that runs along the right side of most windows. You sometimes see scrollbars along the bottom of a window, too.

- **Tablet.** Use your finger to slide an empty area of the Start screen to the left, which shifts everything to the right. Slide to the right to shift everything back to where it was originally.

Figure 2.3: *Move the mouse pointer to the bottom of the Start screen to reveal the scrollbar.*

Here are two other Start screen navigation techniques you need to memorize:

- To return to the Start screen after you've launched an app, press the **Windows** key. Press the **Windows** key again to return to the app.

- To display the Charms menu, press **Windows+C**.

App City: Using the Apps Screen

The Start screen makes it a breeze to launch apps, but unfortunately it's home to only the Windows 8-style apps that are installed on your computer, plus the File Explorer tile. However, Windows 8 is loaded with other programs, such as WordPad (word processing) and Paint (graphics). How the heck are you supposed to launch (or even know about) these extra programs?

Fortunately, Windows 8 comes with the Apps screen, which is a more-or-less complete list of the programs on your computer. To get there, right-click an empty chunk of the Start screen, and then click the **All Apps** icon that appears in the lower-right corner of the screen. (From the keyboard, you can press **Windows+Q** and then press **Esc**.)

LOOK OUT!

If you're a tablet user, you might think that you can "right-click" the Start screen by tapping and holding it. Nope, sorry. For some—I'm sure illogical—reason, that doesn't work. Instead, you have to swipe down from the top edge of the screen. Go figure.

You end up face-to-face with the Apps screen. Use the scrollbar (or slide if you have a tablet) to shift the Apps screen to the left, and you'll come upon the list of Windows programs shown in Figure 2.4. From there, just tap any program you want to launch.

Figure 2.4: *The Windows 8 Apps screen: So that's where the other programs are!*

Searching for a Program

The Apps screen sure has a lot of apps! If you find it hard to locate the program you want in that vast tile sea, I feel your pain. Instead of wading through screens full of tiny tiles, you can call up the program you want right from the Start screen with just a few keystrokes.

To give this a whirl, follow these steps:

1. Return to the Start screen. (Technically, this also works from the Apps screen, so feel free to stay put if that's where you are.)

2. Type the first letter of the program you want to launch. Windows 8 immediately switches to the Apps screen, displays the Search box (which now includes the letter you typed), and displays a list of all programs that begin with the letter you typed.

3. To narrow your search even more, type the second letter of the program's name. Windows 8 now displays only those programs that begin with the letters you typed.

4. Repeat step 3 until you see the program you want.

5. Click the program's tile to launch it.

The beauty of this technique is that it often takes just a couple of keystrokes to locate the program you want. For example, in Figure 2.5 you can see that I only had to type *wo* to bring up the WordPad tile.

Figure 2.5: *In the Start (or Apps) screen, type the first few letters of the program name to locate it lickety-split.*

Now What? Getting a Program to Do Something Useful

Okay, so I know how to get a program running. What's next?

Ah, now you get to go on a little personal power trip, because this section shows you how to boss around your programs. Specifically, you learn how to work with the app bars that come with Windows 8 apps, and the pull-down menus, toolbars, ribbons, and dialog boxes that come with desktop apps.

Making Windows 8 Apps Move

The Windows 8 apps that populate the Windows Start screen are designed to be simple and straightforward. If you're looking for bells and maybe even the odd whistle or two, you won't find them here. That simplicity is a welcome change in a world of maddeningly complex software, but sometimes Windows 8 apps can appear to be a bit *too* simple.

For example, Figure 2.6 shows a screen from the Finance app. There's a big photo in the background, and superimposed on that image you see what appears to be a headline as well as recent index values from the Dow, the S&P 500, and the NASDAQ. So far so good, but is that all there is?

Figure 2.6: *The Finance app is a bit of a head-scratcher when you first launch it.*

The secret is that the Finance app, like many (but by no means all) of the Windows 8 apps, is actually a series of side-by-side screens, and to navigate the program you slide each screen to the left to bring the next screen into view. How you do this depends on whether you're using a regular PC or a tablet:

- **Regular PC.** Move the mouse to the bottom of the screen to display the scrollbar, and then drag the scroll box to the right.

- **Tablet.** Use your finger to slide the screen to the left.

As you drag or slide, the current screen scrolls out to the left and the next screen scrolls in from the right, as shown in Figure 2.7. You can return to a previous screen by either dragging the scroll box left or sliding right.

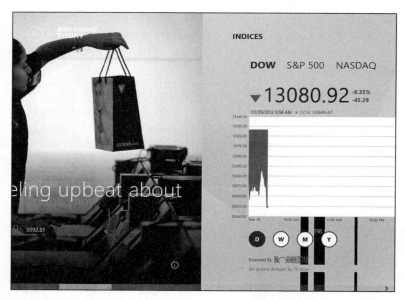

Figure 2.7: *You navigate many Windows 8 apps by scrolling the screens left and right.*

In all Windows 8 apps, you can initiate commands and choose program features using a creature called the app bar. To display the app bar, right-click the app; with a tablet, swipe down from the top edge of the screen (or swipe up from the bottom edge). Figure 2.8 shows the Finance app bar, which offers several icons that represent app features. For example, click **Watchlist** to add a stock to watch, or **Rates** to see a list of current interest rates.

The app bar

Figure 2.8: *The app bar in the Finance app.*

Depending on the app, the app bar will appear either at the top of the screen or the bottom. Some apps have it both ways.

Selecting Commands from Pull-Down Menus

Each program you work with has a set of commands and features that define the majority of what you can do with the program. Most of these commands and features are available via the program's pull-down menus. Oh sure, there are easier ways to tell a program what to do (I talk about some of them later in this chapter), but pull-down menus are special because they offer a complete road map for any program. This section gets you up to speed on this crucial Windows topic.

I'm going to use the Windows Fax and Scan program as an example for the next page or two. If you feel like following along, go ahead and launch the program by typing **fax** in the Start screen and then clicking the **Windows Fax and Scan** tile that appears.

The first thing you need to know is that a program's pull-down menus are housed in the *menu bar*, the horizontal strip that runs across the window, as pointed out in Figure 2.9. Each word in the menu bar represents a pull-down menu.

When you click **Edit**...   The menu bar

...Windows
pulls down
this Edit menu

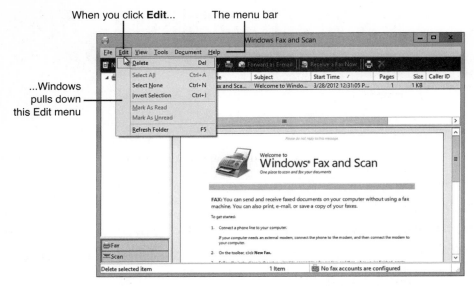

Figure 2.9: *Windows Fax and Scan's File menu.*

WINDOWS WISDOM

If I didn't know better, I'd swear that Windows 8 is a bit embarrassed to be seen with its pull-down menus. That's because many Windows 8 programs operate with the menu bar hidden away like some crazy aunt. If you open a program and you see neither hide nor hair of the menus, pressing the **Alt** key should bring the menu bar out into the light of day.

The various items that run across the menu bar (such as File, Edit, and View in Windows Fax and Scan) are the names of the menus. To see (that is, *pull down*) one of these menus, use either of the following techniques:

- Use your mouse to click the menu name. For example, click **Edit** to pull down the Edit menu.

- Notice in Figure 2.10 that each menu name has an underline under one letter. (If the program you're using doesn't show the underlines, press **Alt** to force them into the open.) That underline tells you that you can pull down the menu by holding down **Alt** and pressing the underlined letter on your keyboard. For example, the *E* in *Edit* gets underlined when you hold down Alt, so you can pull down this menu by pressing **Alt+E**.

The various items you see in the menu are called *commands*. From here, you use either of the following techniques to select a command:

DEFINITION

A **command** is a menu item that initiates some kind of action.

- Use your mouse to click the command you want.
- From your keyboard, use the down-arrow key (↓) or the up-arrow key (↑) to highlight the command, and then press **Enter**.

Throughout this book, I tell you to select a pull-down menu command by separating the menu name and command name with a comma (,), like this: "Select the **Edit, Delete** command."

WINDOWS WISDOM

What if you don't want to select any commands from a menu you already opened? You can get rid of the menu by clicking any empty part of the program's window, or by pressing **Alt** by itself. Alternatively, you can choose a command from a different menu by clicking the menu's name in the menu bar, or by pressing **Alt** plus the underlined letter of the new menu.

Note, too, that many program commands are also available via *shortcut menus*, which open by right-clicking something within the program window.

DEFINITION

Many Windows programs (and Windows 8 itself) use **shortcut menus** to give you quick access to oft-used commands. The idea is that you right-click something and the program pops up a small menu of commands, each of which is somehow related to whatever it is you right-clicked. If you see the command you want, great—just click it, using the left button this time. If you don't want to select a command from the menu, either left-click an empty part of the window or press **Esc**.

What happens next depends on which command you select. Here's a summary of the various possibilities:

- **The command runs.** This is the simplest scenario: the program carries out the command, no questions asked. For example, clicking the **Edit** menu's **Refresh Folder** command redisplays the current folder.

- **Another menu appears.** In this case, you then click the command you want to execute from the new menu. For example, as shown in Figure 2.11, if you select the **View, Zoom** command, you see a submenu that offers various magnification choices.

- **The command is toggled on or off.** Some commands operate like light switches: they turn certain features of a program on and off. When the feature is on, a small check mark appears to the left of the command to let you know. Selecting the command turns off the feature and removes the check mark. If you select the command again, the feature turns back on and the check mark reappears. For example, you can click the **View** menu's **Status Bar** command to toggle the Windows Fax and Scan status bar on and off (see Figure 2.10).

- **A dialog box appears.** Dialog boxes are pesky little windows that show up whenever the program needs to ask you for more information. You learn more about them in Dealing with Dialog Boxes, later in this chapter.

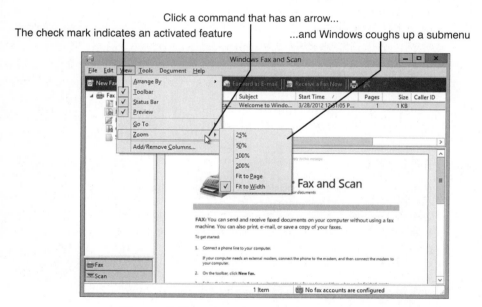

Figure 2.10: *A few pull-down menu features.*

Your Click Is My Command: Toolbar Basics

The computer wizards who build programs have come up with some amazing things over the years, but one of the most useful inventions has to be the *toolbar*. This is a collection of easily accessible icons designed to give you push-button access to common commands and features. No unsightly key combinations to remember; no pull-down menu forests to get lost in.

Toolbars show up all over the place in Windows 8, and you can reap some big dividends if you get to know how they work. If you're following along in Windows Fax and Scan, the toolbar is the horizontal strip that sits just below the menu bar.

Most toolbar icons are buttons that represent the same commands you normally access by using the pull-down menus. All you have to do is click a button, and the program runs the command. In Windows Fax and Scan, for example, one way to start a new document scan is to pull down the **File** menu, click **New**, and then click **Scan**. Not bad, but an even faster way is to simply click the toolbar's **New Scan** button. Easy-peasy, as my British friends would say.

Here's a summary of a few other toolbar-related techniques you ought to know:

- **Button tooltips.** Most toolbar buttons advertise what they do using nothing more than an icon. In this case, you can find out more about a particular button by pointing at it with your mouse. After a second or two, a banner— called a *tooltip*—with the button name pops up (take a peek at Figure 2.11 for an example). Note, too, that lots of programs also display a brief description of the button in the status bar.

- **Hiding and showing toolbars.** In most programs, you toggle a toolbar on and off by selecting the **View, Toolbar** command. If a program offers multiple toolbars, the View menu often includes separate commands for each toolbar. In some other programs, you select the **View, Toolbars** command to display a submenu of the available toolbars, and then select the one you want.

- **Drop-down buttons.** You'll occasionally come across toolbar buttons that are really drop-down menu wannabes. In this case, click the downward-pointing arrow to see a list of commands or options.

This horizontal strip is the toolbar   Point at a toolbar icon…

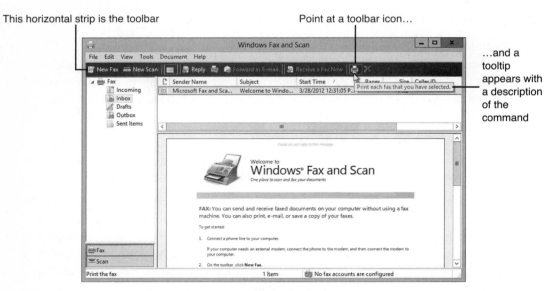

…and a tooltip appears with a description of the command

Figure 2.11: *In most toolbars, you can point your mouse at an icon to find out what it does.*

Getting the Hang of the Ribbon

Just to confuse the issue (Windows 8 has a genius for doing that), several of the programs you may use fairly often have completely different (and potentially baffling) ways to run commands. These programs include Internet Explorer, Windows Live Essentials programs (such as Windows Live Mail), WordPad (a word processor), and Paint (a graphics program). To see what I'm talking about, go ahead and get WordPad onto the desktop by typing **wordpad** in the Start screen and then clicking the **WordPad** icon that appears in the search results. As you can see in Figure 2.12, WordPad is weird in two ways: there's no menu bar (and you can tap **Alt** until your finger falls off), and the toolbar is *huge*. Actually, that's not a toolbar at all, but something called a *ribbon*, which is a kind of toolbar on steroids.

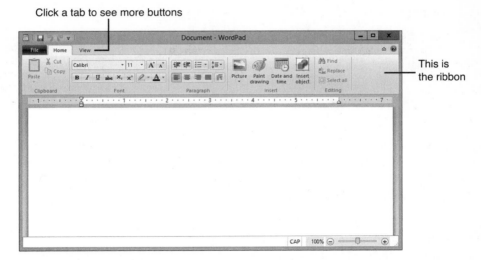

Figure 2.12: *In Windows 8, WordPad—as well as a host of other desktop programs—comes with a newfangled ribbon for faster access to program features.*

The ribbon works basically the same as a regular toolbar, with the major difference being the presence of two tabs: Home and View. Click these tabs to see more buttons. Also, to get to the program's menus, you need to click the **File** tab button in the upper-left corner.

Dealing with Dialog Boxes

I mentioned earlier that after you select some menu commands, the program might require more info from you. For example, if you run a Print command, the program might want to know how many copies of the document you want to print.

In these situations, the program sends an emissary to parley with you. These emissaries, called *dialog boxes*, are one of the most ubiquitous features in the Windows world. This section preps you for your dialog-box conversations by showing you how to work with every type of dialog-box control you're likely to encounter. (They're called *controls* because you use them to manipulate the different dialog-box settings.) Before starting, it's important to keep in mind that most dialog boxes like to monopolize your attention. When one is on the screen, you usually can't do anything else in the program (such as select a pull-down menu). Deal with the dialog box first, and then you can move on to other things.

> **DEFINITION**
>
> A **dialog box** is a small window that a program uses to prompt you for informa-
> tion or to display a message. You interact with each dialog box by using one or
> more **controls** to input data or initiate actions.

Okay, let's get started:

- **Command buttons.** Clicking one of these buttons (see Figure 2.13) executes whatever command is written on the button. The two examples shown in the Options dialog box are the most common. You click **OK** to close the dialog box and put the settings into effect, and you click **Cancel** to close the dialog box without doing anything.

- **Check boxes.** Windows uses a check box to toggle program features on and off (see Figure 2.13). Clicking the check box either adds a check mark (mean- ing the feature will turn on when you click **OK**) or removes the check mark (meaning the feature will get turned off when you click **OK**).

- **Option buttons.** If a program feature offers three or more possibilities, the dialog box will offer an option button for each (see Figure 2.13), and only one button can be selected (that is, have a blue dot inside its circle) at a time. You activate an option button by clicking it.

- **List boxes.** These controls (see Figure 2.13) display a list of items and you select an item by clicking it.

- **Text boxes.** You use these controls (see Figure 2.13) to type text data.

- **Spin boxes.** These controls (see Figure 2.13) enable you to cycle up or down through a series of numbers. The left part of the spin box is a simple text box into which a number can be typed; however, the right part of the spin box has tiny up-and-down-arrow buttons. You click the up arrow to increase the value, and you click the down arrow to decrease the value.

- **Tabs.** Click any of the tabs displayed across the top of some dialog boxes (see Figure 2.14) and you see a new set of controls.

- **Sliders.** Click and drag the slider (see Figure 2.14) to set the value of the control.

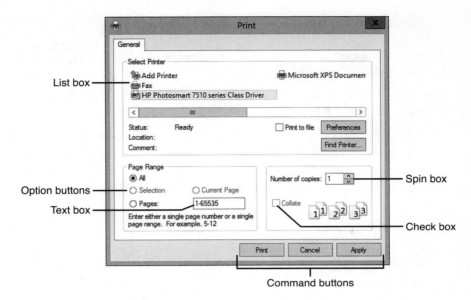

Figure 2.13: *This Print dialog box demonstrates quite a few dialog box features.*

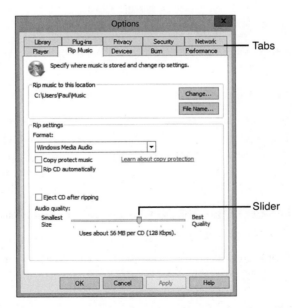

Figure 2.14: *You use tabs to navigate different sets of dialog-box controls, and you click and drag a slider to set a value.*

- **Drop-down list boxes.** These controls represent another example of the list box genre (see Figure 2.15). In this case, at first you see only one item. However, if you click the downward-pointing arrow on the right, the full list appears and it becomes like a regular list box.

- **Combo boxes.** These hybrid controls (see Figure 2.15) combine a list box and a text box. You can either select the item you want from the list or type it in the text box.

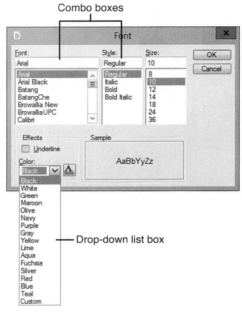

Figure 2.15: *This Font dialog box offers several examples of both combo boxes as well as an example of a drop-down list box.*

Switching from One Program to Another

Windows 8 is totally okay with you opening up two or more programs at the same time (Windows geeks call this *multitasking*). If you do that, however, then you need to know how to switch from one running program to another.

DEFINITION

Multitasking means running multiple programs simultaneously.

How you do that depends on whether you're running a Windows 8 app or desktop program, as the next couple of sections show.

LOOK OUT!

Although it's true that Windows 8 is happy to deal with multiple running programs—think of it as the electronic equivalent of walking and chewing gum at the same time—that doesn't mean you can just start every program you have and leave them running all day. Each open program usurps a chunk of the Windows resources; the more programs you run, the slower each program performs—including Windows itself. The number of applications you can fire up at any one time depends on how much horsepower your computer has. You probably need to play around a bit to see just how many applications you can launch before things get too slow.

Switching Between Windows 8 Programs

If you have multiple Windows 8 apps going, Windows 8 gives you two ways to switch between them using a mouse:

- Maneuver the mouse pointer into the top-left corner of the screen. Windows responds by showing you a teensy version of the next running app (see Figure 2.16); click to switch to that app. If you want to cycle through the apps, leave the mouse pointer in the top-left corner and keep clicking.

Figure 2.16: *Move the mouse pointer to the top-left corner of the screen to see a mini version of the next running app.*

- Move the mouse pointer into the top-left corner of the screen and when the mini version of the next app appears, slide the mouse pointer straight down. Once you get below the next app, Windows 8 displays a list of all running Windows 8 apps, as shown in Figure 2.17. Click the app you want to use.

WINDOWS WISDOM

Notice that the list of running Windows 8 apps includes the Start screen at the bottom, and you can click that to return to the Start screen. Note, too, that you can quickly switch between the current Windows 8 app (including the Desktop app) and the Start screen by pressing the **Windows** key.

Figure 2.17: *Move the mouse pointer to the top-left corner of the screen and then slide it down to see a list of your up-and-running Windows 8 apps.*

HACKING WINDOWS

You can also switch to another Windows 8 app using the keyboard. Hold down the **Windows** key and then tap **Tab**. When you do this, Windows 8 slides in the list of running Windows 8 apps. With the **Windows** key held down, keep pressing **Tab** until the app you want is highlighted, then release the **Windows** key.

Switching between Windows 8 apps really gets fun when you try it on a tablet:

- To switch to the next running app, slide to the right from the left edge of the screen. Your finger drags in the next app, and when you release your finger from the screen the app fills up the screen. Very cool.

- To see the list of running Windows 8 apps, slide in from the left edge again, but this time when you see the next app appear under your finger, reverse course and slide your finger back to the left edge of the screen. As soon as your finger hits the ledge, the app disappears and you see the list of running apps.

Switching Between Desktop Programs

When you fire up a desktop program, Windows 8 marks the occasion by adding a button to the taskbar. If you then coax another program or two onto the screen, each one gets its own taskbar button.

For example, Figure 2.18 shows Windows 8 with two programs running: WordPad and Paint. (To run the latter, type **paint** in the Start screen and then click the **Paint** icon that appears in the search results.) It looks as though Paint has lopped off a good portion of the WordPad window, but in reality Windows 8 is just displaying Paint "on top" of WordPad. In addition, the taskbar has changed in three ways:

- There are now buttons for both WordPad and Paint in the taskbar.

- The buttons for the WordPad and Paint programs have an outline around them to tell you that these buttons represent running programs. This is supposed to help you differentiate these from other taskbar buttons that launch programs. (Yes, this *does* take some getting used to.)

- In the taskbar, the *active* program's button (the Paint button, in this figure) is highlighted. (The active program is the one you're currently slaving away in.)

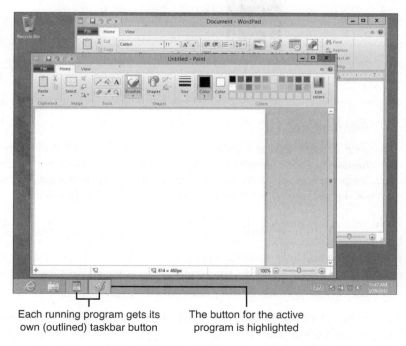

Each running program gets its   The button for the active
own (outlined) taskbar button   program is highlighted

Figure 2.18: *Windows 8 with two programs on the go.*

The taskbar has another trick up its digital sleeve: you can switch from one running program to another by clicking the latter's taskbar button. For example, when I click the WordPad button, the WordPad window comes to the fore, as shown in Figure 2.19.

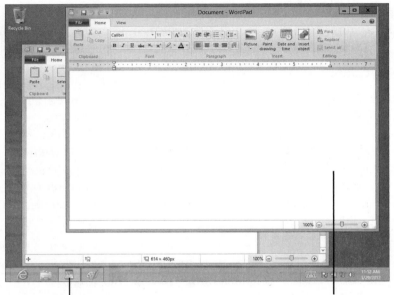

When you click the WordPad taskbar button...   ...the WordPad window elbows its way to the front

Figure 2.19: *You can use the taskbar buttons to switch from one program to another.*

Besides clicking the taskbar buttons, Windows 8 gives you two other ways to leap from one running program to another:

- **Click the program's window.** This is perhaps the simplest and most obvious method. All you do is point the mouse inside the program's window and then click. This method is most useful if your hand is already on the mouse and you can see at least part of the window you want to activate.

- **Hold down Alt and tap Esc.** With each tap of the **Esc** key, Windows 8 brings each running desktop program window to the fore. When you see the program you want, release the **Alt** key.

HACKING WINDOWS

You can switch between any running program—that is, any running Windows 8 app or desktop program—by holding down the **Alt** key and then tapping **Tab**. Windows 8 displays a box that shows each running program. Each time you press **Tab,** the next program gets highlighted. After you highlight the program you want, release the **Alt** key, and Windows 8 switches to the program.

When Enough's Enough: Quitting a Program

Close a program when you're finished using it to keep your screen uncluttered and to reduce the load on Windows' resources.

Shutting Down a Windows 8 Program

How you close down a Windows 8 app depends (as usual) on whether you're doing the regular PC thing or the tablet thing:

- **Regular PC.** Move the mouse pointer to the top of the screen, where it changes to a hand, and then click and drag the hand down. As you drag, the Windows 8 app window shrinks down. Keep dragging the smaller window all the way to the bottom of the screen, and then release the mouse button. If that sounds like an awful lot of work, move the mouse pointer to the top-left corner to display the list of running apps, move the pointer over the app you want to close, right-click it, and then click **Close**. Still too much? Okay, feel free to simply press **Alt+F4** instead.

- **Tablet.** Place your finger at the top edge of the screen, and then slide down until the Windows 8 app window shrinks down. Keep dragging your finger to the bottom of the screen, and then release your finger.

Shutting Down a Desktop Program

The easiest way to ditch a desktop program is to click the **Close** button—the **X** in the upper-right corner of the program's window. You can also use a few other methods, which you may find faster under certain circumstances:

- Press **Alt+F4**.

- Pull down the program's **File** menu and select the **Exit** command (or, more rarely, the **Close** command).

- Right-click the program's taskbar button and then click **Close** in the little menu that appears.

Depending on the program you're closing and the work you were doing with it, you might be asked whether you want to save some files.

SEE ALSO

I tell you how to handle saving documents in Chapter 4. See the section titled The All-Important Save Command.

The Least You Need to Know

- To start a Windows 8 app, click its tile in the Start screen. For all other programs, either use the Apps screen (right-click **Start** and then click **All Apps**) or start typing the program name and then click its tile in the search results.

- To select a pull-down menu command, first display the menu by clicking its name in the menu bar, and then click the command.

- In a dialog box, click **OK** to put dialog box settings into effect; click **Cancel** to bail out of a dialog box without doing anything; click **Help** to view the program's Help system.

- To switch between running programs, click the taskbar buttons. Alternatively, click the program window if you can see a chunk of it, or else press **Alt+Tab**.

- To quit a Windows 8 app, drag from the top edge of the screen to the bottom, or press **Alt+F4**. To quit a desktop program, click the **Close** (**X**) button; you can also usually get away with selecting the program's **File, Exit** command or pressing **Alt+F4**.

Working with Windows 8 Windows

In This Chapter

- Window gadgets and gewgaws
- Minimizing and maximizing windows
- Moving and sizing windows
- How to wield window scrollbars

Windows gets its name because, as you saw in Chapter 2, each desktop program that you launch shows up on the screen in a box, and that box is called a *window*. Why they named them windows instead of, say, *boxes*, I can't imagine. After all, have *you* ever seen a window on the top of a desk? I thought not.

Nincompoop nomenclature concerns aside, you're going to have to build up some window stamina because they'll come at you from the four corners of the screen. Fortunately, such stamina can be had without resorting to smelly workout clothes or a ThighMaster. As you see in this chapter, all that's required is practicing a few handy mouse techniques.

Artfully Arranging Windows 8 Windows

The window idea seems to go out the … well … window when it comes to the Windows 8 apps that launch from the Start screen. After all, when you crank up a Windows 8 app there's no box in sight, so therefore, no window; right? Not exactly. Windows 8 apps do technically appear in a window, it's just that by default these windows take up the entire screen. You can prove this to yourself by revisiting a couple of techniques that I blathered on about in Chapter 2:

- To close a running Windows 8 app, move the mouse pointer to the top of the screen (where it changes to a hand), then drag down. (On a tablet, slide down from the top of the screen instead.) As you drag, the Windows 8 app suddenly shrinks down to a small window, as shown in Figure 3.1.

- To switch to another app using a tablet, swipe in from the left edge of the screen. As you swipe, your finger brings in the next app as a small window.

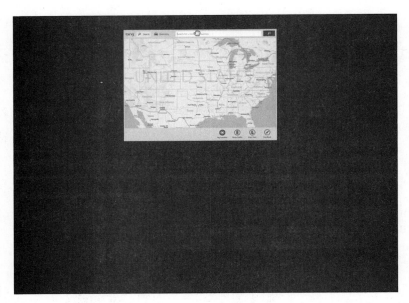

Figure 3.1: *Drag the top edge of a Windows 8 app down, and it suddenly morphs into something distinctly windowlike.*

Okay, so Windows 8 apps have a hidden "windowness." What's in it for you? That you can take advantage of it to show two Windows 8 apps onscreen at the same time. This means you could keep an eye on your stocks while simultaneously surfing the Web, or watch what your Facebook friends are up to while also perusing the Windows Store.

You do this by *snapping* the current Windows 8 app to the left or right side of the screen. This means that the app shrinks down to about a quarter of its normal width and parks itself on the left or right side of the screen, and then the next app takes up the rest of the screen. Figure 3.2 shows the Finance app snapped to the left side of the screen, while the Maps app covers the rest.

Figure 3.2: *You can display two Windows 8 apps at the same time by snapping an app to the left or right side of the screen.*

LOOK OUT!

Before going any further, you should know that you can't do the snap thing unless your monitor's screen resolution is set to at least 1366×768. If what I just said is complete gobbledygook to you, head for Chapter 18 and see Changing the Screen Resolution for a translation.

By now you won't be in the least bit surprised to learn that how you snap a Windows 8 app depends on whether you're using a regular PC or a tablet:

- **Regular PC.** Move the mouse pointer to the top of the screen, where it changes to a hand, and then click and drag the hand down. As you drag, the Windows 8 app window shrinks down. Now drag the smaller window all the way to the left or right side of the screen, and then release the mouse button. An easier method is to move the mouse pointer to the top left corner to display the list of running apps, move the pointer over the app you want to snap, right-click it, and then click either **Snap Left** or **Snap Right**.

HACKING WINDOWS

Yet another way to snap the current Windows 8 app is to press **Windows+.** (period). If you hold down the **Windows** key and tap **.** (period) repeatedly, Windows 8 cycles the app through snap left, snap right, and full-screen.

- **Tablet.** Place your finger at the top edge of the screen, and then slide down until the Windows 8 app window shrinks down. Keep dragging your finger to the left or right side of the screen, and then release your finger.

Warming Up: A Desktop Window Walkabout

Now let's turn our attention to the Desktop app and its very different window experience. As you'll soon see, your average desktop window is a kind of mini Nautilus gym, brimming with various gadgets that you push and pull. The secret to a successful desktop-window workout is to get to know where these gadgets are and how to use them. To that end, let's take a tour of a typical window, as shown in Figure 3.3. This is a Notepad window. To get it onscreen, use the Start screen to type **notepad** and then click **Notepad** in the search results.

Here's a rundown of the various trinkets pointed out in Figure 3.3:

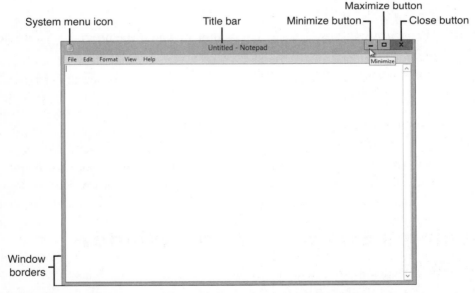

Figure 3.3: *The Notepad window will be your "gym" for this chapter's exercise regimen.*

- **Title bar.** This is the band that forms the top portion of the window. As its name implies, the title bar tells you the name of the currently open document. (In Figure 3.3, the document is new, so it has the temporary—and decidedly uninspiring—name *Untitled*. See Figure 3.9 for a better example.) The title bar also usually shows the name of the program with a dash in between the two names.

- **Buttons galore.** The right side of the title bar is populated with three buttons: the two blue buttons are named *Minimize* and *Maximize*, and the red button is named *Close*. I fill you in on what they do a bit later (see the section Breaking a Sweat: Window Exercises).

- **Borders.** Most windows are surrounded by four borders that you can manipulate, with your mouse, to change the size of the window (I show you how to do this later in this chapter; see Breaking a Sweat: Window Exercises).

- **System-menu icon.** The system menu sports several commands that enable keyboard users to perform routine window maintenance. If you're dealing with a program window, you drop down the system menu by pressing **Alt+spacebar**; for a document window, the system menu sprouts in response to **Alt+-** (hyphen).

Now just hold on a cotton-picking second. What's the difference between a program window and a document window?

Gee, you *are* paying attention, aren't you? Here you go:

- **Program window.** This is the window in which the program as a whole appears.

- **Document window.** This is a window that appears inside the program window; it contains a single, open document. This isn't something you'll have to worry about too much if you run only the desktop programs that come with Windows 8 because most of them are only capable of opening one document at a time. However, lots of other programs—such as those that come with Microsoft Office—are capable of working with two or more documents at once. In this case, each document appears inside its own window.

Breaking a Sweat: Desktop Window Exercises

Before getting to the specifics of using the four main window techniques—*minimizing, maximizing, moving,* and *sizing*—let's see how they can solve some niggling Windows problems and help you work better.

Problem #1: You have an open program that you know you won't need for a while. It's taking up desktop space, but you don't want to close it. The solution is to *minimize* the program's window; which means that it's cleared off the desktop, but remains open and appears only as a taskbar button. You can't move or size a window if it's either maximized or minimized.

Problem #2: You want the largest possible work area for a program. The solution is to *maximize* the program's window; this enlarges the window so it fills the entire desktop area.

Problem #3: You have multiple programs running and their windows overlap each other so some data is covered up. The way to fix this is to *move* one or more of the windows so that they don't overlap or overlap less.

Problem #4: No matter how much you move your windows, they still overlap. In this case, you need to resort to more drastic measures: *sizing* the windows. For example, you can reduce the size of less important windows and increase the size of windows in which you do the most work.

The next few sections discuss these techniques and a few more, for good measure.

Minimizing a Window

When you click a window's **Minimize** button, the window disappears from view. The window isn't closed, however, because its taskbar button remains in place, as you can see in Figure 3.4.

Just the window's taskbar button is visible

Figure 3.4: *When you minimize a program's window, the program remains running, but all you see is its taskbar button.*

Maximizing a Window

Clicking a window's **Maximize** button is a whole different kettle of window fish. In this case, the window grows until it fills the entire desktop, as you can see in Figure 3.5. Note that the Maximize button has, without warning, morphed into a new entity: the Restore button. I talk about this new creature in the next section.

HACKING WINDOWS

The Minimize, Maximize, Restore, and Close buttons are a tad on the small side. Here are some techniques to help you avoid these teensy buttons: minimize the current window by clicking its taskbar button; maximize a window by double-clicking its title bar or dragging the title bar to the top of the screen; restore a maximized window by double-clicking its title bar; close a window by double-clicking its system-menu icon.

The Restore button

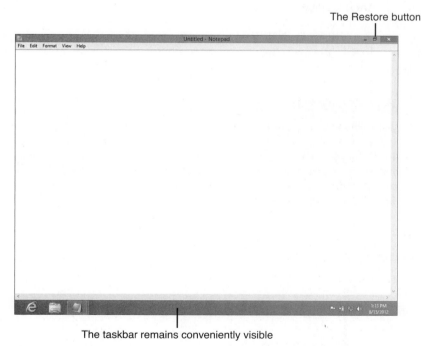

The taskbar remains conveniently visible

Figure 3.5: *When you maximize a window, it takes over the entire desktop.*

Restoring a Window

In Windows parlance, *restoring* a window means that you put the window back exactly the way it was before minimizing it or maximizing it. How you do this depends on what action you inflicted on the window.

- If you minimized the window, click its **taskbar** button.

- If you maximized the window, click the **Restore** button (pointed out in Figure 3.5).

Moving a Window

Moving a window from one part of the desktop to another takes a simple mouse maneuver. Here are the steps to follow:

1. Make sure the window isn't maximized (or that it's not—duh—minimized).

2. Position the mouse pointer inside the window's title bar, but not over the system-menu icon or any of the buttons on the right.

3. Click and drag the title bar. (That is, press and hold down the left mouse button and then move the mouse.) As you drag, the window moves along with your mouse—although it may lag behind slightly if you have a slower system.

4. When the window is in the position you want, release the mouse button.

> **WINDOWS WISDOM**
>
> If you want to move a window so that it takes up, say, the left half of the screen, Windows 8 offers an easy way to do this: click and drag the window title bar until the mouse pointer bumps up against the left edge of the screen. When an outline of the new window position appears, release the mouse button. You can also click and drag to the right edge to move the window so that it takes up the right half of the screen.

Sizing a Window

If you want to change the size of a window instead, you need to plow through these steps:

1. Make sure the window isn't maximized or minimized.

2. Point the mouse at the window border you want to adjust. For example, if you want to expand the window toward the bottom of the screen, point the mouse at the bottom border. When you've positioned the pointer correctly, it becomes a two-headed arrow, as shown in Figure 3.6.

3. Click and drag the border to the position you want.

4. Release the mouse button to set the new border position.

5. Repeat steps 2 through 4 for any other borders you want to size.

HACKING WINDOWS

If you want to change both the height and width of a window, you can save yourself a bit of effort by sizing two sides in one fell swoop. To do this, move the mouse pointer over a window corner. (The pointer will change to a diagonal two-sided arrow.) When you drag the mouse, Windows 8 sizes the two sides that create the corner.

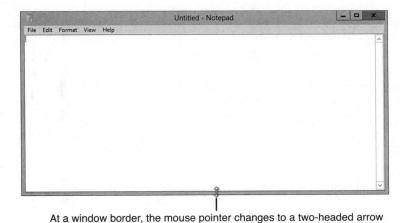

At a window border, the mouse pointer changes to a two-headed arrow

Figure 3.6: *You resize a window by dragging the window borders hither and yon.*

Cascading and Stacking Windows

If you're pressed for time, you can take advantage of some Windows 8 features that can save you a few steps. To get at these features, right-click an empty section of the taskbar. The shortcut menu that slides into view contains (among others) the following commands:

- **Cascade Windows**. This command automatically arranges all your nonmini-mized windows in a diagonal pattern that lets you see the title bar of each window. Figure 3.7 shows three cascaded windows.

- **Show Windows Side by Side**. This feature automatically arranges all your nonminimized windows into horizontal strips so that each of them gets an equal amount of desktop real estate without overlapping each other.

- **Show Windows Stacked.** This command is similar to Show windows side by side, except that it arranges the windows into vertical strips.

Figure 3.7: *The Cascade Windows command arranges your windows neatly in a diagonal pattern.*

Taking a Peek at the Desktop

As your Windows 8 career progresses, you'll no doubt end up with some of your stuff on the desktop. You might create your own icons or you might give a few Windows 8–desktop gadgets a whirl (as described in Chapter 18, Customizing the Desktop). Whatever your desktop ends up looking like, you'll want to take a peek at it from time to time. You normally do that by minimizing each of your open windows, but that might be *way* too much work if you've got a bunch of programs running.

To work around this problem, Windows 8 gives you two options:

- Right-click an empty stretch of the taskbar and then click **Show the Desktop**. This command hides all the nonminimized windows so you can see the full desktop. To get your windows back where they were, right-click the taskbar yet again and then click **Show Open Windows**.

- Move your mouse pointer over the **Show Desktop** button on the far right of the taskbar. Mysteriously, the open windows fade from view—except for their ghostly outlines, as shown in Figure 3.8. Move the mouse pointer off the **Show Desktop** button to make the windows rematerialize; alternatively, click the **Show Desktop** button to minimize the windows.

Show desktop

Figure 3.8: *Move your mouse pointer over the taskbar's **Show Desktop** button to make your windows fade away.*

Window Weight Lifting: Using Scrollbars

Often, depending on the program you're using, the document you're dealing with won't fit entirely inside the window's boundaries—even when you maximize the window. When this happens, you need some way to move to the document parts you can't see.

From the keyboard, you can use the basic navigation keys: the arrow keys, Page Up, and Page Down. Mouse users (as usual) have all the fun, they get to learn a new skill: how to use scrollbars. Using the Notepad window shown in Figure 3.9, I've pointed out the major features of the average scrollbar. Here's how to use these features to get around inside a document.

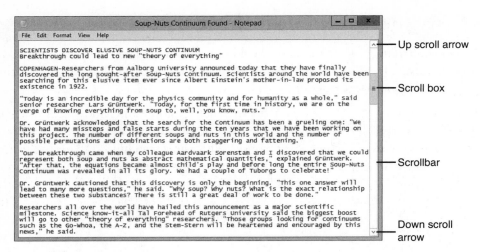

Figure 3.9: *Mouse fans get to use the scrollbar to traipse through a document.*

- To find out where you are in the document, note the position of the **scroll box**. For example, if the scroll box is about halfway down, you know you're somewhere near the middle of the document. Similarly, if the scroll box is near the bottom of the scrollbar, then you know you're near the end of the document.

- To scroll down through the document one line at a time, click the **down scroll arrow**. To scroll continuously, press and hold down the left mouse button on the **down scroll arrow**.

- To scroll up through the document one line at a time, click the **up scroll arrow**. To scroll continuously, press and hold down the left mouse button on the **up scroll arrow**.

- To leap through the document one screen at a time, click inside the scrollbar between the scroll box and the scroll arrows. For example, to move down one screen, click inside the scrollbar between the scroll box and the down scroll arrow.

- To move to a specific part of the document, click and drag the scroll box up or down.

Note, as well, that many of the windows you work in will also sport a second scrollbar that runs horizontally along the bottom of the window. Horizontal scrollbars work the same as their vertical cousins, except that they let you move left and right in documents displaying wider than your screen.

Scrolling with a Wheel Mouse

Most modern mice feature a little wheel between the two buttons. If you have one of these rotary rodents, you can scroll up and down through a document by rotating the wheel forward or backward.

Some applications (such as Microsoft's Internet Explorer and Microsoft Office) also support a feature called *panning* that lets you scroll automatically through a document and control the speed. To enable panning, click the wheel button. The application will then display an origin mark (the position of this mark varies from application to application). Drag the pointer above the origin mark to scroll up; drag the pointer below the origin mark to scroll down. Note also that the farther the pointer is from the origin mark, the faster you scroll. To turn off panning, click the wheel again.

> **DEFINITION**
>
> To **pan** means to use the mouse wheel to scroll automatically through a document.

The Least You Need to Know

- To snap a Windows 8 app into place, drag the top of the app down and then drag it to the left or right edge, or press **Windows+.** (period). On a tablet, slide your finger from the top edge of the screen and then slide the window to the left or right side of the screen.
- To minimize a desktop window means that the window disappears from the desktop, although the program continues to run. You minimize a window by clicking the **Minimize** button in the upper-right corner.
- To maximize a desktop window means that the window expands to fill the entire desktop. You maximize a window by clicking the **Maximize** button in the upper-right corner.
- To move a desktop window, use your mouse to drag the title bar to and fro.
- To size a desktop window, use your mouse to drag any of the window's borders.
- To let Windows do most of the work, right-click an empty part of the taskbar to eyeball several commands for cascading, tiling, and minimizing all windows.

Saving, Opening, Printing, and Other Document Lore

In This Chapter

- Forging a fresh document
- Saving a document for posterity
- Closing a document and opening it up again
- Getting a grip on Windows 8's newfangled libraries
- Handy document-editing techniques
- Printing a document, just for the heck of it

The purpose of the chapters here in Part 1 is to help you get comfortable with Windows 8, and if you've been following along and practicing what you've learned, you and Windows should be getting along famously by now. However, there's another concept you need to familiarize yourself with before you're ready to fully explore the Windows universe: documents.

This chapter plugs that gap in your Windows education by teaching you all the basic techniques for manipulating documents; this includes creating, saving, closing, opening, editing, and printing documents, plus much more.

What on Earth Is a Document?

Most folks think a document is a word-processing file. That's certainly true—as far as it goes—but I'm talking about a bigger picture in this chapter. Specifically, when I say *document*, what I really mean is *any* file you create by cajoling a program into doing something useful.

So yes, a file created within the confines of a word-processing program (such as WordPad) is a document. However, these are also documents: text notes typed into a text editor; images created in a graphics program; email missives composed in an email program; spreadsheets constructed with a spreadsheet program; and presentations cobbled together with a presentation graphics program. In other words, if you can create it or edit it yourself, it's a document.

Manufacturing a New Document

Lots of Windows programs—including WordPad, Notepad, and Paint—are courteous enough to offer up a new, ready-to-roll document when you start the program. This means you can just dive right into your typing or drawing or whatever. Later on, however, you may need to start another new document. To do so, use one of the following techniques:

- If the program has a menu bar, select the **File>New** command.

- If the program has a ribbon, click the **File** tab and then click **New**, as shown in Figure 4.1.

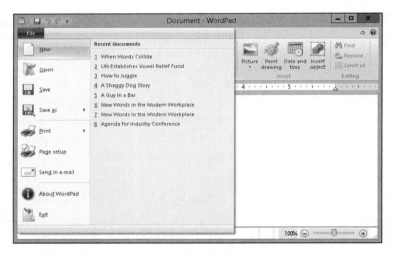

Figure 4.1: *In a ribbon-ready program such as WordPad, you start a new document by clicking the **File** tab and selecting the **New** command.*

- Click the **New** button in the program's toolbar.

- In many Windows programs, you can spit out a new document by pressing **Ctrl+N**.

In most cases, the program will then toss a fresh document onscreen. Some programs display a dialog box that asks you what kind of new document you want.

The All-Important Save Command

Save your work as soon as you can and as often as you can.

Without even a jot of hyperbole, I'm telling you right here and now, this deceptively simple slogan is probably the single most important piece of advice you'll stumble upon in this book.

Why all the fuss? Because when you work with a new document (or with an existing document), all the changes you make are stored temporarily in your computer's memory. The bad news is that memory is a fickle and transient medium that, despite its name, forgets all of its contents when you shut down Windows. If you haven't saved your document to your hard disk (which maintains its contents even when Windows isn't running—and even if your computer is turned off), you lose all the changes you've made and it's impossible to get them back. Scary!

LOOK OUT!

If your computer's memory doesn't go into clean-slate mode until you shut down Windows, you may be wondering why you can't just wait to save until you're ready to close up shop for the night. If a power failure shuts off your system or if Windows crashes—these things happen, believe me—all your unsaved work is toast. By saving regularly, you greatly lessen the chance of that happening.

To guard against such a disaster, remember my saving slogan and keep the following in mind:

- When creating a new document, save it as soon as you've entered any data that's worth keeping.

- After the new document is saved, keep right on saving it as often as you can. When I'm writing a book, I typically save my work every 30 to 60 seconds (I'm paranoid!), but a reasonable schedule is to save your work every 5 minutes or so.

Saving a New Document

Saving a new document takes a bit of extra work, but after that's out of the way, subsequent saves require only a mouse click or two. To save a new document, follow these steps:

1. Pull down the **File** menu or tab and then click the **Save** command, or click the **Save** button in the program's toolbar. The program displays a Save As dialog box like the one shown in Figure 4.2.

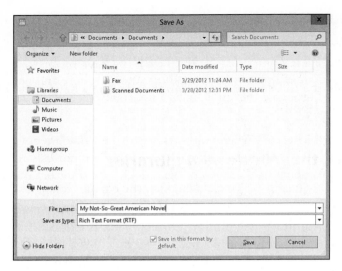

Figure 4.2: *The Save As dialog box appears when you're saving a new document.*

2. Use the **File name** text box to enter a name for your document. Note that the name you choose must be different from any other document in the folder. Also, Windows 8 lets you enter file names that are up to 255 characters. Your names can include spaces, commas, and apostrophes, but not the following characters: \ | ? : * " < > .

3. Now use the **Save as type** drop-down list to choose the type of document you want to create. In the vast majority of cases you won't have to bother with this because the default type is best. Many programs can create different document types, however, and this capability often comes in handy.

4. Click the **Save** button. The program makes a permanent copy of the document on your hard disk.

Saving an Existing Document

After all that hard work, you'll be happy to know that subsequent document saves are much easier. That's because when you select the **File, Save** command, the program simply updates the existing hard-disk copy of the document. This takes just a second or two (usually) and no dialog box shows up to pester you for information. Because this is so easy, there's no excuse not to save your work regularly. Particularly since Windows 8 offers a few even easier methods for saving a document:

- If you're a fan of keyboard shortcuts, here's one to memorize for the ages: press **Ctrl+S**.

- If you're a fan of toolbar buttons, click the **Save** toolbar button.

- Doing the ribbon thing? You can usually find a **Save** button in the Quick Access Toolbar.

Checking Out the Windows 8 Libraries

When you first open the Save As dialog box, the current folder is almost always one of the folders that Windows 8 refers to as a *library*. For example in Figure 4.2, the Save As dialog box shows the Documents library as the current folder; which, as you might figure, is a good place to store documents. Windows 8 comes with three other libraries—Music, Pictures, and Videos—and you can pretty much guess what types of files go in each library.

I highly recommend that you store all the stuff you create in one of these libraries, because they're designed to be a central storage area for all the files you create. Using libraries is a good idea for three reasons:

- It makes your documents easy to find because you know exactly where they are.

- When you want to back up your documents, you need to only select the libraries (rather than hunting around your hard disk for all your documents). (For more information about how to back up your documents, see the section in Chapter 20 titled Step 6—Back Up Your Files.)

- The libraries are easy to get to: click the **File Explorer** icon in the Start screen to open the Libraries folder (see Figure 4.3), then double-click the icon for the library you want. (If you happen to be working in the Desktop app, you can also click the **File Explorer** icon in the taskbar.)

Figure 4.3: *Click the Start screen's **File Explorer** icon to see Windows 8's library collection.*

Using the Save As Command to Make a Copy of a Document

As you slave away in Windows 8, you sometimes find that you need to create a second, slightly different, copy of a document. For example, you might create a letter and then decide that you need a second copy to send to someone else. Rather than re-creating the entire letter from scratch, it's much easier to make a copy of the existing document and then change just the address and salutation.

The easiest way to go about this is to use the Save As command. This command is a lot like Save, except it enables you to save the document with a new name and/or to a new location. (Think of it as the don't-reinvent-the-wheel command.) To use Save As to create a new document, follow these steps:

1. Open the original document—not a new one. (If you're not sure how to go about this, skip ahead to the section titled Opening an Existing Document to find out.)

2. Select the **File, Save As** command. The program displays the same Save As dialog box shown in Figure 4.2.

3. Either select a different storage location for the new document or enter a different file name—or both.

4. Click **Save.** The program closes the original document, makes a copy, and then opens the new document.

5. Make your changes to the new document (see the following section).

Getting It Right: Text Editing for Beginners

As you create your document, you have to delete text, move text to different locations, and so on. To make your electronic writing life easier, it's crucial to get these basic editing chores down pat. To that end, here's a summary of some editing techniques you can use in most any program that deals with text (including Notepad, WordPad, and Windows Live Mail):

- **Highlighting text with the mouse.** Before you can do something to existing text, you need to highlight it. To highlight text with a mouse, click and drag the mouse over the characters you want. That is, you first position the mouse pointer a teensy bit to the left of the first character you want to highlight. Then you press and hold down the left mouse button and move the mouse to the right. As you do, the characters you pass over become highlighted. While you drag, you can also move the mouse down to highlight multiple lines. When you release the mouse button, the text remains highlighted.

- **Highlighting text with the keyboard.** To highlight text by using the keyboard, position the cursor to the left of the first character, hold down the **Shift** key, and then press the **right-arrow** key until the entire selection is highlighted. Use the **down-arrow** key (or even **Page Down** if you have a lot of ground to cover) when you need to highlight multiple lines.

LOOK OUT!

If you highlight some text and then press a character on your keyboard, your entire selection will disappear and be replaced by the character you typed! (If you press the **Enter** key, the highlighted text just disappears entirely.) This is normal behavior that can cause trouble for even experienced document jockeys. To get your text back, immediately select the **Edit>Undo** command or press **Ctrl+Z**.

- **Copying highlighted text.** To make a copy of the highlighted text, select the **Edit>Copy** command. (Alternatively, you can also press **Ctrl+C** or click the **Copy** button on the ribbon or toolbar.) Then position the cursor where you want to place the copy, and select the **Edit>Paste** command. (Your other choices are to press **Ctrl+V** or click the **Paste** button on the ribbon or toolbar.) A perfect copy of your selection appears instantly. Note that you can paste this text as many times as you need.

- **Moving highlighted text.** When you need to move something from one part of a document to another, you *could* do it by making a copy, pasting it, and then going back to delete the original. If you do this, however, your colleagues will certainly make fun of you, because there's an easier way.

After you highlight what you want to move, select the **Edit>Cut** command (the shortcuts are pressing **Ctrl+X** or clicking the **Cut** button on the ribbon or toolbar). Your selection disappears from the screen—but don't panic, Windows 8 saves it for you. Position the cursor where you want to place the text, and then select **Edit>Paste.** Your stuff miraculously reappears in the new location.

- **Deleting text.** Because even the best typists make occasional typos, knowing how to delete is a necessary editing skill. Put away the Wite-Out, though, because deleting a character or two is easier (and less messy) if you use either of the following techniques: position the cursor to the right of the offending character and press the **Backspace** key; or position the cursor to the left of the character and press the **Delete** key. If you have a large chunk of material you want to expunge from the document, highlight it and press the **Delete** key or the **Backspace** key.

WINDOWS WISDOM

All this cut, copy, and paste moonshine is a bit mysterious. Where does cut text (or whatever) go? How does Windows 8 know what to paste? Does Windows 8 have some kind of digital hip pocket that it uses to store and retrieve cut or copied data? Truth be told, that's not a bad analogy. This "hip pocket" is actually a chunk of your computer's memory called the *clipboard.* Whenever you run the Cut or Copy command, Windows 8 heads to the clipboard, removes whatever currently resides there, and stores the cut or copied data. When you issue the Paste command, Windows 8 grabs whatever is on the clipboard and tosses it into your document.

- **To err is human, to undo divine.** What do you do if you paste text to the wrong spot or consign a vital piece of an irreplaceable document to deletion purgatory? Happily, Notepad, WordPad, and many other Windows 8 programs have an Undo feature to get you out of these jams. To reverse your most recent action, select the **Edit>Undo** command to restore everything to the way it was before you made your blunder. And yes, there are shortcuts you can use: try either pressing **Ctrl+Z** or clicking the **Undo** button on the ribbon or toolbar.

It's important to remember that most of the time the Undo command usually only undoes your most recent action. So if you delete something, perform some other task, and then try to undo the deletion, chances are the program won't let you do it. Therefore, always try to run **Undo** immediately after making your error. Note, however, that some programs are more flexible and will let you undo several actions. In this case, you just keep selecting the **Undo** command until your document is back the way you want it.

Closing a Document

Some weakling Windows programs (such as WordPad and Paint) allow you to open only one document at a time. In such programs, you can close the document you're currently working on by starting a new document, by opening another document, or by quitting the program altogether.

However, most full-featured Windows programs let you open as many documents as you want (subject to the usual memory limitations that govern all computer work). In this case, each open document appears inside its own window called a *document window*, not surprisingly. These document windows have their own versions of the Minimize, Maximize, Restore, and Close buttons. Also, the name of each document appears on the program's Window menu, which you can use to switch from one document to another.

Because things can get crowded pretty fast, though, you probably want to close any documents you don't need at the moment. To do this, activate the document you want to close and select the **File>Close** command; or click the document window's **Close** button. If you made changes to the document since last saving it, a dialog box appears asking whether you want to save those changes. Click **Yes** to save, **No** to discard the changes, or **Cancel** to leave the document open. In most programs that support multiple open documents, you also can close the current document by pressing **Ctrl+F4**.

Opening an Existing Document

After you've saved a document or two, you often need to get one of them back onscreen to make changes or review your handiwork. To do that, you need to open the document by using any one of the following techniques:

- **Use the Open dialog box.** Select the **File>Open** command. (Alternatively, press **Ctrl+O** or click the **Open** button on the ribbon or toolbar.) Find the document you want to open, highlight it, and then click **Open**.

- **Use a library.** If you're using a Windows 8 library to store your stuff, you can open a document by displaying the folder (select **Start** and then click your **User name**), opening the appropriate library (such as **Documents** or **Pictures**), and then double-clicking the document's icon. If the appropriate application isn't running, Windows 8 will start it for you and load the document automatically.

- **Use the Files search panes.** In the Windows 8 Start screen, press **Windows+F** to open the Files search pane, then start typing the name of the document. When the name of the document shows up in the search results, click the document to open it.

Sending a Document to the Printer

The nice thing about printing in Windows 8 is that the basic steps you follow are more or less identical in each and every Windows program. After you learn the fundamentals, you can apply them to all your Windows applications. Here are the steps you need to follow:

1. In your program, open the document you want to print.

2. Select the **File>Print** command; this opens a Print dialog box similar to the one shown in Figure 4.4 for the WordPad word processor.

   If your fingers are poised over your keyboard, you may find that in most applications pressing **Ctrl+P** is a faster way to get to the Print dialog box. If you just want a single copy of the document, click the **Print** toolbar button to bypass the Print dialog box and print the document directly.

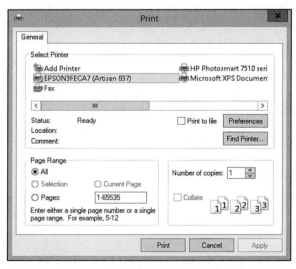

Figure 4.4: *WordPad's Print dialog box is a typical example of the species.*

3. The options in the Print dialog box vary slightly from application to application, but you almost always see three things:

   - A list for selecting the printer to use. In WordPad's Print dialog box, for example, use the **Select Printer** list to select the printer.

   - A text box or spin box to enter the number of copies you want. In the WordPad Print dialog box, use the **Number of copies** text box.

SEE ALSO

Before you can print, you may need to tell Windows 8 what type of printer you have. I tell you how to go about this in Chapter 6. See the section titled Device Advice I: Installing Hardware.

   - Some controls for selecting how much of the file to print. You normally have the option of printing the entire document or a specific range of pages. (WordPad's Print dialog box also includes a Selection option button you can activate to print only the currently highlighted text.)

4. When you've chosen your options, click the **Print** button to start printing (some Print dialog boxes have an **OK** button instead).

Keep watching the information area of the taskbar (the area to the left of the clock). After a few seconds (depending on the size of the document), a printer icon appears, as shown in Figure 4.5. This tells you that Windows 8 is hard at work farming out the document to your printer. This icon disappears after the printer has finished its job. If you have an exceptionally speedy printer, this icon may come and go without you laying eyes on it. If the printer icon shows up with a red question mark icon superimposed on it, it means there's a problem with the printer.

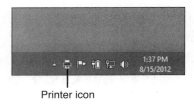

Printer icon

Figure 4.5: *The printer icon tells you that Windows 8 is printing.*

The Least You Need to Know

- To forge a new document, select the **File>New** command; or press **Ctrl+N**; or click the toolbar's **New** button.

- To save a document, select the **File>Save** command; or press **Ctrl+S**; or click the **Save** button. If you're saving a new document, use the Save As dialog box to pick out a location and a name for the document.

- You'll simplify your life immeasurably if you store all your files in the libraries provided by Windows 8.

- Press **Backspace** to delete the character to the left of the cursor; press **Delete** to wipe out the character to the right; press **Ctrl+Z** to undo your most recent mistake.

- To open a document, select the **File>Open** command; or press **Ctrl+O**; or click the **Open** button.

- To print a document, select the **File>Print** command; press **Ctrl+P**; or click the **Print** button.

Fiddling with Files and Folders

In This Chapter

- Exploring your files and folders with File Explorer
- Creating, selecting, copying, moving, renaming, deleting, and searching for files and folders
- Burning files to a CD
- Sending files to the cloud (whatever that is)
- A fistful of useful file and folder factoids

In Chapter 4, you learned that it's off-the-scale crucial to save your documents as soon and often as you can. That way, you preserve your documents within the stable confines of your computer's hard disk. You also learned that it's best to use your user-account libraries as the central storage locations for your stuff.

You learned, in other words, that your hard disk is a vital chunk of digital real estate. So as a responsible landowner, it's important for you to tend your plot and keep your grounds well maintained. That's the purpose of this chapter: it shows you how to use some of Windows 8's built-in tools to work with your hard disk's files, folders, and libraries. You get the scoop on creating new files, folders, and libraries; copying and moving files from one folder to another; renaming and deleting files and folders; and much more.

Navigating with File Explorer

The Windows 8 program you use to explore your computer and its files and folders is called, appropriately enough, File Explorer. There are two main ways to coax this program onto the screen.

* In the Windows 8 Start screen, type **explorer** and then click the **File Explorer** tile.

* If you're currently hanging around in the Desktop app, click the **File Explorer** icon in the taskbar.

Either way, you end up eyeballing a window that looks suspiciously like the one shown in Figure 5.1.

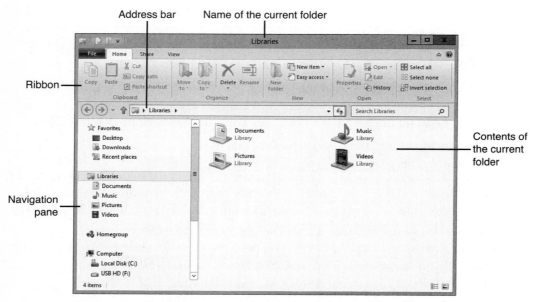

Figure 5.1: *Use File Explorer to check out your computer's files and folders.*

The job of File Explorer is to display the contents of a given folder so that you can check out what's in the folder or muck about with those contents in some way—such as renaming one of your files (see Renaming a File or Folder later in this chapter). File Explorer is set up to help you do just that. First, notice that the address bar shows you the name of the current folder File Explorer is displaying. In this case, the name of the folder is Libraries, which displays the following icons for your user libraries:

* **Documents.** Use this folder to store all the documents that don't fit into more specific folders such as Music and Pictures.

* **Music.** Use this folder to store your music and sound files.

* **Pictures.** Use this folder to store your digital images and photos.

● **Videos.** Use this folder to store your digital videos and movies.

Navigating to a File

One of the most common chores associated with Windows Explorer is navigating through various folders and subfolders (folders within folders) to get to a particular file.

You have a couple of ways to get started:

● If you see the folder you want in the navigation pane, go ahead and click it to display its contents. The Favorites section includes a few common folders, such as Desktop and Downloads; the Libraries section contains your four main user account folders; and the Computer section contains disk drives for your computer. I talk a bit about the Homegroup section in Chapter 12.

● If you see the folder you want in the contents area, double-click it. For example, if you're on the hunt for a video file, you'd double-click the **Videos** folder.

If the file you want resides in the folder you opened, then rest easy because your navigation chores are done. Unfortunately, you rarely get off so easily in Windows 8. That's because it's quite common to have a file squirreled away in a subfolder. For example, take a look at Figure 5.2, where I've opened the Music library on my system. As you can see, this folder consists of nothing but subfolders.

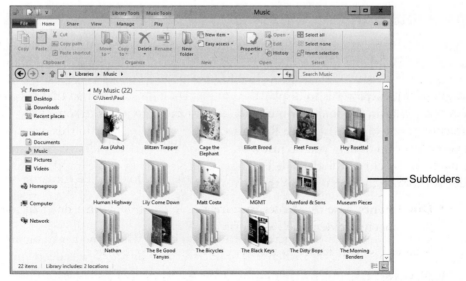

Figure 5.2: *You may need to navigate several subfolders to get to the file you want.*

If the file you want is in one of the subfolders, double-click the subfolder's icon. Repeat this as often as necessary to reach the file you want. For example, Figure 5.3 shows the results on my system after I double-clicked the Human Highway folder (this is the name of a band) and then double-clicked yet another subfolder named Moody Motorcycle (this is the name of a Human Highway album).

Music files

Figure 5.3: *Opening a folder reveals the contents of that folder.*

Getting Around in File Explorer

As you navigate from one subfolder to the next, notice that the File Explorer address bar changes as you do. For example, when I start out in my user folder, the address bar just shows Libraries. If I then open the Music subfolder, the address changes to Libraries > Music (see Figure 5.2). When I open the Human Highway folder and then the Moody Motorcycle folder, the address bar looks like this (see Figure 5.3):

Libraries > Music > Human Highway > Moody Motorcycle

In other words, each time you go down into another subfolder, File Explorer shows you the "path" you've taken to get there by tacking on the name of the current subfolder.

However, the address-bar path isn't just to let you know where the heck you are (although that's welcome info when you're buried three or four levels deep and are up to your digital armpits in subfolders). Even better, you can use the path to navigate your way to other folders. There are two basic techniques:

- **To navigate back.** Click any item in the path to jump directly to that folder. For example, in the path shown in Figure 5.3, clicking Music would take me directly to the Music folder.

- **To navigate sideways (sort of).** Click the little arrow to the right of one of the path folders. This displays a list of all the available subfolders, as shown in Figure 5.4. Click one of those subfolders to jump directly to it.

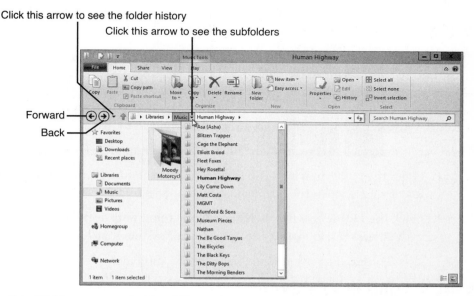

Figure 5.4: *Clicking an arrow beside a folder in the path reveals the available subfolders that you can leap to directly.*

Here are a few other pointers for navigating from folder to folder in File Explorer:

- To go back to the previous folder, you can also click the **Back** button (pointed out in Figure 5.4). There are also a couple of keyboard shortcuts that you can use: **Backspace** and **Alt+Left Arrow**.

- After you've gone back to a previous folder, you can move forward again by clicking the **Forward** button. The keyboard shortcut for this is **Alt+Right Arrow**.

- Rather than stepping back and forward one folder at a time, you can leap over multiple folders in a single bound. To do this, click the **downward-pointing arrow** to the right of the **Forward** toolbar button. In the list that appears, click the folder you want to visit.

Workaday File and Folder Maintenance

Now that you and File Explorer are getting acquainted, it's time to put this digital domestic to good use. Specifically, the next few sections show you how to use File Explorer to perform no fewer than nine workaday chores for files and folders: creating, selecting, copying, moving, renaming, previewing, deleting, compressing, and burning.

Creating a New File, Folder, or Library

If you want to manufacture a shiny new file for yourself, the best way to go about it is to run the appropriate application and select that program's **File>New** command. (Note, too, that most programs—including Windows 8 WordPad and Notepad accessories—create a new file for you automatically when you start them.) You then select the **File>Save** command to save the file to your hard disk.

However, it *is* possible to create a new file within File Explorer. Here's how:

1. Open the folder in which you want to create the file. If you're not sure which folder to use, open the all-purpose Documents folder.

2. Click the **Home** tab and then click **New item**. This displays another menu with at least the following file names (your system may have more):

    - **Folder.** This command creates a new subfolder.

    - **Shortcut.** This command creates a shortcut, which acts as a pointer to a program or document.

    - **Contact.** This command creates a new contact to whom you can send email. (See Chapter 14 for more.)

    - **Journal Document.** This command creates a new Windows Journal file, which you use to jot handwritten notes if you have a digital pen and a tablet-style PC.

    - **Rich Text Document.** This command creates a slightly different type of WordPad file.

    - **Text Document.** This command creates a plain text file that's the same as what you create using the Notepad program.

    - **Compressed (zipped) Folder.** This command creates a special folder that compresses multiple files into a smaller package suitable for sending over the internet. I talk more about this type of file later in this chapter, in the section Creating a Compressed Folder.

3. Select the type of file you want. Windows 8 creates the new file and displays a generic (boring) name—such as "New Text Document"—in a text box.

4. Type a name that makes sense, and then press **Enter** or click some of the blank real estate inside the window.

If you misspell the file name or simply change your mind, just hold tight and I'll teach you how to change the file name later in this chapter. If Windows 8 complains about a particular character that you try to use, leave it out for now. I'll tell you about the rules for file names a bit later. (In both cases, see the section Renaming a File or Folder, later in this chapter.)

What about creating a brand-spanking-new library if you find that the standard-issue Documents, Music, Pictures, and Videos libraries don't cut the digital mustard? Sure, why not? For example, you might want a separate library for recorded TV shows, or a library for files related to some all-important project you're working on. Whatever your need, here are the steps to follow to forge a new library:

1. In any File Explorer window, click **Libraries** in the Navigation pane.

2. Click the **Home** tab, click **New Item**, and then click **Library**. Windows 8 coughs up a new library and displays a generic name.

3. Type a name for the library and then press **Enter**.

Your library is sadly empty right now, but I'll show you a bit later how to fill it up (check out Including a Folder in a Library, later in this chapter).

Selecting Files and Folders

Before getting to the rest of the file-maintenance fun, you need to know how to select the files or folders that you want to horse around with.

Let's begin with the simplest case: selecting a single file or folder. This is a two-step procedure:

1. Open the folder that contains the file or subfolder you want to mess with.

2. In the folder contents list, click the file's icon.

So far, so good. However, there will be plenty of times when you need to deal with two or more files or folders. For example, you might want to herd several files onto a flash drive or memory card. Rather than dealing with the files one at a time, you can do the whole thing in one fell swoop by first selecting all the files and then moving (or copying, or whatever) them as a group. Windows 8 offers the following methods.

- **Selecting consecutive items.** If the files or folders you want to select are listed consecutively, say "Ooh, how convenient!" and then do this: select the first item, hold down the **Shift** key, select the last item, and then release **Shift.** Windows 8 kindly does the dirty work of selecting all the items in between.

- **Selecting nonconsecutive items.** If the files or folders you want to select are listed willy-nilly, say "Oy, why me?!" and then do this: select the first item, hold down the **Ctrl** key, click each of the other items, and then release **Ctrl.** If you click something by accident, don't sweat it: just click it again to deselect it.

- **Selecting all items.** If you want to select everything inside a folder: select the **Organize>Select all** command, or press **Ctrl+A.**

> **WINDOWS WISDOM**
>
> If you're running Windows 8 on a tablet, you can select a single file by tapping it. To select several consecutive files, drag your finger over the files. To select several nonconsecutive files, well, that's a tad tricky because it depends on the current view. For list-like views (such as List and Details), tap to the left of each file to select its check box; for icon views (such as Large Icons and Tiles), tap the top-left corner of each file's icon to select its check box.

Copying and Moving a File or Folder

A copy of a file or folder is an exact replica of the original that you store on another part of your hard disk or on a removable disk (such as a flash drive or memory card). Copies are useful for making backups or if you want to transport a file or folder to another computer.

Note, too, that the location of files and folders you create isn't set in stone. If you're not happy with the current location, there's no problem moving a file or folder somewhere else.

> **WINDOWS WISDOM**
>
> Windows 8 has a special Send To menu that contains commonly used destinations, such as your Desktop or a flash drive. To see this menu, right-click an item and then click **Send to.** Now select the destination you want, and Windows 8 copies the selected items lickety-split.

Here are the steps to follow:

1. Select the files or folders you want to transport.

2. Click the **Home** tab and then click one of the following commands:

   Copy. Choose this if you're copying files or folders.

   Cut. Choose this if you're moving files or folders.

3. Navigate to the destination folder or disk drive.

4. Click the **Home** tab and then click **Paste**.

Including a Folder in a Library

I've mentioned Windows 8's new libraries a few times now, but I haven't bothered to properly introduce them to you. Fortunately, there's not much to know: a library is a special folder that acts as a collection of folders from different parts of your system. For example, a library might include a folder from your hard drive, another folder from an external hard drive connected to your computer, and even a third folder from some other computer on your network! The library displays all the files from the various locations as a single collection, so a library is a handy way to consolidate related files from different places.

It's important to bear in mind that Windows 8 doesn't actually consolidate all those files, in the sense that it moves them into the library. Instead the library just displays the files while leaving them in their original locations. This is why the tall-forehead types at Microsoft insist on referring to libraries as *virtual* folders. This means that when you include a folder in a library, all you're doing is telling Windows 8 to display the contents of the folder in the library; the actual folder isn't tampered with in any way.

To include a folder in a library, navigate to the folder you want to include in the library, click the folder icon, click the **Home** tab, click **Easy access**, and then click **Include in library**. In the list of libraries that appears (see Figure 5.5), click the library you want to use.

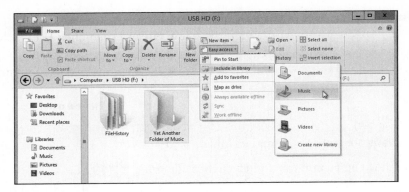

Figure 5.5: *Select the folder and then click* **Include in library** *to add it to one of your Windows 8 libraries.*

Renaming a File or Folder

Windows 8 supports file and folder names up to about 255 characters long, so you don't have to settle for boring monikers on the files and folders you create. If you don't like a name, feel free to rename it. Follow these simple steps to rename a file or folder:

1. Select the file or folder you want to rename. (You can work with only one item at a time for this.)

2. Run the **Home>Rename** command, or press **F2**. Windows 8 creates a text box around the name.

3. Edit the name as you see fit.

4. When you're done, press **Enter**.

Bear in mind that although Windows 8 likes long file names and accepts most keyboard characters (including spaces), there are nine characters that are strictly prohibited: * | \ : " < > ? /.

Previewing a File

When you want to eyeball what's in a file, you normally double-click the file to load it into whatever program is associated with that type of file. That's easy enough, I suppose, but it does seem like overkill if all you want is a quick peek at what's going on inside a file.

Fortunately, Windows 8 understands this and offers a faster way to display a preview of any file. To give this a whirl, click the **View** tab and then click **Preview pane**. Now select the file you want to get a gander at and File Explorer uses the Preview pane to show it to you. Figure 5.6 shows an example of the Preview pane at work.

The Preview pane

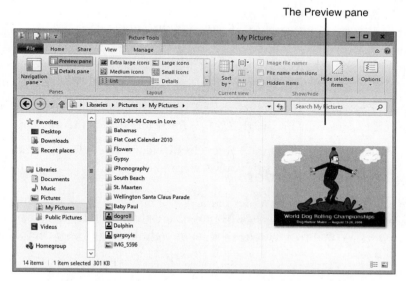

Figure 5.6: *File Explorer with its Preview pane on the job.*

Deleting a File or Folder

Although most of today's hard disks boast a mammoth amount of real estate, you could still run out of room one day if you don't delete the file debris that you no longer use. Deleting unwanted files and folders is fairly easy:

1. Select the files or folders you want to blow away.

2. Click the **Home** tab.

3. Click the top half of the **Delete** button (you can also just press **Delete**). Windows 8 goes right ahead and consigns the poor things to the cold, cruel *Recycle Bin*.

DEFINITION

The **Recycle Bin** is a special storage area that Windows 8 has set aside for deleted files and folders.

HACKING WINDOWS

Another way to delete a file or folder is to drag it from File Explorer and drop it on the desktop's Recycle Bin icon.

What happens if you nuke some crucial file or folder that you'd give your right arm to have back? Assuming you need your right arm, if the deletion was the last thing you did, you don't have to bother with the Recycle Bin. Just press **Ctrl+Z** to salvage the file. (Note that it will be placed back in the folder where you originally deleted it, not necessarily in the folder you are currently in.) In fact, Windows 8 is only too happy to let you reverse the last *10* actions you performed (press **Ctrl+Z** up to 10 times).

If the Ctrl+Z command doesn't get the job done, then Windows 8 offers an alternative method to save your bacon: the *Recycle Bin*. Here's how it works:

1. Double-click the desktop's **Recycle Bin** icon. The folder that appears contains a list of all the stuff you've expunged recently.

2. Select the files or folders you want to recover.

3. Under the **Tools** tab, click **Manage**, and then click **Restore the selected items**. Windows 8 marches the items right back to where they came from. Whew!

How the heck can the Recycle Bin restore a deleted file?

Good question. You can get part of the answer by looking at the Recycle Bin icon on your Windows 8 desktop. It looks like a garbage can, and that's sort of what the Recycle Bin is like. Think about it: if you toss a piece of paper into the garbage, there's nothing to stop you from reaching in and pulling it back out. The Recycle Bin operates the same way: it's really just a special hidden folder (called *Recycled*) on your hard disk. When you delete a file, Windows 8 moves the file into the Recycled folder. So restoring a file is a simple matter of reaching into the folder and pulling out the file. The Recycle Bin handles all this for you (and even returns your file without wrinkles and coffee grounds). However, just like when you hand your trash to the garbage man, after you empty the Recycle Bin (by right-clicking the desktop's **Recycle Bin** icon and then clicking **Empty Recycle Bin**), there is no retrieving lost files.

Creating a Compressed Folder

When you download files from the internet, they often arrive as .zip files. These are files that have been compressed for faster downloading. In Windows 8, a zip file is called a *compressed folder*. Why a folder? Because a zip file contains one or more files, just like a regular folder. As you'll see, this makes it easy to deal with the files within the zippered folder, and it enables Windows 8 to offer a few useful compression and decompression features.

To create a zip file (compressed folder), there are two methods you can use:

- Select the items you want to store in the zip file, right-click any of the selected items, and then click the **Send To>Compressed (zipped) folder** command. Windows 8 creates a zip file with the same name as the last file you selected.

- Create a new, empty zip file by selecting the **Home>New item>Compressed (zipped) Folder** command. Windows 8 creates a new zip file with an active text box. Edit the name and press **Enter**. You can then drag the files you want to archive and drop them on the zip file's icon.

To see what's inside a zip file, double-click it. Windows 8 opens the file as a folder that shows the files within the zipped folder as the folder contents.

To extract all of the files from a zip: click the file, click the **Extract** tab, and then click **Extract all** to display the Select a Destination and Extract Files dialog box. Type the destination for the extracted files, or click **Browse** to select the destination using a dialog box. When you're good and ready, click **Extract**. Windows 8 extracts the files and then displays a new window showing the destination folder.

SEE ALSO

What if you only want to extract one or two of the files? Not a problem. You can do this by copying the file or files in the compressed folder and then pasting them inside the destination folder. See Copying and Moving a File or Folder, earlier in the chapter, for the details.

Burning Files to a CD or DVD Disc

In the world before Windows 8, burning files to a CD was an exercise in utter confusion: you had to know the difference between CD-R and CD-RW (and even CD±RW, just to be cruel), what types of discs your CD burner could take, the subtle differences between recordable and rewritable discs, and on and on. And burning DVDs with those older versions of Windows? In your dreams!

Windows 8 changes all that by enabling you to burn files to any type of disc you want—and you can even add and remove files from any type of disc at any time. Is this a miracle? No, it's just that Windows 8 has figured out a way to treat a CD or DVD disc like a hard disk, flash drive, or any other file-storage medium.

So if you have a CD or DVD burner attached to your computer, Windows 8 should recognize it and be ready to burn at will. To try this out, you first have to set up the disc by following these steps:

1. Insert a CD disc into your CD burner—or a CD or DVD into your DVD burner. (If a notification shows up, move the mouse pointer over the message and then click **X** to get rid of it.)

2. In File Explorer, open the **Computer** branch in the Navigation pane and then click the CD or DVD drive. The first time you do this, the Burn a Disc dialog box appears.

3. Type a disc title, make sure the **Like a USB flash drive** option is selected, and then click **Next**. Windows 8 formats the disc to make it ready to receive files. This may take a while, so groom your dog while you wait.

When all that malarkey is done (again, if you're pestered by a notification, say "Grrr" and click **X**), you're ready to get down to the burning thing by following these steps:

1. In File Explorer, select the files or folders you want to burn to the disc.

2. Click the **Share** tab and then click **Burn to disc**. Windows 8 copies the files to the disc.

3. Repeat steps 1 and 2 until you've sent all the files you want to the disc.

4. In the File Explorer Navigation pane, click the disc.

5. Click the **Drive** tab and then click **Close session**. Windows 8 finalizes the disc, which can take a minute or two.

6. Click **Eject**. Windows 8 spits out the disc.

Finding a File in That Mess You Call a Hard Disk

Bill Gates, Microsoft's co-founder, used to summarize his company's mission of easy access to data as "information at your fingertips." We're still a long way off from that laudable goal, but there are a few things you can do to ensure that the info you need is never far away:

- **Store stuff in your user profile.** The most inefficient way to store documents is to scatter them around your hard disk. A much better approach is to plop everything in a single place so you always know where to look for things. The perfect place for this is your user profile (that is, your Windows 8 user account), which consists of all your libraries.

- **Use subfolders to organize your documents.** Stuffing stuff into your user folder is a good idea (if I do say so myself), but you shouldn't just cram all your files into that one folder. Instead, create subfolders to hold related items. As you saw earlier, Windows 8 starts you off with subfolders (actually, libraries) named Documents, Pictures, Music, and Videos. Feel free to add other subfolders for things such as letters, memos, projects, presentations, spreadsheets, tirades to the editor, bad poetry, and whatever other categories you can think of.

- **Give your files meaningful names.** Take advantage of Windows 8's long file-name capability to give your documents names that tell you exactly what's inside each file. A document named "Letter" doesn't tell you much, but "Letter to A. Gore Re: Inventing the internet" surely does.

- **Dejunk your folders.** Keep your folders clean by deleting any files that you'll never use again.

If you're like most people, then you'll probably end up with hundreds of documents, but if you follow these suggestions, finding the one you need shouldn't be a problem. Even so, there will be times when you don't remember exactly which document you need, or you want to find all documents containing a particular word or phrase. For these situations, Windows 8 offers a Search feature that can help you track down what you need.

Start Screen Searching

One of the nifty features in Windows 8 is the capability to perform quick-and-not-even-remotely-dirty searches from the friendly confines of the Start screen. Really! Just start typing a word or phrase that more or less identifies the item you seek. It could be part of the file name, some text from a document, the name of a band, and so on. Windows 8 switches immediately into search mode and displays the results of its labors, which fall into four categories:

- **Apps** that include your search text.

- **Settings** and options with names that include your search text.

- **Files** in your user account—documents, music, photos, and videos—with names or contents that include your search text.

- **Specific Windows 8 apps.** These are icons that enable you to apply your search text to the app you choose. For example, you can choose Mail to search your email, People to search your contacts, or Internet Explorer to run a web search.

Figure 5.7 shows an example search, in this case, for "calc." A search pane appears on the right, which includes the Search box at the top, into which Windows 8 automatically adds your search text. Below that you see the Apps, Settings, and Files search categories; you click the one you want to use (such as Files in Figure 5.7). If you want to apply the search to a specific Windows 8 app, click the app's icon in the search pane.

WINDOWS WISDOM

You can specify the kind of search you want to perform in advance. For a settings search, press **Windows+W**; for a file search, press **Windows+F**.

Figure 5.7: *Windows 8 lets you perform on-the-fly searches right from the Start screen.*

If you see the program or file you want, click it to open it. To run another search, type your text in the Search box and press **Enter**.

As-You-Type Searching

The Start screen search scours *all* of your PC's apps, settings, and user account files. However, you may need to perform a more targeted search. For example, suppose you have thousands of music files or hundreds of digital images. How do you find a document needle in such an electronic haystack?

Windows 8's solution is to also enable you to perform as-you-type searches in any folder by using the Instant Search box that appears to the right of the address bar. Again, you just type your search word or phrase in the box, and then File Explorer displays those files in the current folder with names, contents, or properties that match your search text, as shown in Figure 5.8.

Figure 5.8: *You can also run as-you-type searches in any folder window.*

SEE ALSO

You can also run as-you-type searches in some Windows 8 programs, including Windows Live Photo Gallery (see Chapter 8), Windows Media Player (see Chapter 10), and Windows Live Mail (see Chapter 14).

Shipping a File to Your SkyDrive

When systems geeks create diagrams of their networks, they usually include relatively faithful renderings of tangible objects such as computers, routers, and modems, but the amorphous, intangible, and opaque nature of the internet has long been represented by a cloud.

This cloud metaphor is a pervasive one, and it's the reason why nowadays, when people talk about using internet-based software and hardware, they say they're working (playing, sharing, or whatever) in the *cloud*. It's also the source of the phrase *cloud computing*. This is a new type of computing, in which our data—and even the software we use to work with that data—resides within the cloud; we access everything not only with our PCs, but also with cloud-friendly devices such as tablet PCs and smartphones, such as Windows phones.

Windows 8 is designed with the cloud in mind, so if you log in using a Microsoft account, it uses the cloud to synchronize your settings with any other PC using the same account. It also means you can store some of your files in the cloud, which allows you to access them from anywhere. The Microsoft version of cloud storage is called *SkyDrive*, and you follow these steps to ship a file there:

1. In the Start screen, click the **SkyDrive** tile. The SkyDrive app loads and displays your SkyDrive folders (see Figure 5.9).

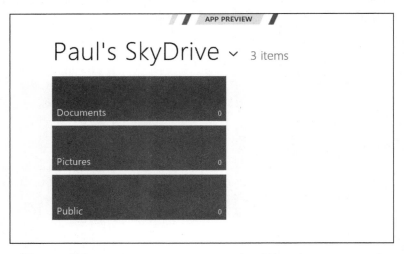

Figure 5.9: *Your SkyDrive comes with a few folders to get you started.*

2. Click the folder you want to use. SkyDrive opens the folder and displays its contents.

3. Right-click the screen and then click **Add** in the Application bar. The Files screen appears.

4. Use the **Files** list to choose the folder that has the file you want to ship.

5. Click the file.

6. Click **Add to SkyDrive**. The SkyDrive app uploads the file to the cloud.

The Least You Need to Know

- You select a file or folder by clicking it. To select multiple files or folders, hold down **Ctrl** and click each item.

- To move stuff, select the files or folders and then click **Home>Cut**. Alternatively, to copy, select the files or folders and then click **Home>Copy**. Display the destination folder and then click **Home>Paste** to complete the move or copy.

- To burn data to a formatted CD or DVD, select the files and folders and then click **Share>Burn to disc**.

- To search for a file, type your search word or phrase in the Search screen or in a folder-window Search box.

- To send a file to your SkyDrive, click the **SkyDrive** tile, open SkyDrive folder, right-click the screen, and then click **Add**.

Installing and Removing Programs and Devices

In This Chapter

- Installing and removing chunks of Windows 8
- Installing and removing software programs
- Step-by-step procedures for installing all kinds of devices
- Installing specific devices such as printers, modems, joysticks, and scanners
- Saying *adios* to devices you no longer need

It's one thing to understand that the PC is a versatile beast that can handle all kinds of different programs and devices, but it's quite another to actually install stuff. This chapter will help by showing you exactly how to install Windows 8 components, software programs, and devices on your machine. For good measure, you also learn how to uninstall all those things, just in case they don't get along with your computer.

The Welcome Wagon: Installing a Program

As you work through this book, you'll see that Windows 8 comes stocked with a decent collection of programs, some of which are first-rate (such as Internet Explorer and Windows Media Player) and some of which are merely okay (such as Paint and WordPad). Also, most PC manufacturers are kind enough to stock their machines with a few extra programs.

However, it's a rare computer owner who's satisfied with just these freebies—or even wants them in the first place. Most of us want something better or faster or just plain *cooler*. If that describes you and you decide to take the plunge on a new program, this section shows you how to install it in Windows 8.

Installing from the Windows Store

As you see a bit later, one way to install a program is to purchase it from a retail store and use the disc that comes with the package to load the program onto your PC. It all seems rather primitive, doesn't it? In recent years we've been able to reach out and grab programs from the web and install them by running a downloaded file. That has a more modern feel to it, but unless you know exactly what you're looking for, it's often hard to find new programs online.

Microsoft aims to change all that—that is, to make it easier to find and install programs—by offering the Windows Store. The Windows Store is an app that comes with Windows 8 and its sole purpose in life is to offer a slick and simple way to find new apps and install them with as little fuss as possible.

To see how it works, click the **Store** tile on the Start screen. The Windows Store app loads, and on the initial screen is the Spotlight section, which highlights a few recent apps. Scroll (or swipe, if you're using a tablet) to the right and you see all kinds of app categories: Games, Social, Entertainment, Photos, and many more. You have three ways to deal with these categories:

- If you see an app you'd like to learn more about, click it.

- Click a category's **Top free** tile to see a list of the most popular free apps in that category, and then click an app.

- Click a category name to see a complete list of the apps in that category, and then click an app.

Whichever method you choose, you end up at an app info screen, which will look something like the one shown in Figure 6.1. Click the **Overview**, **Details**, and **Reviews** tabs to get the scoop on the app. From there, you can usually either click **Try** (to install a trial version of the app) or click **Buy** (to purchase the app and install it); many free apps come with an **Install** button instead of Buy. Windows 8 busies itself installing the app, and then displays a notification in the upper-right corner of the screen to let you know when the installation is complete.

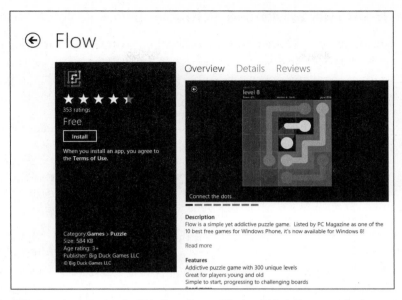

Figure 6.1: *Window shopping in the Windows Store. Use an app's info page to learn more about it and then either try it or buy it.*

Installing Windows Live Essentials

Windows Live Essentials is a collection of programs that Microsoft makes available on the web for downloading to your computer. These programs include Mail (for working with email; see Chapter 14, Sending and Receiving Email with Windows Live Mail), Photo Gallery (for viewing and editing digital photos; see Chapter 8, Managing Your Pictures with Windows 8), and Movie Maker (for editing digital video; see Chapter 11, Making Movies with Windows 8).

To get your mitts on these programs, you need to connect to the internet (as explained in Chapter 7), download them, and then install them. Fortunately, Windows 8 uses an installation program to handle most of the dirty work for you automatically, so you need only follow these steps:

1. In the Start screen, click **Internet Explorer**. The Windows 8 version of Internet Explorer opens up. (If this is the first you've seen of this Internet Explorer business, see Chapter 13 for a crash course.)

2. In the Address box at the bottom of the screen, type **download.live.com** and press **Enter**. Internet Explorer whisks you to the Windows Live Essentials page.

3. Click **Download now**. Internet Explorer asks what you want to do next.

4. Say "Chill, dude!" and click **Run**. User Account Control wonders if you really know what you're doing.

5. Slap your forehead in mock exasperation and click **Yes**. At long last the Windows Live Essentials installation program shows up.

6. Click **Choose the programs you want to install**. The Select Programs to Install dialog box appears, as shown in Figure 6.2.

Figure 6.2: *Use this window to decide which Windows Live Essentials programs you want to shoehorn into your PC.*

7. Activate the check box beside each program you want to install. (If you're not sure about a particular program, move the mouse pointer over it to see a description.)

8. Click **Install**. Windows 8 installs your selected programs.

Installing a New Program

What if you're looking to fill in a software niche that Windows 8 doesn't cover, either via the Windows Store or the Windows Live Essentials programs? In that case, you need to go outside the Windows box (literally!) and purchase an appropriate program. This often means going to a computer store, but you can also purchase software on the internet.

After you have the program, your next chore is to install it. This means you run a setup routine that makes the program ready for use on your computer. Most setup procedures perform the following tasks:

- Create a new folder for the program.

- Copy any files that the program needs to run to the new folder and to other strategic folders on your hard disk.

- Tweak Windows 8 as needed to ensure that the program runs properly.

WINDOWS WISDOM

I recommend that you accept the default values offered by the install program unless you *really* know what you're doing. In particular, if the program gives you a choice of a "typical" or a "custom" installation, go the "typical" route to save yourself time and hassle. You can always go back and install additional components for the specific program later. (See the following section, Changing a Program's Installed Components.)

How you launch this setup routine depends on how the program is distributed:

- **The program is on a disc.** After you insert the disc, Windows 8 automatically looks for an installation program. If it finds one, it displays a notification that says **Tap to choose what happens with software and games**. Click the notification to display a list that includes an option that says something like "Run SETUP.EXE." Click that option to get the installation underway.

- **You downloaded the program from the internet.** In this case, you end up with the downloaded file on your hard disk. Be sure this file resides in an otherwise-empty folder and then double-click the file. This either launches the setup routine or it extracts a bunch of files into the folder. If the latter happens, look for an application file named Setup (or, more rarely, Install), and then double-click that file.

- **All other cases.** If you have a disc-based program for which Windows 8 can't find an installation program, or a program distributed on some other removable medium (such as a flash drive), use the Start screen to click **File Explorer**, open the drive, and then double-click the installation program (usually called Setup or Install).

From here, follow the instructions and prompts that the setup routine sends your way. (This procedure varies from program to program.)

> **HACKING WINDOWS**
>
> Sometimes installing a program can wreak havoc on your system. The quickest way to recover from a bad installation is to restore your system to the way it was before you ran the setup program. The only way to do that is to set a restore point just before you run the setup program. A *restore point* is a kind of digital snapshot of your computer's current configuration. If things go awry, you can tell Windows 8 to consult that snapshot and return the system to what it was before the rogue program did its damage. To learn how to set and use restore points, see Chapters 20 and 22.

Changing a Program's Installed Components

When you install most programs, the setup software puts the entire program onto your computer. However, some larger programs (such as Microsoft Office) will only install some of their components. If you find you're missing something when working with the program, follow these steps to install the component you need:

1. In the Start screen, press **Windows+W** to open the Settings search pane.

2. Type **uninstall**. (Yup, I know you're not uninstalling the program, but this is just the easiest way to get where we're going.)

3. Click **Change or remove a program**. Windows 8 displays a list of the programs installed on your computer.

4. Click the program you want to work with.

5. Click the **Change** button (or, in some cases, the **Uninstall/Change** button).

6. What happens from here depends on the program. For example, you may be asked to insert the program installation disc. Eventually, you should see an option that says something like **Modify** or **Add or Remove Features**. Make sure you select that option, which means you'll eventually see a list of features that you can add to the program. Look for the feature you want and select it.

That last step lacks detail, I know, but every program has its own way of doing things; you'll just have to see what the program throws your way.

The Bum's Rush: Removing a Program

Most programs seem like good ideas at the time you install them. Unless you're an outright pessimist, you probably figured that a program you installed was going to help you work smarter, be more efficient, or have more fun. Sadly, some programs don't live up to expectations. The good news is that you don't have to put up with a loser program after you realize it's not up to snuff. You can uninstall a program—completely remove it from your computer—so that it doesn't clutter up your Start screen, desktop, hard disk, or any other location where it might have inserted itself.

Getting Rid of a Windows 8 App

You saw earlier that the Windows Store makes it a breeze to install a Windows 8 app. Even better, Windows 8 makes it even easier to uninstall a Windows 8 app that has outlived its usefulness. In fact, it takes but three measly steps:

1. On the Start screen, right-click the Windows 8 app you want to uninstall.

2. In the application bar that slides up, click **Uninstall**. Windows 8, ever cautious, asks you to confirm it.

3. With no malice in your heart, click **Uninstall**.

Uninstalling a Windows Live Essentials Program

Okay, so you installed Windows Live Mesh or Messenger Companion and you *still* don't know what the heck they do. No problem! You can ditch them and any other Windows Live Essentials program that's dead to you. Here's how:

1. In the Start screen, press **Windows+W** to open the Settings search pane.

2. Type **uninstall**.

3. Click **Uninstall a program**. Windows 8 displays a list of the programs installed on your computer.

4. Click **Windows Live Essentials**.

5. Click the **Uninstall/Change** button. The Windows Live Essentials window appears after a moment or two.

6. Click **Remove one or more Windows Live programs**. Windows Live displays a list of the Essentials programs on your computer.

7. Activate the check box beside each program you want to throw out.

8. Click **Uninstall**. Windows Live sends the selected programs packing.

Giving a Program the Heave-Ho

If you have a Windows application that has worn out its welcome, this section shows you how to uninstall the darn thing so that it's out of your life forever. The good news is that Windows 8 has a feature that enables you to vaporize any application with a simple click of the mouse. Here's how it works:

1. In the Start screen, press **Windows+W** to open the Settings search pane.

2. Type **uninstall**.

3. Click **Uninstall a program**. Windows 8 displays a list of the programs installed on your computer.

4. Click the program you want to uninstall.

5. Click the **Uninstall** button (or perhaps **Uninstall/Change**).

6. What happens next depends on the program. You may see a dialog box asking you to confirm the uninstall, or you may be asked whether you want to run an "Automatic" or "Custom" uninstall; be sure to select the **Automatic** option. Whatever happens, follow the instructions on the screen until you return to the Add or Remove Programs window.

> **WINDOWS WISDOM**
>
> Don't be surprised if the uninstall routine doesn't wipe out absolutely everything for a program. If you created any documents or customized the program, the uninstall program may leave behind a few scraps.

Device Advice I: Installing Hardware

Software installation is usually a painless operation that often requires just a few mouse clicks on your part. Hardware, however, is another story. Not only must you attach the device to your machine—which might even require that you remove the cover to get inside the computer—but you also have to hope Windows 8 will recognize the device and set it up correctly.

To ensure that your device and Windows 8 get along famously, check the box it came in to see whether it says anything about being compatible with Windows 8. If it is, then you shouldn't have any problems. If the box tells you that the device was designed for Windows 7, then you're still probably okay.

Understanding Hardware Types

Although thousands of devices are available in dozens of device categories, I like to organize devices according to how you attach them to the computer. From this point of view, there are three types:

- **External plug-in devices.** These are devices that use some kind of cable to plug into a *port* in the back of the PC. These devices include keyboards, mice, joysticks, modems, printers, speakers, and monitors. These kinds of devices are easy to install if you remember one thing: the computer's ports each have a unique shape, and the cable plug has a shape that matches one of those ports, so there's usually only one possible place into which any cable can plug. The exception to this is if the back of the computer has two ports with identical configurations. That just means your machine offers two of the same port type, so you can plug your device into either one.

> **DEFINITION**
>
> A **port** is a computer receptacle into which you plug the cable for a device.

- **Internal disk drives.** These are the toughest devices to install, not only because you have to get inside your computer, but also because there are many steps involved. Your best bet here is to take the machine to a computer service center or bribe a nearby computer geek into doing the job for you.

- **Internal circuit boards.** These are cards that plug into slots inside your computer. There are circuit boards for all kinds of things, including sound cards, graphics cards, and network cards. Again, you should get someone who knows what he or she is doing to install these kinds of devices for you.

Installing a Device Driver

Your device and your computer are now shacked up, but they're not married yet. To get a full relationship going, Windows 8 has to install a tiny bit of software called a *device driver*. This miniprogram has code that operates (drives) the device, so it acts as a kind of middleman between the device and Windows 8.

In the best of all possible worlds, after you've attached the device, Windows 8 recognizes the new limb and proceeds to install the device driver and any other software required to make the device run. This is automatic for the most part, and when all is said and done—well, done, anyway; nothing much is said during this procedure—your device is ready for action.

How do you know? The easiest way is just to start using the device. Otherwise, you can see for yourself by opening the Devices screen: Press **Windows+W**, type **devices**, and then click **Devices**. As you can see in Figure 6.3, if Windows 8 recognized your device and set it up properly, you either see no message under the device name, or you see the word **Ready**.

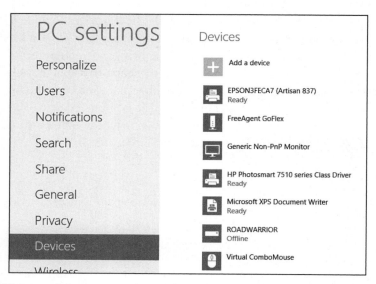

Figure 6.3: *When you plug in and turn on your device, ideally Windows 8 will recognize it right away and add it to the Devices list with either no message or the word Ready.*

What happens from here depends on the device, and you might have to jump through a hoop or two. For example, if you're installing a wireless keyboard, you're usually given a code to type to complete the "pairing." Follow the instructions that show up on the screen.

On the other hand, if Windows 8 is still scratching its digital head over a device, it displays some sort of error message in the Devices screen. For example, in Figure 6.4 you can see that the USB-modem device shows the dreaded message "Driver is unavailable."

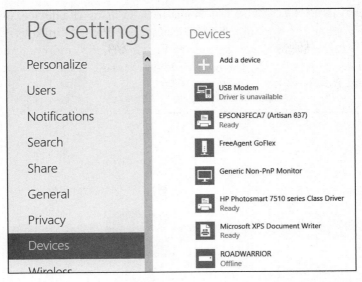

Figure 6.4: *When Windows 8 can't do its device-driver duty, you see the message "Driver is unavailable."*

If, for some reason, Windows 8 doesn't automatically recognize your new device, all is not lost. If your device came with an installation disc, insert the disc and run the setup program.

If you don't have a disc, there's still hope for your device. That's because Windows 8 comes with a hardware troubleshooter called Add a Device Wizard, which scours every nook and cranny of your system to look for new stuff. Here's how it works:

1. In the Start screen, press **Windows+W** to open the Settings search pane.

2. Type **devices** and then click **Devices and Printers**. The Devices and Printers window shows up with a list of the major hardware doodads connected to your computer (see Figure 6.5).

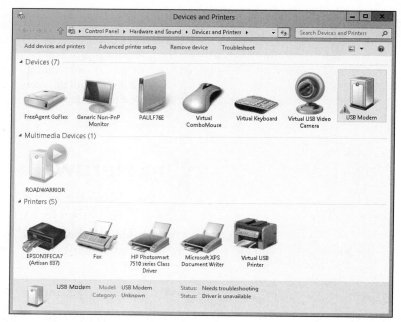

Figure 6.5: *Windows 8's Devices and Printers window gives you a handy list of your PC's major hardware bits and pieces.*

3. Click the device you're having trouble with and then click **Troubleshoot**. The troubleshooter leaps into action and analyzes the device. When it's done, it will hopefully display a solution, such as offering to install a device driver, as shown in Figure 6.6.

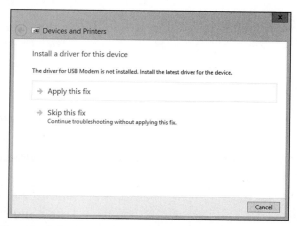

Figure 6.6: *If the troubleshooter offers a solution, go for it!*

4. Click the solution—and cross your fingers, just in case!

If the troubleshooter fails in its quest to locate a device driver, don't give up hope just yet. Open up the nearest web browser and surf to the device manufacturer's website. Look for a link to a section named "Support" (or perhaps "Software" or "Downloads" or, ideally, "Device Drivers"), locate your device, and then download the driver that works with Windows 8 (or Windows 7, if no Windows 8 driver is available).

Device Advice II: Removing Hardware

If you have a device you no longer use, or if you get a better device for your birthday, you need to remove the old device from your computer and then let Windows 8 know that it's gone. The exception to this is if the device supports Plug and Play. If it does, then Windows 8 recognizes that the device is gone and it adjusts itself accordingly. Otherwise, you need to do it by hand:

1. In the Start screen, press **Windows+W** to open the Settings search pane.

2. Type **devices** and then click **Devices and Printers** to return to the Devices and Printers window.

3. Click the device you're no longer using.

4. Click **Remove device**. Windows 8 asks if you're sure.

5. Say "Sure, I'm sure!" and click **Yes**. Windows 8 wastes no more of your time and removes the device.

6. If the device is an internal component, shut down your computer and then remove the device. Otherwise, just unplug the device.

The Least You Need to Know

- Most software discs support AutoPlay, so the installation program runs automatically after you insert the disc.
- Click the **Store** tile on the Start screen to launch the Windows Store and peruse the available Windows 8 apps.
- Use the **Programs and Features** window in Control Panel (in the Start screen, press **Windows+W**, type **uninstall**, and then click **Change or remove a program**) to help you change or uninstall non–Windows 8 apps.

- To ensure the easiest hardware configuration, buy only devices that are both Plug and Play–compatible and Windows 8–compatible.

- When installing an external device, remember that its cable can plug into only a single, complementary port on the back of the computer.

- If Plug and Play doesn't work, insert the disc that came with the device.

Getting Onto the Internet

In This Chapter

- How to choose an internet service provider
- What you need to know to get an account and start surfing
- Understanding the difference between dial-up and broadband
- Getting connected to the internet
- Getting disconnected from the internet

The internet's tentacles have insinuated themselves into every nook and cranny of modern life. Businesses ranging from corner-hugging mom-and-pop shops to continent-straddling corporations are online; web pages are now counted in the billions; and people send far more email messages than postal messages.

It truly is a wired—which is just *weird* spelled "sideways"—world. If you feel like you're the only person remaining who isn't online, this chapter will help. I'll tell you exactly what you need to make it happen, and then I'll take you through the connection process, step by finicky step.

What to Look for in an Internet Service Provider

The route to the internet isn't a direct one. Instead, you can only get there by engaging the services of a middleman or, more accurately, a middle company: an *internet service provider* or *ISP* for short.

> **DEFINITION**
>
> An **internet service provider (ISP)** takes your money in exchange for providing an internet account, which you need in order to get online.

An ISP is a business that has negotiated a deal with the local telephone company or some other behemoth organization to get a direct connection to the internet's highways and byways. These kinds of connections cost thousands of dollars a month, so they're out of reach for all but the most well-heeled tycoons. The ISP affords it by signing up subscribers and offering them a piece of the ISP's internet connection. After you have an account with an ISP, the connection process works as follows:

1. You use your modem to connect to the ISP.

2. The ISP's computer verifies that you're one of their subscribers.

3. The ISP's computer sets up a connection between your computer and the internet.

4. You go, girl—or boy, as the case may be!

So before you can do anything on the internet, you have to set up an account with an ISP and then you need to give Windows the details. Before we get to that, let's take a second to run through a few pointers to bear in mind when deciding which ISP to choose.

The first thing you have to decide is what type of connection you want. There are three basic connection types:

- **Broadband.** This type of connection uses a special external modem to connect to the ISP. Broadband connections are usually a bit more expensive than dial-up, but they are many times faster. Most folks use broadband these days.

- **Dial-up.** This type of connection uses your computer's modem to dial a phone number that connects the modem to an ISP's system. In general, dial-up connections are slow, but cheap.

- **Wireless.** This type of connection uses wireless networking technology to connect to a nearby device that has an internet connection—usually a broadband connection.

The next few sections take you through some specific ISP pointers for each type of connection, but here are four general ones to bear in mind when you're ISP shopping:

- Connection speeds are measured in either thousands of bits (kilobits) per second—usually abbreviated as *Kbps*—or millions of bits (megabits) per second—usually abbreviated as Mbps. (A *bit* is the fundamental unit of computer information. For example, it takes eight bits to define a single character, such as *a* or even *ä*.)

- Make sure the ISP offers a local or toll-free number for technical support.

- I recommend dealing with only large ISPs. There are plenty of fly-by-night operations out there and they're just not worth the hassle of dropped connections, busy signals, lack of support, or going belly-up when you most need them.

- If you can't decide between two (or more) ISPs, see what extra goodies they offer: space for your own web pages, extra email accounts, internet software bundles, and so on.

Heading Down the Broadband Highway

Most people use broadband nowadays for a simple reason: it's *way* faster than dial-up. Depending on the connection speed, it can be 20, 100, or even *500* times faster. That's a lot of fast. (Another broadband bonus: you don't tie up your phone line when you're connected.) Here are some things to put on your broadband-shopping-notes list:

- Most ISPs charge a monthly fee, which typically ranges from $15 to $60.

- Broadband requires a different kind of modem, which you usually rent from the ISP. Make sure you find out the rental fee.

- When comparing prices, remember there is usually a trade-off between price and connection speed. For example, a cheap plan might get you a 1-Mbps connection, while a more expensive plan might max out at 25 Mbps.

- When you look at broadband speed, you usually see two numbers, one higher than the other. The higher number is the download speed—which is the speed at which stuff from the internet is sent to your computer; the lower number is the upload speed—which is the speed at which you send stuff from your computer to the internet. Most internet connections spend way more time downloading than uploading, so download speed is really the one to watch.

- It's important to note that most plans put a monthly limit on the amount of data you can send back and forth, or the *bandwidth*. If you exceed that amount, you get charged extra (be sure to find out how much).

I mentioned earlier that broadband uses a special ISP-supplied modem. Here are the basics for getting it set up:

- Run a phone line or a cable line (which kind you use depends on the ISP) from the wall jack to the port in the back of the modem.

- Run a networking cable from the network port in the back of the modem to the network card port in the back of your computer.

Going Wireless

If you want to set up a wireless internet connection for your computer, this isn't usually something you get from an ISP—at least not directly. (Having said that, there are ISPs who can help you do the wireless thing, so ask.) Instead, you need to establish an internet connection first—this is almost always a broadband connection—and then set up wireless internet on a separate device.

This separate device is usually a wireless router. Here's how to set things up:

- Run a phone line or cable from the wall jack to the port in the back of the broadband modem.

- Run a networking cable from the network port in the back of the modem to the special port (labeled *Internet* or *WLAN* or something similar) in the back of the wireless router.

If you haven't yet configured your wireless router or gateway for internet access, see Chapter 12 for details.

Doing It with Dial-Up

Here are some things to mull over if you're thinking about a dial-up connection:

- Most ISPs charge a monthly fee, which typically ranges from $5 to $30. Decide in advance the maximum that you're willing to shell out each month.

- Remember that ISP plans usually trade off between price and hours of connection time—the lower the price, the fewer the hours you get.

- It's important to note that most plans charge you (by the minute or by the hour) if you exceed the number of hours the plan offers. These charges can be exorbitant (a buck or two an hour), so you don't want to get into that. Therefore, you need to give some thought to how much time you plan to spend online. That's hard to do at this stage, I know, but you just need to ballpark it. If in doubt, get a plan with a large number of hours (say, 100 or 150). You can always scale back later on.

- Most major ISPs offer an unlimited-use plan. This means you can connect whenever you want for as long as you want, and you pay a set fee per month— usually around $20. This is a good option to take for a few months until you figure out how often you use the internet.

- All modems made in the past few years support a faster connection speed called *56K* (or sometimes *V.90*), which offers a maximum speed of 56 Kbps. If you have such a modem (if you're not certain, it's probably safe to assume that you do), make sure the ISP you choose also supports 56K—almost all of them do nowadays.

- Make sure the ISP offers a local-access or toll-free number to avoid long-distance charges. Note: watch out for extra charges for the use of a toll-free line. Even better, some nationwide ISPs offer local access in various cities. This is particularly useful if you do a lot of traveling.

If you use a dial-up internet connection, your telephone and modem will probably share the same line. In this case, you don't have to switch the cable between the phone and the modem all the time. Instead, it's possible to get a permanent, no-hassle setup that'll make everyone happy. The secret is that many modems have two telephone-cable jacks in the back:

- **Line jack.** This one is usually labeled *Line* or *Telco*, or has a picture of a wall jack.

- **Telephone jack.** This one is usually labeled *Phone* or has a picture of a telephone.

Follow these directions to set things up:

1. Run a phone cable from the wall jack to the modem's line jack.

2. Run a second phone cable from the telephone to the modem's telephone jack.

> **WINDOWS WISDOM**
>
> If you have a modem that has just a single jack, you need to get a phone-line splitter that turns a single phone line into two separate lines. Run the phone cable from the wall to the splitter, and then run one line from the splitter to the modem and the other from the splitter to the phone.

This setup lets you use the phone whenever you need it—the signal goes right through the modem (when you're not using it, of course)—and lets you use the modem whenever you need it.

Getting Ready to Rumble: Gathering Information

As you'll see in just a sec, you can build your internet connection with your bare hands, but you need to gather some raw materials first. Whether it's a dial-up or broadband connection to your internet account, you need to have the proper bits of information from your ISP. In the bad old days (way back in the previous century), you needed reams of the most obscure and incomprehensible gobbledygook you ever laid eyes on. Things are much more civilized nowadays (insert prayer to your higher power of choice here), so you need to have just the following tidbits to log on:

- For dial-up and broadband, you need your user name (which might also be called your *log-on name*) and password that you use to log on to the ISP.

- For a wireless connection, you need to know the name of your wireless network (sometimes called the SSID) and the security key or password, if the network requires one.

- For a dial-up connection, you need the phone number you have to dial to connect to the ISP.

With that info at your side, you're now ready to set up the account.

Getting Started on the Road to the Internet

Depending on who set up your computer, there's a chance your computer is already net-friendly. To find out, click the **Internet Explorer** tile in the Start screen to crank up the Internet Explorer web browser. If you end up on a web page, then your internet connection is a going concern. If you see the sad message: "Internet Explorer cannot display the webpage," you've got a few hoops you still need to jump through.

There's a good chance that your ISP sent you some kind of CD that contains the bits and pieces you need to get your connection running. If so, insert the CD and follow whatever instructions come your way to let the ISP handle all the hard stuff for you.

No CD? No problem. Whether your internet path is a dial-up road or a broadband highway, you start things off by following these steps:

1. In the Start screen, press **Windows+W** to open the Settings search pane.

2. Type **connection**.

3. In the search results, click **Set up a connection or network**. (You might need to click an empty section of the screen to see this tile.) The Set Up a Connection or Network dialog box shows up.

4. Click **Connect to the Internet** and then click **Next**. At long last, you see the dialog box shown in Figure 7.1.

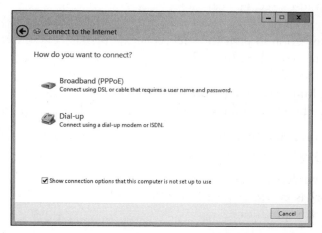

Figure 7.1: *The inevitable fork in the internet road: select Broadband or Dial-up.*

5. Click the connection type you long for:

- **Broadband.** If you click this type, you see the dialog box shown in Figure 7.2. You use this dialog box to type in the user name and password supplied by your ISP. Figure 7.2 shows a completed version of this dialog box.

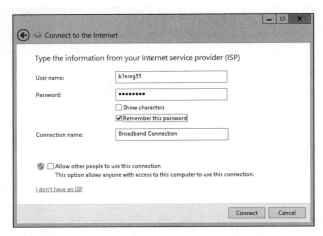

Figure 7.2: *Type in the info your ISP sent you.*

HACKING WINDOWS

For broadband and dial-up connections, you can save yourself having to type the password every time you log on by activating the check box for **Remember this password**.

- **Dial-up.** If you click this type, you see a dialog box that's pretty much a carbon copy of the one shown in Figure 7.2. The only difference is that you also have to type in the dial-up phone number.

6. Click **Connect**. Windows 8 creates the new connection.

SEE ALSO

Wait! What about wireless? Ah, that's a slightly different kettle of connecting-to-the-internet fish; head to Chapter 12 to get the scoop.

If all goes well, you're on the internet! You think there'd be music and fireworks but, alas, no. You just get a rather ho-hum dialog box that says **You are connected to the Internet,** shown in Figure 7.3. If you're not quite ready to do the internet thing right away, you should disconnect your dial-up connection, as described a bit later in the section Severing the Connection.

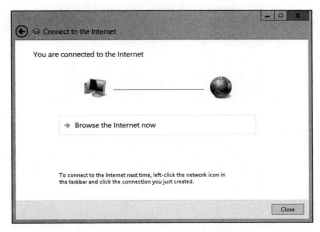

Figure 7.3: *You see this dialog box if your internet connection is successful.*

Making the Connection

Windows 8 is considerate enough to establish a connection to the internet automatically after you set up your account. If you're using a broadband connection, then you'll probably want to keep it running full time, for convenience. You can't do that with dial-up, so you need to disconnect after you're done, and then reconnect later when you're looking for more internet action.

To reconnect to the internet, you have a couple of choices:

- **Make the connection by hand.** Press **Windows+I** to open the Settings pane, click the **Network** icon (it's the one above Notifications), click the internet connection you created, and then click **Connect** (see Figure 7.4).

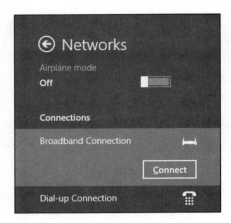

Figure 7.4: *Click the **Network** icon, click your connection, and then click **Connect**.*

- **Start an internet program.** If you launch a program that requires an internet connection—such as Internet Explorer or Windows Live Mail—Windows 8 displays the Dial-up Connection dialog box shown in Figure 7.5. Click **Connect** to make things happen.

Figure 7.5: *When you launch internet-friendly programs such as Internet Explorer or Windows Live Mail, Windows 8 automatically prompts you to connect to the internet.*

HACKING WINDOWS

For even faster service in the future, activate the check box **Connect automatically**. This tells Windows 8 to bypass the Dial-up Connection dialog box and make the connection without pestering you.

Setting Up a Microsoft Account

Now that you're connected to the internet, you probably have a million places to check out. Be my guest! But before you do (or between your sessions), you might want to take a minute or three to configure Windows 8 with a Microsoft account. When you connect a Microsoft account to your Windows 8 user account, many previously secret and hidden Windows 8 features magically become available. For example, you can use the Mail app to access your email and the Messages app to exchange text messages with other Microsoft-account users. You can also download apps from the Windows Store, access your photos and documents anywhere online, and even sync your settings with other PCs where you use the same account.

WINDOWS WISDOM

Most of the time, a Microsoft account means a Live.com or Hotmail.com email address from Microsoft. However, if you have an email address that you use regularly, you're free to use that same address with your Windows 8 account.

It's pretty useful, so if you're up for it, let's run through the steps required to get set up.

1. Press **Windows+W** to open the Settings search pane.

2. Type **microsoft**.

3. In the search results, click **Connect to a Microsoft account**. Windows 8 opens up the PC Settings window and selects the Users tab for you.

4. Click **Switch to a Microsoft Account**. Windows 8 asks you to verify your current account password.

5. Type your password and then click **Next**. Windows 8 now pesters you for your email address.

6. Type your email address, keeping the following in mind:

   • If you have an existing Microsoft address—that is, an address that ends with live.com or hotmail.com—type in that address.

   • If you want to use a non-Microsoft address, type the address you want to use.

   • If you want to create a new account using either Live.com or Hotmail. com, type the user name you prefer to use, followed by either live.com or hotmail.com. Assuming the user name has not been taken, Windows 8 will recognize that this is a new address, and it will create the new account automatically.

7. Click **Next**.

How you proceed from here depends on whether you are creating a new account or using an existing account.

- **Creating a new Microsoft account.** In this case, Windows 8 asks you to enter a bunch of info, including the password you want to use (twice), your first and last name, your country, and your ZIP code.

- **Using an existing Microsoft account.** In this case, you just have to type your Microsoft-account password.

Click **Next** and you end up staring at the screen shown in Figure 7.6, which asks you for all kinds of oddball info, including your mobile phone number, an alternate email address, a secret question, and the answer to that question.

Figure 7.6: *When you connect your user account to a Microsoft account, Windows 8 requests some info for security purposes.*

What's all this about? Actually, it's just to help you if you forget your account password and can't log in. For example, if you forget your password: by forking over your mobile phone number, Microsoft can send you a text message to help you reset your password. You can also give Microsoft an alternative email address, or you can provide the answer to a secret question.

WINDOWS WISDOM

You don't have to fill in all these fields, but Windows 8 does require that you choose at least two of these three methods before it will let you complete your account.

Okay, we're getting there: click **Next**. If you're creating a new account, Windows 8 asks you to jump over one last hoop, which involves choosing the month, day, and year of your birth; specifying your gender; and typing some weird-looking characters to prove that you're a human and not a robot (I kid you not). Click **Next** and then, at long last, click **Finish**.

Windows 8 connects the Microsoft account to your user account, which means that the next time you start Windows 8, use your Microsoft-account email address and password to log in.

Severing the Connection

When you've stood just about all you can stand of the internet's wiles, you can log off your dial-up connection by pressing **Windows+I** to open the Settings pane, clicking the **Network** icon (remember, it's the one above Notifications), clicking the dial-up internet connection, and then clicking **Disconnect**.

The Least You Need to Know

- If you are setting up your connection by hand, your ISP should provide you with the settings and data you need: the access phone number (for dial-up), and your user name and password.

- If you're using a dial-up connection, keep both your phone and your modem available for use by running a phone cable from the wall jack to the modem's line port, and running a second cable from the phone to the modem's telephone jack.

- Making the leap to the internet is as easy pressing **Windows+I**, clicking the **Network** icon, clicking your connection, and then clicking **Connect**.

- It's a good idea to connect a Microsoft account to your Windows 8 user account because it enables you to share photos, shop the Windows Store, and sync your settings across multiple PCs.

- To return to the real world, press **Windows+I**, click the **Network** icon, click your connection, and then click **Disconnect**.

Having Fun with Windows 8

It wasn't all that long ago when computers were viewed as "business-only" beasts, and only the most geeklike among us actually had a personal computer at home. Now (this being the twenty-first century and all), the digital domicile is a reality and computers in the home are as common as weeds in your neighbor's yard. Just think: all that cursing and fuming you direct toward your work computer can now be continued in the privacy of your own home—but that's not the only advantage to having a home machine. Now you can perform many fun tasks that aren't appropriate at the office: making drawings, manipulating photos, playing and copying music, and making digital movies. And the best news is that Windows 8 is set up to handle all of those leisure-time activities right out of the box. The chapters in Part 2 show you how to perform these and other more-fun-than-a-barrel-full-of-monkeys tasks.

Importing Images from a Scanner or Digital Camera

In This Chapter

- Telling Windows 8 about your scanner or digital camera
- Importing images from the digital camera to your computer
- Scanning images to your computer
- Getting the hang of memory cards
- Working directly with photos stored in a digital camera

It used to be that the only way to get an image onto your computer was either to create it yourself or to grab a pic from a clip-art collection or photo library. If you lacked artistic flair or if you couldn't find a suitable image, you were out of luck.

Now, however, getting images into digital form is easier than ever, thanks to two graphics gadgets that have become more affordable: A *document scanner* acts much like a photocopier; it creates an image of a flat surface, such as a photograph or a sheet of paper. The difference is that the scanner saves the image to a graphics file instead of on paper. A *digital camera* acts much like a regular camera; it captures and stores an image of the outside world. The difference is that the digital camera stores the image internally in its memory instead of on film. It's then possible to connect the digital camera to your computer and save the image as a graphics file on your hard disk.

The big news is that Windows 8 understands both types of doohickeys and often identifies them by a single generic name: *imaging devices* (since both produce image files). Windows 8 comes with support for a variety of scanners and cameras, so getting your digital images from "out here" to "in there" has never been easier, as you see in this chapter.

Installing a Scanner or Digital Camera

Windows 8 offers a number of options for installing scanners and digital cameras. Make sure the device is turned on and connected to your computer, and then try the following:

- **Plug and Play.** Most of today's crop of scanners and cameras are plug-and-play compatible. This means that as soon as you turn on and connect the device to your computer, Windows 8 should recognize it and set it up for you automatically. In most cases, you'll see a notification that looks suspiciously like the one shown in Figure 8.1. Click the notification and then click **Import pictures and videos**.

Figure 8.1: *In most cases, once you plug in your scanner or camera, Windows 8 will welcome it with open arms and display a notification like the one shown here.*

- **Use the Scanners and Cameras window.** If Windows 8 doesn't recognize your scanner or camera, it may just need a bit of convincing. In the Start screen, press **Windows+W** to open the Settings search pane, type **scanners**, and then click **View cameras and scanners** in the search results. When the Scanners and Cameras window shows up, click **Add Device** (you need to enter your Windows 8–administrator credentials at this point; see Chapter 12) to get the Scanner and Camera Installation Wizard on the job. Click **Next** to see a list of scanner and digital camera manufacturers and models. Find your camera or scanner in this list, click **Next**, and follow the instructions on the screen.

- **Install the device software.** Any scanner or digital camera worth its salt will come with software for setting up the device. If the first two options don't work, try installing the software.

Once your scanner or camera is installed you'll probably see an icon for it, not only in the Scanners and Cameras window, but also in the Devices and Printers window (press **Windows+W**, type **devices**, and then click **Devices and Printers**), as shown in Figure 8.2. Note, however, that if you turn off or disconnect the device, then it no longer appears in either window.

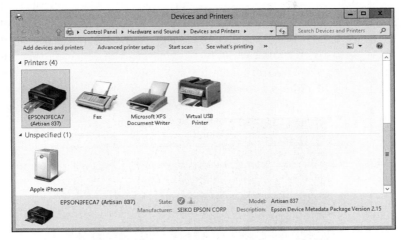

Figure 8.2: *The Devices and Printers window contains an icon for each imaging device installed on your system.*

 LOOK OUT!

Bear in mind that, despite its name, the Scanners and Cameras window doesn't show some digital cameras, for some reason. So don't panic if your camera doesn't show up there.

You should also know that Windows 8 considers a digital camera to be a type of file-storage device. This makes sense because a digital camera uses some kind of memory module or disk to store the digital photos you've taken. The kicker is because the camera stores files, Windows 8 treats it as a folder attached to your computer, so it appears in the Computer folder (on the desktop, click **File Explorer** and then click **Computer**), as shown in Figure 8.3. Later in this chapter I'll show you how to use the Computer folder to get at the images stored in your camera.

Figure 8.3: *Windows 8 considers a digital camera just another folder, so the camera shows up in the Computer folder.*

Getting Images from Your Scanner or Camera

The whole point of a scanner or digital camera is to transfer an image of something from the device to your computer hard drive. From there you can edit the image, email it to a friend or colleague, publish it to the web, or simply store it for safekeeping. This section shows you how to make a hard-disk copy of an image.

Importing Pictures from a Digital Camera

Although it's occasionally fun to browse photos on your digital camera, the images are too tiny to be satisfying. If you want to take a good peek at your handiwork, you need to get those pics onto your computer.

To get started, you have two choices:

- Select **File Explorer** and then click **Computer** to open the Computer window. Right-click the camera, and then click **Import Pictures and Videos**.

- If you downloaded Windows Live Essentials Photo Gallery (as I yammered on about back in Chapter 6), launch the program (in the Start screen, type **live** and then click **Windows Live Photo Gallery**). In the **Home** tab, click **Import**, use the Import Pictures and Videos dialog box to click the camera you want to use, and then click **Import**.

HACKING WINDOWS

If you've just connected your camera and you're eyeballing the notification shown earlier in Figure 8.1, you can also get things started by clicking **Import Pictures and Videos**.

Either way, Windows 8 offers up the Import Photos and Videos dialog box, shown in Figure 8.4.

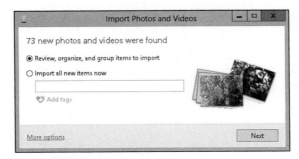

Figure 8.4: *Use this dialog box to get your Windows 8–digital camera import underway.*

In just a second Windows 8 will ask you to enter a name for your imported photo. Before we get to that, you need to understand how Windows 8 uses that name:

- It creates a subfolder in the Pictures folder, and the name of the new subfolder is today's date followed by your tag. For example, if today is August 23, 2013, and your tag is Lampshade on My Head, then the new subfolder will have the name: 2013-08-23 Lampshade on My Head.

- It gives the file (photo) the same name as the tag with the number 001 after it: Lampshade on My Head 001.jpg. If you're importing a bunch of photos from your digital camera, then the number gets bumped up for each photo: 002, 003, and so on.

With that out of the way, you come to yet another fork in the photo-importing road:

- **Import everything from the camera.** This is the easiest way to go; you tell Windows 8 to go ahead and grab everything from the camera. (Technically, you're just importing photos you haven't imported in the past.) In this case, click the **Import all new items now** option, use the text box to type a name for the import, and then click **Import**.

- **Import selected groups of photos.** This is the road to take if you only want to import a subset of your camera's photos. For example, if you have photos of a wedding and your most recent keg party, you probably want to import those separately! In this case, select the **Review, organize, and group items to import** option and click **Next**. Windows 8 presents your photos in groups by date. For each group you want to import, activate the group's check box and type a name for the group. When you're ready to roll, click **Import**.

Windows 8 starts importing the photos from the camera to your computer. If you want Windows 8 to delete the photos from the camera when the dust clears, activate the check box **Erase after importing**. When the import is complete, Windows 8 drops you off in the Imported Pictures and Videos folder.

Scanning an Image

Windows 8 comes with its own Scanner and Camera Wizard to give you a step-by-step method for capturing images. Let's see how it works. First, place the picture or document or whatever on the scanner glass. Then launch the Scanner and Camera Wizard using one of the following methods:

- If your device is a scanner and it has some kind of scan button, press that button.

- In the Start screen, press **Windows+W**, type **devices**, click **Devices and Printers**, click your scanner, and then click **Start scan**.

- In the Start screen, type **scan,** and then click **Windows Fax and Scan**. In the Windows Fax and Scan window, select **File>New>Scan**, click your scanner, and then click **OK**.

- In Windows Live Photo Gallery (type **live** in the Start screen and then click **Windows Live Photo Gallery**), select the Home tab's **Import** button, click your scanner, and then click **Import**.

Whichever method you choose, you see the New Scan dialog box. Feel free to click the **Preview** button to see what your image will look like before fiddling with any of the options or committing yourself to the scan. A preview of your scan appears as shown in Figure 8.5.

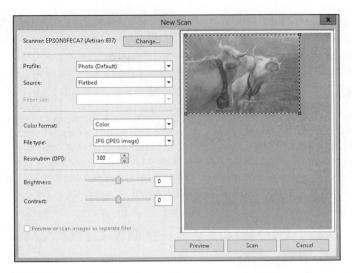

Figure 8.5: *You use the New Scan dialog box to grab an image from a scanner.*

If the dotted rectangle in the preview area isn't the same size as the image, click and drag the bottom-right corner of the rectangle to make it the same size (as I've done in Figure 8.5).

Before getting to the scan, you might want to make a few adjustments. For example, the **Color Format** list offers three options:

- **Color.** Choose this option if the document you're scanning is a color photograph or drawing.

- **Grayscale.** Choose this option if your document is a picture that renders colors using different shades of gray.

- **Black and white.** Choose this option if your document uses only black and white—for example, if it's a page of text.

You can also use the **File Type** list to select the image format you prefer: JPEG, Bitmap, PNG, or TIFF. Finally, you can also mess about with the Resolution spin box to set your preferred *resolution*, which determines the quality of the scan.

DEFINITION

The **resolution** determines the overall quality of the scanned image; the higher the resolution, the higher the quality and (on the downside) the bigger the resulting file. Resolution is measured in dots per inch (DPI).

When you're ready to get the scanning show on the road, click **Scan**. After Windows 8 scans the image, the Importing Pictures and Videos dialog box shows up; type a name for the image in the text box and then click **Import**.

> **WINDOWS WISDOM**
>
> Windows 8 gives you another way to scan pictures: in Paint, select the **File> From scanner or camera** command. If the Select Device dialog box shows up, select the imaging device you want to use and then click **OK**. Note that any decent graphics program also comes with support for scanning stuff. So if you have a better program than Paint, check to see if you can use it to scan pictures.

Dealing with Memory Cards and Other Removable Media

Many digital cameras store images using a special kind of doohickey called a memory card. These miniature memory modules come in many different shapes and sizes, including CompactFlash (CF) cards, MultiMedia cards (MMC), Memory Sticks, SecureDigital (SD) cards, and more. They're handy little devils because after you transfer your images to your computer, you can wipe out the card and start all over again. Although you usually get at the card's images by connecting the camera directly to your computer as described in the previous section, there are special devices called memory card readers into which you can insert one or more memory cards and then connect the unit to the computer.

Windows 8 treats each slot in a memory card reader as a disk drive, and they show up in the Computer folder as Removable Disk drives. You're then free to insert a memory card and browse its images directly, as described in the next section. In Figure 8.6, you see four Removable Disk drives created by my card reader—drives E:, F:, G:, and H:—and only drive E has a card inserted.

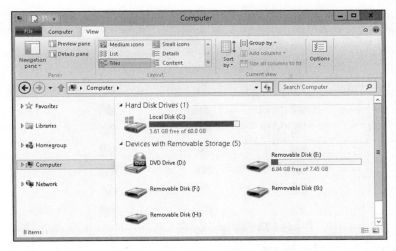

Figure 8.6: *When you insert a memory card, Windows 8 creates a few temporary removable disk drives for the reader's slots.*

Browsing Digital Camera Images

One of Windows 8's nicer features is the capability to parley directly with a digital camera using File Explorer. This is possible because, as I mentioned earlier, Windows 8 treats whatever the camera uses to store the digital photos as an honest-to-goodness folder. This means you can open the folder and get your hands dirty by working with the images yourself.

To do this, launch File Explorer, click **Computer**, and then double-click the camera icon (see Figure 8.2 earlier in this chapter; remember that this technique also applies to memory cards). Windows 8 connects to the camera and displays the following folders the camera uses for storage:

- **Removable storage.** Open this folder if your pictures are stored on a memory card that you plug into the camera.

- **Internal storage.** Open this folder if your pictures are stored on a teensy hard drive or similar internal-storage doodad.

Open the folders to get to your pictures (you may have to wade through a few levels of subfolders). Windows 8 then displays the images thumbnail-style, as shown in Figure 8.7. To copy an image from the camera to your hard disk, click and drag the image, and then drop it onto the **Pictures** library.

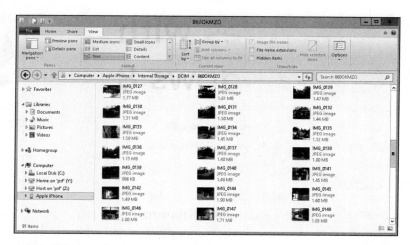

Figure 8.7: *Windows 8 is happy to show your camera's digital photos in a folder window.*

Note, too, that you can also clear out the camera's photos by selecting all the images (press **Ctrl+A**) and then pressing **Delete**.

The Least You Need to Know

- To see your installed imaging devices, use the Start screen to type **devices**, and then click **Devices and Printers**.

- To get pictures from a camera, select **File Explorer**, click **Computer** to open the Computer window, right-click the camera, and then click **Import Pictures and Videos**.

- To scan an image, either press the device's scan button or open **Devices and Printers**, click your scanner, and then click **Start scan**.

- To import pictures using Windows Live Photo Gallery, select the **Home** tab's **Import** command.

- To access your stored images on your digital camera via File Explorer, click **Computer** and then double-click the camera's icon.

Managing Your Pictures with Windows 8

In This Chapter

- GIF, JPEG, and other image format acronyms
- A quick peek at the Photos and Camera apps
- Viewing image thumbnails and slide shows
- Converting an image from one format to another
- Printing images
- Taking a stroll through the Windows Live Photo Gallery

Windows has enabled us to go beyond the workaday world of letters and memos to documents that positively cry out for image enhancement: business presentations, flyers, newsletters, and web pages, to name only a few. Fortunately, Windows has various tools that let you create images from scratch, mess around with existing images, and capture digital images from an outside source (such as a digital camera or scanner; see Chapter 8). None of these tools are good enough for professional artists, but they're more than adequate for amateur dabblers whose needs aren't so grandiose. This chapter gives you a bit of background about images and tells you how to work with image files.

The Alphabet Soup of Picture File Formats

There's certainly no shortage of ways that the world's computer geeks have come up with over the years to confuse users and other mere mortals. But few things get the man (and woman) on the street more thoroughly bamboozled than the bewildering array of file formats (also known as *file types*) that exist in the digital world. Perhaps the worst culprit is the picture-file category, which boasts a frighteningly large number of formats. My goal in this section is to help you get through the thicket of acronyms and minutiae that characterize picture-file formats, and to show you how to simplify things so that they actually make sense.

> **WINDOWS WISDOM**
>
> Throughout this chapter and in other parts of the book I'll use the terms *picture, image,* and *graphic* interchangeably.

Before you go any further into this file-format business, you might enjoy taking a step or two in reverse to consider the bigger picture: what is a file format and why do we need so many of them? I like to look at file formats as the underlying structure of a file that's akin to a car's underlying structure. The latter is a collection of metal and plastic bits that form the frame, axles, suspension, engine, and other innards that determine how the car performs. A file format is similar in that it consists of a collection of bits and bytes that determines how the picture is viewed. As you'll see, some formats are better suited for displaying photos, while others have a better time with line drawings.

The sigh-of-relief-inducing news is that even though the computing world is on speaking terms with dozens of different image formats, Windows 8 is conversant with only five:

- **Bitmap.** This is the standard image file format used by Windows 8. It's good for color drawings, although its files tend to be on the large side. Bitmap image files use the extension .bmp, so these files are also referred to as *BMP* files.

- **GIF.** This is one of the standard graphics file formats used on the web. It's only capable of storing 256 colors, so it's suitable for relatively simple line drawings or for images that use only a few colors. The resulting files are compressed, so they end up quite a bit smaller than bitmap files.

- **JPEG.** This is the other standard graphics file format that you see on the web. This format can reproduce millions of colors, so it's suitable for photographs and other high-quality images. JPEG (it's pronounced *JAY-peg*) stores images in a compressed format, so it can knock high-quality images down to a manageable size while still retaining some picture fidelity. (However, the more you compress the image, the poorer the image quality becomes.)

- **PNG.** This is a relatively new file format that's becoming more popular on the internet. It's a versatile format that can be used with both simple drawings and photos. For photos, PNG supports compression to keep images relatively small and, unlike JPEG, PNG compression doesn't reduce the quality of the image.

- **TIFF.** This format is often used with image scanners and digital cameras because it does a great job of rendering photos and other scanned images. The downside is that this format doesn't usually compress the images in any way, so it creates *huge* files. (Note that this file format may go by the extension .tif or .tiff.)

So which one should you use when creating your own image files? That depends:

- If you're creating a drawing to print out or work with only on your computer, use the bitmap format.

- If you're creating a simple drawing to publish on the web, use GIF.

- If you're creating a more complex drawing to publish on the web, use PNG.

- If you're scanning an image or downloading a photo from a digital camera to print or to edit on your computer, use TIFF.

- If you're scanning an image or downloading a photo from a digital camera to email or publish to the web, use JPEG.

Fooling Around with the Photos App

Now that you've stuffed a few photos into your Windows PC (assuming you've done the importing or scanning thing I went on about in Chapter 8), you probably want to take a gander at your newly digitized pics. Windows 8 gives you a fistful of ways to go about this, as you see in this chapter. If you want to start things off simply (always a laudable goal when it comes to computers), look no further than Photos, a Windows 8 app that resides on the Start screen. With Photos, you can view your images or even fire up a slide show.

To get started, go right ahead and click **Photos** on the Start screen. If you see the Photos screen, click the **Pictures library** tile. This gets you face to face with the Pictures Library, which includes a tile for each photo album (that is, a subfolder within your Pictures folder) as well as for any individual photos that aren't part of any album (see Figure 9.1).

SEE ALSO

If you're on the Photos screen, you might be wondering about the three other tiles you see there: SkyDrive photos, Facebook photos, and Flickr photos. These are internet-based photo services. To use them, you need a Microsoft account (see Chapter 7) and then you need to connect these social networks, as I describe in Chapter 15.

Figure 9.1: *The Pictures library as displayed by the Photos app.*

Click the album you want to peruse, and then double-click a photo to open it up full screen. From here, you navigate the photos like so:

- **Display the next photo.** Move the mouse pointer over the current photo and then click the **right arrow** or press the **Right arrow** on the keyboard; on a tablet, slide the current photo off to the left.

- **Display the previous photo.** Move the mouse pointer over the current photo and then click the **left arrow** or press the **Left arrow** key on the keyboard; on a tablet, slide the current photo off to the right.

- **Jump to any photo.** Press **Esc** to return to the album, use the scroll bar to locate the photo, and then double-click the photo.

- **Start a slide show.** To see a slide show of the photos in the current album, right-click the screen and then click **Slide show.**

Getting Creative with the Camera App

In Chapter 8 I show you three ways to get images into your PC: a digital camera, a scanner, and a memory card. Those are the best ways to go, but Windows 8 offers a fourth way: the Camera app. This is a Windows 8 app that can take advantage of your PC's camera (either one that's built in or that you've connected yourself) to take a quick picture of your smiling mug.

Here's how it works:

1. On the Start screen, click **Camera**. Not surprisingly, the Camera app loads. The first time you do this, Windows 8 politely asks if the Camera app can use your *webcam* and microphone.

> **DEFINITION**
>
> A **webcam** is a PC camera—either one that's built-in or that you've attached manually—that is capable of taking your picture (or even a video).

2. Click **Allow**. Now the Camera app appears in earnest, and you see a live shot of yourself (or something near you, depending on where your webcam is pointing).

3. Put your wig hat on your head, or do whatever it is you normally do to get ready for a photo.

4. Aim your camera as needed.

5. If you'd like the Camera app to delay slightly before taking the shot (so you can get into some comically complex position, for example), click **Timer**. (Note: this button is "on" when it has a white background.)

6. If you want to take a video instead of a photo, click the **Video Mode** button. (Again, this button is "on" when it has a white background.)

7. Click the screen. The Camera app makes a cameralike noise and snaps a photo. If you turned on Timer mode, there is three-second delay. If you're recording a video, the app beeps in a most uncameralike way and then begins the recording.

8. If recording a video, click the screen when you're done.

The Camera app tosses your photo or video into a new album called Webcam that it adds to your Pictures library.

A Tour of the Pictures Library

Back in Chapter 4, I told you about your main user-account folder and mentioned that it's the perfect spot to store documents you create. If you've been doing that, then you have noticed that your user folder includes a library named Pictures, and you probably guessed that this is where you ought to be hoarding your picture files. That's certainly true, but not just because of the library's name. Pictures is the place to squirrel away your images because it's a special library that "understands" picture files and offers you some extra features designed specifically for messing around with images:

- It offers *thumbnail* versions of each image that give you not only the name of each file, but also a miniature preview of what each image looks like.

> **DEFINITION**
>
> A **thumbnail** is a scaled-down preview of an image or other file.

- It enables you to see a preview of any image, from which you can then rotate, print, and perform a few other tasks on the image.
- It enables you to view all your images, one by one, in a slide show.
- It enables you to set up a particular image as your Windows 8 desktop background.

Most of the rest of this chapter takes you through the specifics of these features. Before getting to them, however, it's probably a good idea to review just how you get to the Pictures library. Windows 8 offers two methods:

- In the Screen, type **pictures** and then click the **Pictures** icon when it shows up.
- Run File Explorer and then click **Pictures** in the navigation pane.

If you have a subfolder within the Pictures library that you'd like to check out, double-click it.

HACKING WINDOWS

The features available with the Pictures library (discussed in the next section) can also be applied to other folders where images are stored. To do this, launch File Explorer and open the folder you want to work with. Click the **Home** tab's **Properties** command to display the Properties dialog box. In the Customize tab, the group **What kind of folder do you want?** enables you to apply a template to a folder. This means you can convert your folder into a special folder that uses the same features as Pictures—as well as other special folders, such as Music. In the **Optimize this folder for** list, choose the template type that best suits the content of your folder. For example, if your folder contains mostly images, choose the **Pictures** template. Note, too, that you can tell Windows 8 to use the template with that folder's subfolders by activating the check box **Also apply this template to all subfolders**.

All Thumbs: Using the Thumbnail View

When you arrive at the Pictures folder (or one of its subfolders), you'll see the files arranged something like those shown in Figure 9.2; that is, instead of a boring (and only marginally useful) icon, each file shows a thumbnail of the image contained in the file.

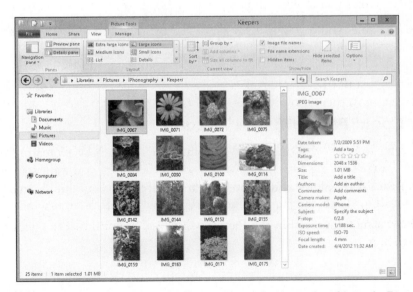

Figure 9.2: *By default, Windows 8 displays a thumbnail of each graphics file in the Pictures folder.*

Windows 8 displays image thumbnails no matter which view you use (even Details).

If you want to know details about an image—such as its height and width in pixels, its file type, and its size—click the file and then click the **View** tab's **Details** pane button. The details then appear in the Preview pane on the right side of the window (see Figure 9.2).

You should also note at this point that when you click an image file to select it, the folder window displays several image-related commands in the Manage tab (which appears under Picture Tools), including **Rotate left** and **Slide Show** (see Figure 9.3). I'll talk about these commands as you work through this chapter.

Figure 9.3: *The ribbon buttons in the Picture Tools–Manage tab magically come alive when you select one or more images.*

A Closer Look: Previewing a Picture

If you prefer to work with one image at a time, the image-preview feature might be just what you're looking for. To activate it, select the image you want to work with and then click the **Home** tab's **Open** button (an alternative method is to double-click the image). This loads the picture into the Windows Photo Viewer window, shown in Figure 9.4.

Previous Picture ⎯
Play Slide Show ⎯
Next Picture
Rotate Clockwise
Rotate Counterclockwise
Delete

Figure 9.4: *Click **Home>Open** to display the selected file in the Photo Viewer.*

This window shows you a larger version of the image and is also festooned with a few icons at the bottom:

> **WINDOWS WISDOM**
>
> You can also jump to the previous picture by pressing the **left-arrow key** on your keyboard. For the next picture, press the **right-arrow key**. Note, too, that you can rotate the image counterclockwise by pressing **Ctrl+,** (comma) and you can rotate the image clockwise by pressing **Ctrl+.** (period).

- **Previous.** Click this icon to display the previous image in the Pictures folder or subfolder.

- **Play Slide Show.** Click this icon (or press **F11**) to start a slide show of the files in the Pictures folder (more on this later in the chapter).

- **Next.** Click this icon to display the next image in the Pictures folder or subfolder.

- **Rotate Clockwise.** Click this icon to rotate the image clockwise 90 degrees. This rotation doesn't apply only to the preview; Windows 8 applies it to the file itself.

- **Rotate Counterclockwise.** Click this icon to rotate the image counterclockwise 90 degrees. Again, this change is applied to the file itself.

- **Delete.** Click this icon (or press **Delete**) to send the image to the Recycle Bin.

Setting Up an Image Slide Show

For its next trick, the Pictures library also offers a slide-show view. This means that Windows 8 displays a full-screen version of the first file, waits a few seconds, displays the second file, and so on. To activate the slide show, you have two choices:

- In the Pictures folder under the Picture Tools tab, select the **Manage** tab's **Slide show** button.

- In the Windows Photo Viewer window, click the **Play Slide Show** icon.

Once the slide show is up and showing, note that you can also control the slide show by hand by right-clicking the screen to display the following commands:

- **Play.** Restarts a paused slide show.

- **Pause.** Pauses the slide show.

- **Next.** Displays the next image (you can also press **right arrow**).

- **Back.** Displays the previous image (you can also press **left arrow**).

- **Shuffle.** Shows the pictures in random order.

- **Loop.** When the slide show has run through all the pictures, it starts over at the beginning.

- **Slide Show Speed.** These commands control the playback speed: Slow, Medium, or Fast.

- **Exit.** Stops the slide show (you can also press the **Esc** key).

Printing Pictures

Printing a picture—particularly a digital photo—is a bit different from printing a text document; in most cases, you will want a different print layout than a text document—depending on the size of the image and the size of the print you want. For that reason,

Windows 8 includes a special photo-printing feature that makes it easy to print your photo. Here's how it works:

1. Open the Pictures folder.

2. Select the pictures you want to print.

3. Click the **Share** tab's **Print** button. Windows 8 displays the Print Pictures dialog box.

4. If you have more than one printer, use the **Printer** list to select the printer you want to use.

5. Use the **Paper size** list to select the size of the paper you're using.

6. Use the **Quality** list to select the printout quality, in dots per inch (DPI); the higher the DPI number, the better the quality, but the more ink it uses.

7. Use the **Layout** list to select the print size you want. When you select a different layout, the **Print preview** box shows you what your printed image will look like (see Figure 9.5).

8. Click **Print**. Windows 8 sends your image (or images) to the printer.

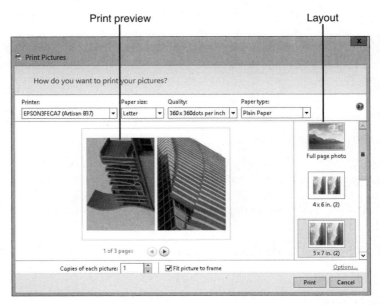

Figure 9.5: *Use this dialog box to set up your photo-printing options.*

Browsing Images in the Windows Live Photo Gallery

Over the past few years, digital cameras have become the photography tool of choice for everyone from novices to professionals. And it's no wonder, since digitals give photographers tremendous freedom to shoot at will without having to worry about processing costs or running out of film. If there's a downside to all this photographic freedom, it's that most of us end up with a huge quantity of photos cluttering our hard drives. The result has been a thriving market for third-party programs to import, view, and manage all those digital images.

The bad news is that Windows 8 doesn't come with such a program. Boo! Ah, but wait, it *does* offer a new program called Windows Live Photo Gallery as part of Windows Live Essentials. (I droned on about it back in Chapter 6, Installing and Removing Programs and Devices.) This program can import images and videos from a camera, a scanner, a removable media device, your local network, or the web. You can then view the images, add metadata such as captions and tags, rate the images, search for images, and even apply common fixes to improve the look of images. You can also burn selected images to a DVD disc. It's actually a really good program, so head back to Chapter 6 (specifically, the section Installing Windows Live Essentials Programs) to learn how to get Windows Live Photo Gallery onto your system.

Once you've done that, launch the program by clicking the Start screen's **Windows Live Photo Gallery** tile. Windows Live Photo Gallery immediately begins making a list of all the images that are stored in your Pictures library. (If you see a dialog box asking if you want to use Windows Live Photo Gallery to open certain file types—such as JPG and GIF—select **Yes**.) You can also import images by hand using the following **File** menu commands:

- **Import photos and videos.** This command launches the Scanner and Camera Wizard, which takes you step by step through the process of importing images from a digital camera, document scanner, or removable media device (see Chapter 8 for more info).

- **Include a folder.** This command displays the Pictures Library Locations dialog box, which enables you to add another folder to your Windows 8–Pictures library.

Grouping Images

By default, Windows Live Photo Gallery groups the images by month according to the date each image was created. To change that, select the **View** tab and then click an item in the Arrange List gallery. For even more options, right-click any empty part of the Windows Live Photo Gallery window and then click the command **Group By**, which enables you to group images by a number of properties, including Date Taken, File Size, Image Size, and Camera.

Tag, You're It: Image Metadata and Tagging

You can also create your own metadata for each image. Windows Live Photo Gallery enables you to change four properties: People Tags (the names of people in the image), Geotag (the location where the image was created), Caption (a description or title for the image), and Descriptive Tags (add one or more descriptive keywords). Figure 9.6 shows an image with some metadata added.

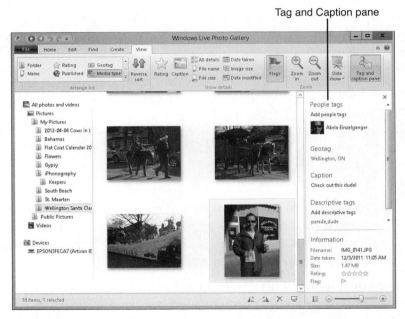

Figure 9.6: *You can apply descriptive tags and a caption to each of your images.*

Follow these steps to add one or more tags to an image:

1. Click the image you want to work with.

2. Click the **View** tab's **Tag and caption pane** button to display—you guessed it—the Tag and Caption pane.

3. Click **Add descriptive tags**.

4. Type the tag and press **Enter**.

5. Repeat steps 3 and 4 to add more tags to the image.

Quick Fixes: Making Image Adjustments

Windows Live Photo Gallery also comes with a limited set of tools for altering images. Double-click the image you want to work with and then click the **Edit** tab to display the image in the window shown in Figure 9.7.

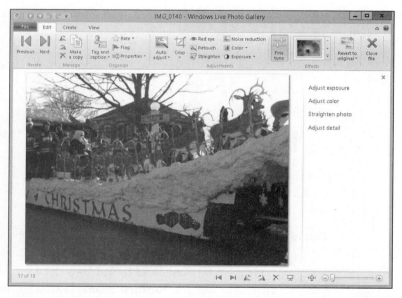

Figure 9.7: *Double-click the photo and then select the **Edit** tab to perform some photo-fixing chores.*

Here you get the following tools:

- **Crop.** Click this tool if you want to remove some extraneous material from your photo, particularly around the edges. Click and drag the corners or sides of the box that appears over your image so that the box encloses just the part of the image you want to keep. Click the bottom half of the **Crop** button and then click **Apply crop**.

- **Red eye.** Click this tool to get rid of that crazed red-eye look that mars an otherwise good photo. Click and drag the mouse over the red eye and Windows Live Photo Gallery will fix it for you automatically. Thanks!

- **Retouch.** Click this button to have Windows Live Photo Gallery identify and remove unsightly blemishes from the photo.

- **Straighten.** Click this tool to straighten a slightly lopsided photo.

- **Noise reduction.** Click this button to make any unnecessary pixels (called *noise*) in the image less noticeable.

- **Color.** Click this tool to automatically adjust the photo's colors.

- **Exposure.** Click this tool to automatically adjust the photo's exposure.

- **Fine tune.** Click this button to display the following four advanced tools:

  - **Adjust exposure.** Click this tool to expose (bad pun intended) sliders for **Brightness**, **Contrast**, **Shadows**, and **Highlights**.

  - **Adjust color.** Click this tool to see sliders for **Color Temperature**, **Tint**, and **Saturation**.

  - **Straighten photo.** Click this tool if you want to straighten your photo by hand. Click and drag the slider to tilt the photo a wee bit one way or the other until your image is straight and true.

  - **Adjust detail.** Click this tool if you want to fine-tune a small piece of the image. Click and drag the image to bring the problematic part into view, and then use the **Sharpen** slider to sharpen the area. You can also click **Analyze**, and then use the **Reduce Noise** button to remove noise from the detail.

If, like me, you really don't know what the heck you're doing when it comes to things like color temperature and contrast, you can also click **Auto adjust** to have Windows Live Photo Gallery make the adjustments for you.

When you're done, click **Close file** to return to Windows Live Photo Gallery.

Setting a Picture as the Desktop Background

The Windows 8 desktop usually comes with a fairly spiffy background image. However, you may find that you get bored with it after a while or that you have a picture of your own that you'd prefer to use. Either way, it's no problem to change the desktop background to any picture on your system. In fact, it takes just three measly steps:

1. In the Windows Live Photo Gallery, double-click the file that contains the image you want to use.

2. Select the **Create** tab.

3. Click **Set as desktop**.

The Least You Need to Know

- If you're working only on your computer, the best formats to use are bitmap for drawings and TIFF for photos. If you're going to email pictures or publish them on the web, use GIF for drawing and JPEG for photos.

- If you just want a quick look at your photos or to run a slide show, click the Start screen's **Photos** app.

- In the Pictures folder, double-click an image to see a preview of it in Windows Photo Viewer.

- To run a slide show, either select the **Manage** tab's **Slide show** button or open Windows Photo Viewer and click the **Play Slide Show** icon.

- In the Start screen, click **Windows Live Photo Gallery** to run the Windows Live Photo Gallery program.

Sights and Sounds: Windows 8's Digital Media Tools

In This Chapter

- Playing multimedia files
- Listening to audio CDs and watching DVD movies
- Ripping music tracks from an audio CD
- Burning music tracks to a CD or DVD
- Connecting your PC and a TV for use with Media Center

The graphics you gawked at in the last two chapters represent only a selection of Windows 8's visual treats. There are actually quite a few more goodies that fall into the sights-for-sore-eyes category, and even a few that could be called "sounds for sore ears." In this chapter, you see that Windows 8 turns your lowly computer into a multimedia powerhouse capable of showing videos, playing audio CDs, watching slick DVD movies, and more.

Playing and Buying Music with the Music App

With the Music app that resides on the Start screen, you can play your own music as well as fork over some not-so-big bucks to purchase songs or albums. (I may as well point out here that to buy stuff through the Music app, you need to be using a Microsoft account to sign in to Windows 8. I showed you how to set up a Microsoft account back in Chapter 7.) Feel free to click the **Music** tile any time you want to get the concert started.

You start off in the Spotlight screen, so if you're really just interested in spinning a tune or two, scroll right to bring up the My Music screen, which will look a bit like the one shown in Figure 10.1. If you see the album you want to play, click it; otherwise, click **my music**, click an album, and then click **Play** to crank up the album.

(If you only feel like listening to one song, click the song and then click the song's **Play** button.)

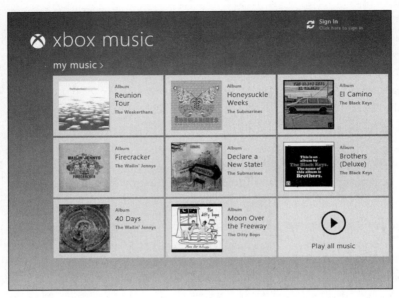

Figure 10.1: *Launch the Music app and then scroll over to the Collection screen to see your albums (some of them, anyway).*

Right-click the screen to display the playback controls. You can then click the **Pause** button to stop playback (and **Play** to resume it); **Next** to skip to the next track; **Previous** to return to the previous track; **Shuffle** to play the songs randomly; or **Repeat** to play the album continuously.

To spend your hard-earned cash on some new tunes, click the screen and then click the **back arrow** (the right-pointing arrow in the upper-left corner) until you reunite with the main Music app screen. Scroll right and then click either **xbox music store** or **most popular**. Use the Featured, Genres, Albums, or Artists tabs to find an album you're interested in, and then click it. You now have two ways to proceed:

- To preview the album, click **Preview**. If you're convinced you want to own it, click **Buy Album**.

- To preview a song, click the song, and then click **Preview**. If you just want to purchase that song, click **Buy Song**.

Seeing What the Video App Can Do

The Video app is your Windows 8 door to all things movielike, including any of your own digital video files, movies, and TV shows. You can play your digital videos, and you can buy or rent movies and TV episodes. (As with music, you need a Microsoft account to buy and rent.) To stop talking and start watching, click the Start screen's **Video** tile.

To play a video: Scroll right to bring up the My Videos section. If you see the video you want, click it. Otherwise, click **my videos**; click **Movies**, **TV**, or **Other**; click a video; and then click **Play**.

To control the playback: Right-click the screen. You can then click the **Pause** button to stop playback (and **Play** to resume it); **Next** to skip to the next chapter of the video (if any); **Previous** to return to the previous chapter; or **Repeat** to start the video all over again once it ends.

If you feel like splurging for a movie or TV show, click the screen and then click the **back arrow** (the right-pointing arrow in the upper-left corner) until you return to the main Video app screen. Scroll right to either the Movies Store section or the TV Store section and then click either **movies marketplace** or **tv marketplace**. Use the tabs—Featured, New Releases, Top Selling, Genres, and Studios for the Movies Marketplace; Featured, Last Night's Shows, Free TV, Top Selling, Genres, and Networks for the TV Marketplace—to find a movie or show that interests you, and then click it. You now have two ways to proceed:

- For movies, click **Buy/Rent**.

- For TV shows, click **View Seasons**, click a season, click an episode, and then click **Buy**.

Getting There from Here with the Maps App

Windows 8 comes with an app called *Maps* that lets you locate addresses on a map and will even give you directions on how to get there. Sweet! Before you use the app, however, you need to configure Windows 8 to allow apps to use your current location. Here's how you go about that:

1. Press **Windows+I** to open the Start settings pane. (On a tablet, swipe in from the right edge and then tap **Settings**.)

2. Click **Change PC Settings**.

3. Click **Privacy**.

4. Click the **Let apps use my location** switch to the **On** position.

With that map malarkey out of the way, return to the Start screen and click **Maps**. Figure 10.2 shows the Maps screen that appears (I've right-clicked to show the application bar, too). There are three main things you can do with the Maps app:

- To mark your current locale on the map, click **My location**.

- To find a location, press **Windows+C** to open the Charms menu, click **Search**, type the address or name in the **Search for a location or business** box and then click the **Search** icon (the magnifying glass) or press the **Enter** key.

- To get directions, click **Directions** and then use the two text boxes to enter your starting point (which, by default, is your current location) and your destination. Press **Enter** to mark the trip on the map and display detailed instructions for the journey.

Figure 10.2: *Use the Maps app to search for locations and get directions from here to there.*

Making Multimedia Whoopee with Media Player

Windows supports all kinds of multimedia formats, including sound files, digital video files, audio CDs, DVD movies, and more. The good news is that rather than messing around with various Windows 8 apps, you can play all these formats using only a single program: Windows Media Player. This clever chunk of software is a true one-stop multimedia shop that's capable of playing sound files, music files, audio CDs, animations, movie files, and even DVDs. It can also copy audio CD tracks to your computer, burn music files to a CD, tune in to internet radio stations, and more.

To try Media Player, you have a bunch of ways to proceed:

- Use the Start screen to type **media** and then click the **Windows Media Player** tile in the results.

> **WINDOWS WISDOM**
>
> The first time you start Windows Media Player, you'll probably see the Welcome to Windows Media Player dialog box. This is a one-time-only wizard that will get Media Player set up and ready to rock (or whatever). I heartily encourage you to use the default setup, so select the option **Recommended settings** and then click **Finish** to move on with your life.

- Insert an audio CD in your CD drive, or insert a DVD disc in your DVD drive. (Note that most DVD drives are also happy to play audio CDs for you.) If Windows displays a notification asking you what you want it to do with the audio CD, click it and then click **Play audio CD: Windows Media Player.**

- Use File Explorer to find a media file and then double-click the file. Remember that your user profile folder has a library named Music, which is the default folder that Windows 8 uses when you save music files.

- Download media from the internet. In most cases, Media Player will launch right away and start playing the sound or movie or whatever. (This is called *streaming* the media.) Sometimes, however, you may have to wait for the entire file to download before Media Player will spring into action.

Figure 10.3 shows what the Media Player window looks like when you launch the program without also starting some media. Your window will look a bit different unless you have precisely the same musical tastes as I do, in which case there are probably some larger issues we need to discuss.

Location within the library

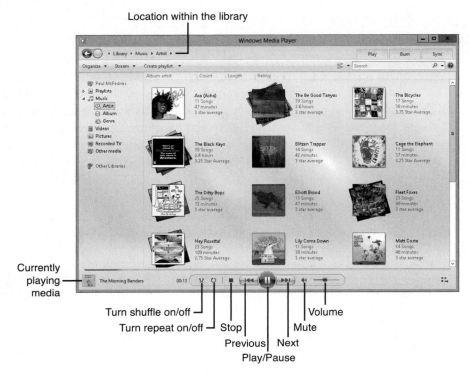

Currently
playing
media

Turn shuffle on/off
Turn repeat on/off   Stop
                    Previous   Next
                        Play/Pause
                                     Mute
                                 Volume

Figure 10.3: *This is the window you see when you launch Media Player.*

The first thing we should do here is ward off a potential area of confusion. In Chapter 5, you learned that Windows 8 organizes your user profile stuff into various libraries: Documents, Pictures, Music, and Video. No big whoop, except that Media Player *also* uses the library metaphor, but just to keep folks scratching their heads, it's not in any way related to libraries in your Windows 8 user profile. Thanks a lot, Microsoft!

So just to try to keep things straight here, I'll use the phrase *Media Player Library* to refer to the various media knickknacks that Media Player makes available to you.

To get around in the Media Player Library, you need to know two things:

- The navigation pane on the left side of the window shows the contents of the Media Player Library, and you see five categories: Playlists, Music, Video, Pictures, and Recorded TV. Double-click a category to open it, and then click a subcategory (such as Artist, Album, or Genre for Music).

HACKING WINDOWS

If you don't see the navigation pane, you can resurrect it by pressing **Alt** and selecting **View>Library,** or by pressing **Ctrl+1**.

- The links just below the title bar show your current location within the Media Player Library. (These are called *breadcrumb links* since they're sort of like breadcrumbs that you can use to retrace your steps.) In Figure 10.3, you can see I'm in the Library > Music > Artist section. Click the arrows to jump to other sections and other categories within the Media Player Library.

I should also point out the tabs that appear on the right side of the window, just below the title bar. You use these tabs to switch from one Media Player function to the other. Let's take a second to run through each tab so you know what you'll be getting yourself into:

- **Play.** This tab displays info about whatever album and track is currently playing, and you can use it to create your own playlists of songs. See the section Becoming a Program Director: Creating a Custom Playlist later in this chapter.

- **Burn.** This section enables you to copy music from your computer to a recordable CD, a process known as *burning*. The scoop on this is in the section Rollin' Your Own Music: Burning Tracks to a CD, later in this chapter.

- **Sync.** This section enables you to synchronize media files on a removable media device or memory card.

Giving Media Player Some Media to Play

I mentioned earlier that Media Player will launch and start playing automatically if you double-click or download a media file or insert an audio CD or DVD disc. However, if you open Media Player directly or if you want it to play something else, then you need to learn how to load media from within the program.

To open a media file, you have two possibilities:

- **Open a file on your computer.** Press **Alt** and select the **File>Open** command (or press **Ctrl+O**), use the Open dialog box to highlight the file, and then click **Open**.

- **Open a file from the internet.** Press **Alt** and select **File>Open URL** (or press **Ctrl+U**), use the Open text box to enter the internet address of the file, and then click **OK**.

Let's Make Some Noise: Playing Media

To control the playback of your media, the Media Player program offers the following buttons (see Figure 10.3):

- **Play/Pause.** Starts the media file or pauses the file when it's playing. Alternatives: select **Play>Play/Pause** or press **Ctrl+P**.

- **Stop.** Stops the media file and returns to the beginning of the file (or to the beginning of the current audio CD track). Alternatives: select **Play>Stop** or press **Ctrl+S**.

- **Previous.** Plays the previous file or track. Alternatives: select **Play>Previous** or press **Ctrl+B**.

> **WINDOWS WISDOM**
>
> If you want to fast-forward through a video, press and hold down the left mouse button over **Next**. (If the mood strikes, you can also Press **Alt** and select **Play>Fast Forward** or press **Ctrl+Shift+F**.) To rewind, instead, press and hold down the left mouse button over **Back**. (Alternatives? You bet: Press **Alt** and select **Play>Rewind** or press **Ctrl+Shift+B**.)

- **Next.** Plays the next file or track. Alternatives: Press **Alt** and then select **Play>Next** or press **Ctrl+F**.

- **Mute.** Turns off the sound playback. Alternatives: Press **Alt** and then select **Play>Volume>Mute** or press **F7**.

- **Volume.** Controls the playback volume. Drag the slider to the left to reduce the volume, or to the right to increase the volume. Alternatives: To increase the volume, press **Alt** and then select **Play>Volume>Up** or press **F9**; to decrease the volume, press **Alt** and select **Play>Volume>Down** or press **F8**.

- **Turn shuffle on/off.** Toggles shuffle mode on and off. Shuffle mode means that your library files or audio CD tracks play in random order. Alternatives: Press **Alt** and then select **Play>Shuffle** or press **Ctrl+H**.

- **Turn repeat on/off.** Toggles repeat mode on and off. When repeat mode is on, Media Player plays a media file over and over until you can't take it anymore. Alternatives: Press **Alt** and then select **Play>Repeat** command or press **Ctrl+T**.

And here are a few juicy tidbits you might want to keep in mind:

- To get a DVD, Video CD (VCD), or audio CD up and running, Press **Alt**, select **Play**, and then choose the **DVD, VCD, or CD Audio** menu option. (If you have multiple drives in your system, select the drive that contains the disc from the menu that appears.)

> **LOOK OUT!**
>
> Some audio CDs do double-duty as data CDs and come with programs you can run. In some cases, the program will run automatically when you insert the CD. So be forewarned that after you insert an audio CD, you may see something other than (or in addition to) Media Player on the screen.

- If you started a video playing, but you don't see it onscreen, Press **Alt** and then select **View>Now Playing**, or press **Ctrl+3**.

- You can eject a DVD, VCD, or audio CD right from Media Player, so you can avoid having to fumble around for the drive's often-hard-to-find eject button. To do this, Press **Alt** and then select **Play>Eject**, or press **Ctrl+J**. (If you have multiple drives in your system, use the menu that appears to select the drive that contains the disc.)

Trying Out Media Player's Audio CD Features

If you like to listen to music while you use your computer, it's possible to convince Media Player to crank up an audio CD. No joke. Audio CDs use the same dimensions as CD-ROM discs, so any audio CD will fit snugly inside your CD drive (or your DVD drive, if you have one).

When you first slide an audio CD into the drive, Windows 8 wakes up and displays a notification asking what you want to do with audio CDs each time. Click the notification and then click **Play Audio CD**. Windows 8 passes the message along to Media Player, which opens its Now Playing window. Move the mouse pointer into the Now Playing window and the playback controls pop up, as shown in Figure 10.4. If you'd rather control things from the main Media Player window, click the **Switch to Library** icon (pointed out in Figure 10.4) to make it so.

Rip CD

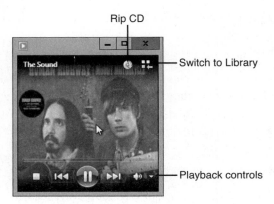

Switch to Library

Playback controls

Figure 10.4: *When you insert an audio CD, Media Player offers up the Now Playing window to control the playback.*

When you play audio CDs in Media Player, bear in mind that Media Player can access information about a CD from the internet. If your computer is connected to the internet when you insert the disc, Media Player will automatically reach out and grab various bits of data about the CD: its title, the name of the performer or group, the name and length of each track, and more. If you connect to the internet after the disc is already playing, you can get the disc info by switching to the main Media Player window, clicking the audio CD in the navigation pane, right-clicking the album or any track, and then clicking **Find Album Info**.

HACKING WINDOWS

As an added and slightly surprising bonus, the list of tracks is customizable. If Media Player can't get the name of a track, or if you want to change the existing name, right-click the track and then click **Edit**. Type in the new name and then press **Enter**.

Hard Disk Rock: Ripping Tracks from a CD

Media Player's audio CD playback is flexible, for sure, but playing audio CDs suffers from two important drawbacks:

- Shuffling discs in and out of the drive can be a hassle.

- There isn't any way to mix tunes from two or more CDs into a single playlist, even if your system has multiple CD and DVD drives.

To solve these dilemmas, Media Player enables you to copy—or *rip*, as the kids say—individual tracks from one or more CDs and store them on your computer's hard disk. From there, you can create a custom playlist that combines the tracks in any order you like.

Before I show you how you go about ripping tracks from an audio CD, let's take a second to set a few options related to track copying. In the Media Player window, select the **Organize>Options** command to display the Options dialog box and then select the **Rip Music** tab.

There are two main things you can do in this tab:

- **Change the file format.** Use the **Format** list to select the audio file format you want to use for the ripped tracks. There are lots of options here, but MP3 is the best way to go.

- **Change the audio quality.** The quality of the copied files is proportional to the acreage they consume on your hard disk. That is, the higher the quality, the fatter the file. Use the **Audio quality** slider to choose which quality level you want. Each level is measured in kilobits per second (Kbps), where there are 8 bits in a byte and 1,024 bytes in a kilobyte (KB).

WINDOWS WISDOM

To save a bit of time, Media Player offers a faster way to choose the format and audio quality. In the navigation pane, click the audio CD, and then click **Rip Settings** in Media Player's taskbar to display a menu. Select either **Format** (to select an audio file format) or **Audio Quality** (to select a quality level).

Click **OK** when you've made your choices.

To do the actual ripping, you have a couple of ways to go. The no-muss-no-fuss method is to insert the audio CD you want to rip, wait until you see Media Player's Now Playing window, move your mouse over the window to display the controls, and then click **Rip CD** (which I pointed out earlier in Figure 10.4).

If you want more control over the ripping process, then you need to put up with a bit of muss and fuss (but just a bit). In this case, you need to follow these steps:

1. Insert the audio CD you want to rip. If you see the Media Player's Now Playing window, click **Switch to Library** (or press **Ctrl+1**) to switch to the Media Player Library.

2. You should see the contents of the CD. If not, click the audio CD in Media Player's navigation pane.

3. For each track that you don't want to rip, deactivate the check box to the left of the track number. (They're all activated by default.)

4. Click **Rip CD**.

Media Player starts the copy process, which you can monitor by watching the **Rip Status** column (see Figure 10.5).

Figure 10.5: *You can use Media Player to rip audio CD tracks to your hard disk.*

Becoming a Program Director: Creating a Custom Playlist

Once you've copied a mess of CD tracks to your hard disk, you're free to combine these tracks and play them in any order. If you just want to play an individual track, here is the easiest way to go about it:

1. Display the **Library>Music** section.

2. In the **Music** branch, select one of the sub-branches: Album, Artist, or Genre.

3. Double-click the album, artist, genre, or whatever that contains the track you want.

4. Double-click the track.

Rather than playing single tracks using this method, you might prefer to combine multiple tracks into a playlist. You can then select the playlist and Media Player will play all the tunes for you automatically.

> **WINDOWS WISDOM**
>
> The techniques in this section apply equally to MP3 files and other music files that you download from the internet.

The first thing you need to do is create a new playlist:

1. Click **Create Playlist**. Media Player adds a new playlist to the Playlists section of the Library and creates a text box around the playlist name.

2. Type a descriptive name in the text box and press **Enter**.

3. Display the track or tracks you want to add to the playlist.

4. Click and drag the track (or tracks) and then drop the selection on the playlist name in the Playlists section. (If your click-and-drag skills aren't what they used to be, you can also right-click the track or tracks, click **Add to**, and then click the name of your playlist in the menu that appears.)

5. Repeat steps 3 and 4 to add all the tracks you want in your playlist.

6. Click the playlist to review your handiwork (see Figure 10.6).

Figure 10.6: *Click and drag tracks from the Library and drop them on the playlist to create a custom playlist.*

Rollin' Your Own Music: Burning Tracks to a CD

Listening to music while working on your computer is loads of fun, but I certainly hope you don't spend every waking minute in front of your PC. When it's time to get away, why not take some of your digital music with you? Media Player can perform the neat trick of copying—say *burning* when you're on the street—music files from your computer to a recordable CD or DVD. Here's how it works:

1. Select the **Burn** tab.

2. Display the track or tracks you want to burn.

3. Click and drag the track or tracks and drop the selection inside the Burn List. (Alternatively, right-click the selected tracks and then click **Add to>Burn list**.)

4. Repeat steps 2 and 3 to add all the tracks you want to burn.

5. Click **Start burn**. Media Player begins burning the tracks to the disc.

> **LOOK OUT!**
>
> Remember that once Media Player finishes writing to a CD-R or DVD-R disc, it "closes" the disc, which means that you can never write anything else to the disc. Therefore, make sure you have enough music available to fill up the CD-R (about 70 minutes) or DVD-R (about 500 minutes) so as not to waste space on the disc.

Movies, Tunes, and More: Running Media Center

Proving that digital media is a big deal these days, some versions of Windows 8 come with yet another digital media tool called Media Center. As its name implies, Media Center is meant to act as a kind of hub for your home entertainment center.

In a basic setup, you connect your computer to your TV and you can then use Media Center to play DVDs or downloaded movies, listen to music, watch digital slide shows, view TV listings, and even record TV programs.

A more space-age approach is to set up a wireless network and add an *extender*—such as an Xbox 360 game console—that enables you to stream movies, music, tunes, and TV to other devices on the network, even if they reside in another room or floor of your house.

DEFINITION

A Media Center **extender** is a device that enables you to watch or listen to your computer's media using other devices on your network.

As you can imagine, all of this is a bit complex and would require another book to learn how to connect everything, configure it, and then use it. So this section just provides you with a bit of an overview so you can at least get some idea of what Media Center is all about.

Making the Connection

There are many ways to configure a Media Center PC as an entertainment hub, but the simplest and most common is to connect the PC to a TV, which enables you to "watch" what's on the PC using the TV instead of a regular computer monitor. In particular, it means that whatever you do with the Media Center program—watch a DVD, run a digital slide show, and so on—appears on the TV.

How you connect your computer to the TV depends on the configuration of both, but there are two basic concepts you need to know:

- You attach one end of a cable to a port on your computer's video card and the other end to an input port in back of your TV.

- The video card port and the TV port must be the same type.

For example, if you have a newer TV and PC, then you most likely need an HDMI cable. If your equipment's a bit older, then you most likely need an S-Video cable instead. Even older than that and you'll most likely be using a cable with RCA connectors, which are the red, white, and yellow jacks that used to be commonly used with audiovisual equipment.

Looking at things the other way around, you might want to use Media Center to watch TV and record programs. In this case, you also need to connect your TV–set-top box to your computer:

- You attach one end of a coaxial cable to the output port (usually labeled *Cable Out* or *Out to TV*) in back of your set-top box, and the other end to a port on your computer.

- The computer connection must be a coaxial cable port on either your computer's video card or on a separate TV tuner device.

Firing Up Media Center

Once you've gone through all that rigmarole, get Media Center on the job by typing **media** in the Start screen and then clicking **Media Center**. The first time you launch Media Center, the program leads you by the hand through a series of configuration screens, some of which are optional. By judiciously skipping the unimportant parts of the process, you can get through it in just a few minutes. For even faster service, click **Continue** and then click **Express** to let Media Center handle the details.

Taking a Look Around

Figure 10.7 shows the initial Media Center screen that appears after you've handled the program's setup chores.

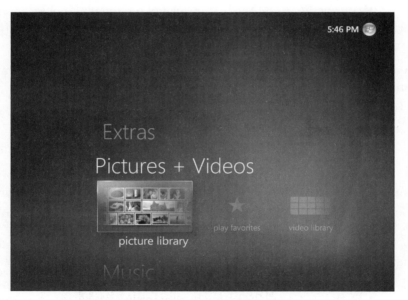

Figure 10.7: *The initial Media Center screen.*

Media Center starts off by displaying a list of the main tasks you can perform, which include the following:

- **Pictures + Videos.** Use this task to access your picture and video libraries. Second-level tasks here are Picture Library, Play Favorites, and Video Library. (I'm not sure why Microsoft chose to combine these rather different medias into a single task, but it does take some getting used to.)

- **Music.** Use this task to work with music and radio. Second-level tasks are Music Library (a list of the music files on your system), Play Favorites, Radio (listen to radio either through a tuner or via the internet), and Search (search your system for music).

- **Movies.** Use this task to work with DVD movies. Second-level tasks are Movie Library (a list of the DVD movies you've watched) and Play DVD.

- **TV.** Use this task to work with your TV tuner. Second-level tasks are Recorded TV (a list of TV shows you've recorded to your hard disk), Guide (what's on and when), and Live TV Setup (configuring TV options).

- **Tasks.** Use this task to run other Media Center features. Second-level tasks are Shutdown (close Media Center), Settings (configure Media Center), Learn More (get help with Media Center), Burn CD/DVD, Sync (synchronize content with an external device), Add Extender (add networked devices—such as Xbox 360—to view your content on those devices), and Media Only (locks Media Center in full-screen mode).

The Least You Need to Know

- Windows 8's new media marvels include the Music, Video, and Maps apps.

- The Media Player program can handle almost any kind of multimedia file. To use it, type **media** and then click **Windows Media Player** or double-click a media file.

- In most cases, you'll see the AutoPlay notification automatically after you insert an audio CD or DVD movie disc. The dialog box usually gives you a choice between playing the disc in Media Player and playing it in Media Center.

- Before using Media Player to rip audio CD tracks to your computer, your first task should be to choose the quality setting you want. To do this, select **Tools>Options**, and then use the **Rip Music** tab's **Audio quality** slider.

- Before using Media Center, make sure your PC is connected to your TV via an HDMI, S-Video, or RCA cable. If you want to record and watch TV on your computer, connect your PC's TV tuner and the set-top box with a coaxial cable.

Making Movies with Windows 8

In This Chapter

* Movie Maker's hardware hurdles
* How to capture video from a webcam
* Getting comfortable with video clips
* Inserting clips into a movie
* Editing a movie by trimming clips, adding transitions, and more

In the magical multimedia tour of the past three chapters, you've seen how Windows 8 handles images and sounds. In this chapter, you take all of that to its logical conclusion by learning how to string together multiple images and sounds. In other words, you learn how to record and edit videos on your computer. The tool that will turn you into a veritable videographer is Windows Live Movie Maker—a scaled-down, but still quite functional, video recording and editing program.

Introducing Movie Maker

Movie Maker can capture video from a camcorder, VCR, desktop camera, or even a TV, and save it on your computer. From there, you can cut out the bits you don't want, rearrange the footage, add narration and between-scenes transitions, and perform other Spielbergian tasks. You can then save your creation to a recordable CD or DVD, plop it onto your website, or email it to an unsuspecting friend or co-worker (or even to a suspecting one, for that matter).

As you might have surmised by now, the *Live* portion of Windows Live Movie Maker means you must download and install this program from the Windows Live Essentials website, as described back in Chapter 6. I'll wait here while you go ahead and do that.

Done? Good. The next section tells you what equipment you need for Movie Maker to do its thing, how to record footage, how to edit it into a crowd-pleasing shape, and how to distribute the final product.

What Hardware Do You Need to Use Movie Maker?

Before I answer the question that forms the title of this section, first let me say that you don't necessarily need *any* extra hardware to use Movie Maker. That's because the program is perfectly happy to work with existing digital video files. As you see a bit later, it's possible to import video files into Movie Maker and then play with them as you see fit. In fact, Movie Maker can deal with video files in all of the following formats (and a few more obscure ones, too):

- Advanced Systems Format (also known as ASF)
- Apple QuickTime (MOV or QT)
- Motion Picture Experts Group (MPEG or MPG)
- Video for Windows (AVI)
- Windows Media (WM)
- Windows Media Video (WMV; this is the format that Movie Maker uses when it saves your movies)

Besides all that, Movie Maker can also import many image and audio file formats. However, if it's your own video footage you're after, then you need to attach a video device to your computer. How you do this depends on what type of device you have and what type of connectors your computer has:

- **If you have a digital camcorder or desktop video camera (also called a web camera or webcam) and your computer has a USB port:** If your camcorder or camera supports USB, it should come with a USB cable that you attach directly to the computer.
- **If you have a digital camcorder or desktop video camera and your computer has an IEEE 1394 (FireWire) port:** IEEE 1394 is still a relatively uncommon method for getting digital video (and other kinds of data) into a computer. IEEE 1394 is one of those names that only a geek could love; fortunately, there's a more fun synonym that the rest of us can use: *FireWire*.

A few new computers are now shipping with FireWire ports, and there are also FireWire boards and PC cards that you can install. If your digital camera supports FireWire, it should come with a FireWire cable that you attach directly to the computer's FireWire port.

- **If you have an analog camcorder or VCR and your computer has a USB port:** There are products—known affectionately as *video dongles* in the trade—available that have the yellow, red, and white RCA jacks on one end (or the red, green, and blue RGB component jacks) and a USB connector on the other. In this case, you run an RCA (or RGB) cable from the camcorder or VCR to the dongle and then attach the dongle to your computer's USB port.

A Tour of the Movie Maker Screen

With all that out of the way, it's time to start making some digital movies. To get Movie Maker rolling, head over to the Start screen and click the **Windows Live Movie Maker** tile. Windows 8 releases the Windows Live Movie Maker window onto the desktop. Figure 11.1 shows the Movie Maker window with a movie project already on the go to help you understand the various parts of the program.

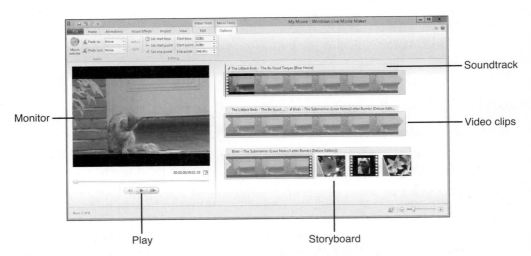

Figure 11.1: *The Movie Maker window with a movie project in progress.*

Let's run through the various Movie Maker "actors" and the roles they play:

- **Storyboard.** This is the area that holds the clips for your current movie project and is where you edit the movie.

- **Video clips.** These thumbnails represent the video clips that you've added to your project. Each clip shows the first *frame* of the video segment.

> **DEFINITION**
>
> A **frame** is a single image from a movie. All movies simulate motion by playing a rapid sequence of still images. The more images displayed per second, the better the quality of the movie. This measure is called *frame rate* and it's measured in frames per second (fps). Low quality is about 8 fps and high quality is 30 fps.

- **Monitor.** You use this area to play a clip or play your movie.

- **Play.** Click this button to play the current clip.

- **Soundtrack.** If you add a music soundtrack to your project, it appears here.

Importing Footage from a Video Camera

In previous versions of Movie Maker you could use the program to import video from a camera. This chore is now handled by Windows 8 itself, so I'll handle it here separately, too. As the next two sections show, you can import either existing footage or a live feed.

Importing Existing Footage from a Video Camera

First, some good news: Importing video footage from a digital camera is exactly the same as importing images from a digital camera. Why is that good news? Because it means that the technique I told you about in Chapter 6 for importing photos (see Importing Pictures from a Digital Camera) also works like a charm for importing videos. To ensure a smooth import, here are two things to bear in mind:

- It's likely you won't want to import everything from the camera, just the video (or videos) you want to use in your Movie Maker project. So when you get to the Import Photos and Videos dialog box, be sure to select the **Review, organize, and group items to import** option and click **Next**.

• In the dialog box that shows the groups of photos and videos, deactivate the **Select all** option and click **Expand all** so that you can see everything, particularly the video you want to import. How can you tell what's a video and what's a photo? A video appears with a filmstrip icon, as pointed out in Figure 11.2.

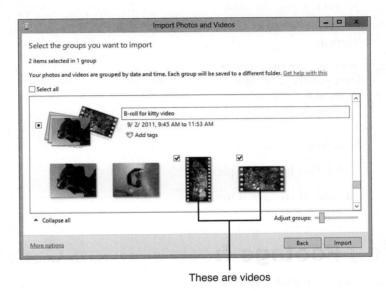

These are videos

Figure 11.2: *Digital camera videos appear with a filmstrip icon.*

That's about it. Type a name for the imported video and then click **Import**.

Importing Live Footage from a Video Camera

If you want to import a live feed, follow these steps:

1. If you're using an external camera, turn it on, switch it into record mode, and then attach the camera to your computer.

2. In Movie Maker, select **Home>Webcam video**. Movie Maker connects to your camera and opens the Webcam tab, which displays a live feed.

3. Give yourself a wave, say "Lights! Camera! Action!" and then click **Record**.

4. Mug for the camera as you see fit, and then click **Stop**. The Save Video dialog box appears.

5. Type a name for the video and then click **Save**. Movie Maker saves the video and then adds it to the Storyboard.

Starting a Fresh Movie Maker Project

In Movie Maker, the files you work with are called *projects*, and they consist of video clips, still images, music and sound effects, scene transitions, and titles.

Movie Maker starts a new movie project for you automatically when you crank it up. However, you can start a fresh project at any time by selecting the **File>New project** command (or by pressing **Ctrl+N**).

From Projector to Project: Creating Your Movie Project

Your footage is safely ensconced on your hard disk and you've got a piping hot project ready to go. Now what? Now it's nitty-gritty time as you start constructing your movie piece by piece.

Creating a movie in Movie Maker roughly involves the following steps:

1. Add a video clip to the storyboard.

2. Use the storyboard to move the video clip into the section of the movie where you want it to be seen.

3. Cut out unwanted sections of the video clip.

4. Add a transition effect between the previous clip and the new clip.

5. Apply a video effect to the clip.

6. Repeat steps 1 through 5 until you're done.

7. Insert a soundtrack.

The rest of this section takes you through each of these steps.

Adding a Video Clip to the Storyboard

Your first step in any Movie Maker project is to get some video "in the can" (as they say in the movie biz). That is, you need to add a collection of clips to the project to use as your editing raw materials. Here's how it works:

1. Click the **Home** tab.

2. In the **Add** section, click **Add videos and photos**. Predictably, the Add Videos and Photos dialog box appears.

3. Select the media file you want to add. You can select either a video file or a photo. If you go with the latter, note that Movie Maker sets up the photo as a video clip that displays the photo for 7 seconds.

4. Click **Open**. Movie Maker adds the media to the storyboard.

Using the Storyboard to Juggle Clips

When you insert your clips into the project, you don't need to worry too much about the order the clips appear because the order is easy to change by using any of the following techniques:

- To move a clip, use your mouse to drag the clip to a new position within the storyboard. A black vertical bar tells you where the clip will appear when you drop it.

- To copy a clip, hold down the **Ctrl** key, drag the clip to the position where you want the copy to appear (again, the black vertical bar lets you know where the clip will end up), and then drop the clip.

- To delete a clip, click it, and then press **Delete**.

HACKING WINDOWS

You can work with multiple clips in the storyboard, if that suits your fancy. To select multiple clips in a row, click the first clip, hold down **Shift**, and click the last clip. To select clips willy-nilly, hold down **Ctrl** and click each clip.

Trimming a Clip

When you add a video clip to the storyboard, Movie Maker adds the entire clip, including those first few seconds when the camera was pointing at your feet. Nobody wants to see your feet (although you know your audience best), so how do you get rid of that unwanted footage? The secret is to trim the bad footage from the clip's beginning or end—or both. Here's how:

1. In the storyboard, click the clip you want to trim.

2. Display the **Edit** tab.

3. Click **Trim tool**. Movie Maker displays the Trim tab and the trim controls, as shown in Figure 11.3.

Trim the beginning of the video

Trim the end of the video

Figure 11.3: *Use Movie Maker's trim controls to lop off unsightly video clip footage.*

4. Drag the **Trim the beginning of the video** bar to the right to set the start point of the good footage. As you drag the bar, the current clip position appears in the monitor, so you can see exactly where you are within the clip.

HACKING WINDOWS

Another way to set the start point for a clip is to play the clip until you get to the point you want to start, click **Pause**, and then click **Set start point**. You can also play to the end point, pause, and then click **Set end point**.

5. Drag the **Trim the end of the video** bar to the left to set the end point of the good footage.

6. Click **Save trim**.

WINDOWS WISDOM

I mentioned earlier that Movie Maker sets up a photo to display as a "clip" for 7 seconds. To change that, click the photo in the storyboard, click the **Edit** tab, then use the **Duration** control to set the time, in seconds, that you want the photo to stay onscreen.

Adding a Transition Between Two Clips

In video editing, a transition is an effect that accompanies the change from one scene to another. In Movie Maker, the default transition from one clip to another is a jump cut: an immediate scene change from the first clip to the next. However, you don't have to settle for something so plain. Movie Maker has dozens of other transitions you can use to make people sit up and take notice. Here are the steps to follow to add transitions between scenes:

1. Select the **Animations** tab.

2. Select the second of the two clips that you want involved in the transition.

3. In the **Transitions** group, click the transition you want to use. Movie Maker adds the transition between the selected clip and the one before it.

4. Repeat steps 2 and 3 to add other transitions to your project.

Adding Video Effects

A video effect is a visual treatment applied to a clip. For example, Sepia Tone effect makes a clip look as though it is quite old. Movie Maker comes with more than two dozen effects that you can apply. Here are the steps to follow to apply an effect to a clip:

1. Select the **Visual Effects** tab.

2. Select the clip that you want to work with.

3. In the **Effects** group, click the visual effect you want to use. Movie Maker applies the effect.

4. Repeat steps 2 and 3 to add other effects to your project.

Adding a Soundtrack

If you choose to record both video and audio when capturing your footage, your clips will come with an audio track that represents the audio portion of the video. You can supplement this track with a separate audio track that can play narration, background music, sound effects, or whatever other auditory marvels your project needs.

Here's how it works:

1. Display the **Home** tab.

2. In the **Add** section, click the top half of the **Add music** button. The Add Music dialog box shows up.

3. Click the music file you want to use as a soundtrack.

4. Click **Open**. Movie Maker adds the track to the movie and displays the Options tab under Music Tools, as shown in Figure 11.4.

5. To control the relative volume between the clip audio and the soundtrack audio, click **Music volume** and then drag the slider either left (to reduce the music audio) or right (to increase the music audio).

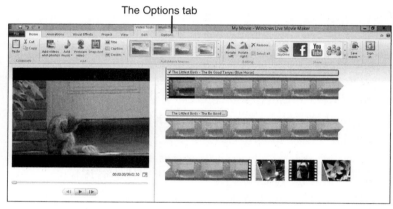

Figure 11.4: *Under Music Tools, the Options tab offers several tools for working with your audio track.*

Outputting Your Project to a Movie File

If you want to watch your movie in Movie Maker itself, just click the **Play** button. If you want to watch your movie elsewhere, then you need to output the project to a movie file.

Follow these steps to output your project to a file:

1. Display the **Home** tab.

2. In the **Share** group, click **Save movie**.

3. Click the output format you want to use, such as a high-definition display, a computer monitor, or a Windows Phone. Movie Maker displays the Save Movie dialog box.

4. Type a name for your movie and select a location.

5. Click **Save**. Movie Maker lives up to its name by making the movie. (This may take a while, depending on the length of your movie and the number of transitions and effects you used.)

6. When the movie is at long last complete, you can either click **Play** to give it a whirl, or click **Close** to move on to other pursuits.

The Least You Need to Know

- If you have an analog camcorder, VCR, or TV, you need a video capture card (or a graphics card that supports video capture) and you need the proper composite or S-Video cable to make the attachment. If your device supports USB, attach it to one of your computer's USB ports.

- For a digital camcorder or camera, attach the device to either a USB port or to an IEEE 1394 (FireWire) port.

- To record live video footage in Windows 8, put your external camera in record mode, click the **Home** tab, and then click **Webcam video**.

- To add clips to the storyboard, display the **Home** tab, and then click **Add videos and photos** in the **Add** group.

- To add a soundtrack to your project, display the **Home** tab, and then click **Add music** in the **Add** group.

- To turn your project into an honest-to-goodness digital movie file, display the **Home** tab, click **Save movie**, and then click the movie format you prefer.

Getting Things Done with Windows 8

Playing around with images, videos, and music can be a heck of a lot of fun, but one of these days you've got to get some work done. (Insert groan of disappointment here.) When the time comes for your nose and the grindstone to get reacquainted, Windows 8 will be there for you with some competent tools for getting things done. The chapters in Part 3 look at the most commonly used of these tools. You learn how to work with user accounts in Chapter 12, how to surf the web in Chapter 13, and how to do the email thing in Chapter 14. Chapter 15 covers the new social networking features in Windows 8, Chapter 16 covers faxing, and Chapter 17 covers notebook features. Don't work too hard!

Sharing Your Computer with Others

In This Chapter

- Creating accounts for each person who uses your computer
- Setting up accounts with passwords and custom pictures
- Sharing and hiding your documents
- Keeping an eye on the kids with parental controls
- Setting up your very own wireless network

Do you share your computer with other people, either at work or at home? Then you've probably run smack dab into one undeniable fact: people are individuals with minds of their own! One person prefers Windows in a black-and-purple color scheme; another person just loves changing the desktop background, the wackier the better; yet another person prefers to have a zillion shortcuts on the Windows desktop; and, of course, *everybody* uses a different mix of applications and creates their own documents. How can you possibly satisfy all these diverse tastes and prevent people from coming to blows?

Well, it's a lot easier than you might think. Windows 8 enables you to set up a different *user account* for each person who uses the computer. These accounts keep your stuff separate from everyone else's stuff, including documents and programs, desktop and Start-menu configuration, Internet Explorer favorites, and more. This means everyone can customize Windows 8 to their heart's content without foisting their tastes on anyone else. This chapter shows you how to set up, maintain, and use Windows 8's user accounts. You also learn how to set up a simple network so you can share your stuff without sharing your computer.

Understanding These User-Account Doodads

In a sense, a user account gives everyone their own version of Windows 8 that they can muck around with as they see fit. This includes the following:

- All the customization stuff covered in Part 4 of the book. This means each user can set up his or her own colors, desktop background, screen saver, and Start-screen customizations.

- Favorite websites defined in Internet Explorer.

- Email accounts set up in the Mail app or Windows Live Mail.

Not only that, Windows 8 also supports a feature called *fast user switching*; what this means is that different users can switch in and out of Windows but leave their programs running. For example, suppose little Alphonse is blowing away some aliens and Dad needs to check his email. In the old days, Alphonse would have to shut down his game so that Dad could log on and run his email program. In Windows 8, Alphonse can leave his game running while Dad switches to his account and does his email duties. Alphonse can then switch back right away and resume doing nasty things to strange creatures.

The last thing you need to know before getting started is that Windows 8 offers two different user account types:

- **Administrator.** This type of account has wide (but not complete) access to the computer. An administrator can install any type of program or device; make changes that affect the entire system; and add, change, and delete user accounts. Note, however, that the administrator can't examine the private documents of any other user.

- **Standard user.** This type of account has access to only some of the computer's features. A standard user can view his own files, view those files that have been set up to be shared with other users, perform his own customizations, and change his password.

In Windows 8, there's only one administrator account, and that's whatever account you set up when you went through the initial Windows 8 configuration. Every other account you create (as described next) is automatically a standard user.

Creating a New Account

When you or some suitably savvy geek set up Windows 8 on your computer, the installation program asked for the name of a user. Windows 8 then set up an administrator account for that person. If you're the administrator, then you're free to add more accounts as you see fit.

Here are the steps to follow:

1. Press **Windows+W** to open the handy Settings search pane.

2. Type **users** and then click **Users** in the search results. The PC Settings app shows up and courteously displays the Users tab for you.

3. Click **Add a user**. This launches the Add a User screen.

4. Click **Sign in without a Microsoft account**.

SEE ALSO

This section assumes you just want to set up your new user as a local account. Later, if you want to switch the user to a Microsoft account, no problem. See Setting Up a Microsoft Account in Chapter 7.

5. Click **Local account**.

6. Use the **User name** text box to enter a name for the user.

7. Use the **Password** text box to type the password for the user. (Note that you see a bunch of dots, instead of the actual characters you type. This is a security feature to prevent someone from spying the password.)

LOOK OUT!

Yes, as a matter of fact, you *can* create a standard user account without a password. However, just because you can, it doesn't follow that you should. If you don't protect an account with a password, any Tom, Dick, or Hacker can sign on to that account just by selecting it on the sign-on screen! Doh! To avoid this, give the account a password.

8. Use the **Reenter password** text box to type the password once again. If you're not sure if you typed the password exactly the same, click and hold the **Display Characters** icon pointed out in Figure 12.1, which displays your characters. Release the mouse button to restore the security dots.

9. Use the **Password hint** text box to enter a password hint. This word or phrase is accessible in the sign-on screen and is visible to all; therefore, make the hint as vague as possible while still being useful to you if you forget your password.

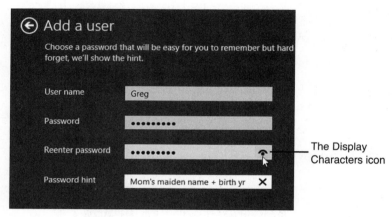

Figure 12.1: *Use this screen to type the new user's name and password.*

10. Click **Next**. Windows 8 creates the new account.

11. If you're setting up an account for one of your kids, consider activating the **Is this a child's account?** check box. This will save you a step down the road when you set up Family Safety for your kids. See "Protecting Your Kids with Family Safety," later in this chapter.

12. Click **Finish**.

Logging On to an Account

Once you have two or more user accounts on the go, then each time you crank up Windows 8 and press a key to get past the Lock screen, you end up at the sign-on screen, which displays an icon for each user account (see Figure 12.2 for an example).

Click your user icon (or the icon of whatever account you want to use), enter the account password, and then press **Enter**.

Figure 12.2: *The sign-on screen displays an icon for each user account.*

Once you're logged on to an account, you can return to the sign-on screen by following these steps:

1. In the Start screen, click your user account tile, which appears in the upperright corner of the screen. Windows 8 displays the menu shown in Figure 12.3.

Figure 12.3: *Click your user account tile to see this menu of account-related commands.*

2. Select one of the following:

    *   **Lock.** Click this command to leave all your programs running and display the Lock screen. This is a good choice when you'll be leaving your desk for a bit and you don't want some snoop seeing what's on your screen. You can't return to the Start screen without signing back on to your account.

- **Sign out.** Click this command if you prefer to shut down all of the current user's windows and programs. Windows 8 drops you off at the Lock screen.

- **A user icon.** Click this command if you want to leave the current user's windows and programs open and running. (This is the fast user-switching feature that I mentioned earlier in the chapter.) At the sign-on screen, Windows 8 displays *Logged on* under the user's name.

Making Changes to an Existing Account

You'll be happy to hear that your main Windows 8–administrator account, and any standard accounts you conjure up, are not set in stone. In fact, you can change quite a few things about an account, including its picture and password. You can also delete any accounts you no longer use. The next few sections run through the instructions for the most common user account tasks.

Changing the Account Picture

The user account isn't the most exciting topic in the computing world, so it's a welcome relief that Windows 8 includes a feature that lets you have a bit of fun: you can assign a picture to each user. This picture is visible on the sign-on screen and on the user account tile that appears in the top-right corner of the Start screen. Windows 8 supplies a generic picture when you create an account, but here's how you change it to something with a bit more pizzazz:

1. Log in as the user you want to change.

2. Click the user account tile and then click **Change account picture**. The PC Settings app loads and offers you the Personalize tab with the Account Picture section selected.

3. Now you come to a fork in the account picture road:

   - **Use an existing picture.** This is the way to go if you have just the picture you want lying around in your PC somewhere. Click **Browse** to display a screen for selecting files. Click **Files** and then click a folder that has the pic you want to use (such as **Pictures**). Click the picture and then click **Choose image**.

- **Take a new picture.** If you're looking particularly good today (no surprise there), you can use your PC's built-in or attached webcam to take a snap of your smiling mug. Click **Webcam** to launch the Camera app, put your best face forward, and then click the screen to take the picture. Click **OK** if you look awesome, or click **Retake** to try again.

4. Click the picture you want to use. If you have your own picture, click **Browse for more pictures**, use the Open dialog box to find the image you want, and then click **Open**.

5. Click **Change Picture**.

Changing the Account Password

If you store sensitive data on your computer (or just don't want someone to snoop), then you should think carefully about the password you choose. That is:

- Don't use an obvious word, such as your name, the number "1234", or the word *password*.

- Make sure the password is at least 8 characters in length (the longer the better).

- Make sure the password uses at least 1 character from at least three of the following four sets: lowercase letters, uppercase letters, numbers, and symbols (such as @ and #).

If you're starting to perspire profusely because your account (or any account you created) doesn't even come close to these criteria, sweat not, my friend. You can fix things lickety-split by changing the password:

1. Log in as the user you want to change.

2. Press **Windows+W** to open the Settings search pane.

3. Type **users** and then click **Users** in the search results. The PC Settings app loads and displays the Users tab.

4. In the Users tab of the PC Settings app, click **Change your password**.

5. Use the **Old password** text box to type your existing password.

6. Use the **New password** and **Re-enter password** text boxes to type the fresh password.

7. Click **Next**. Windows 8 changes the account's password, just like that.

8. Click **Finish**.

Creating a Picture Password

Are you using Windows 8 on a tablet? If you've armed your user account with a long and complicated password, then you might find that it takes you a teeth-gnashingly long time to sign in to Windows 8 using your tablet's touch keyboard.

If so, then here's a bit of good news for you: you can switch to a picture password instead. In this case, your "password" is a series of three gestures—any combination of a tap, a straight line, or a circle—that you apply to a photo. Windows 8 displays the photo at startup, and you repeat your gestures—in order—to sign in to Windows. It's *way* easier than wrestling with the onscreen keyboard.

LOOK OUT!

Using a picture password is a lot easier, but there's a catch. (You just knew there'd be a catch, didn't you?) Unlike a regular text password where the characters appear as dots to prevent someone from seeing them, your gestures have no such protection. Therefore, it's possible (at least in theory) for some evildoer to view and possibly even record your gestures using a camera. Curses!

If you're game to try, follow these steps to set it up:

1. Log in as the user you want to change.

2. Press **Windows+W** to open the Settings search pane.

3. Type **users** and then click **Users** in the search results. The PC Settings app displays the Users tab.

4. Click **Create a picture password**. Ever paranoid, Windows 8 asks you to verify your account password.

5. Type your password and then click **OK**. Satisfied, Windows 8 opens the Welcome to Picture Password screen.

6. Click **Choose picture**. Windows 8 prompts you to select a picture to use for the password.

7. Click the picture you want to use and then click **Open**. The How's This Look? screen appears.

8. Drag the picture so that the image is positioned where you prefer, and then click **Use this picture**. Now the Set Up Your Gestures screen makes an appearance.

9. Use your finger (or stylus or even a mouse) to draw three gestures. Remember that you can use any combination of a tap, a line, and a circle. As you complete each gesture, Windows 8 displays it on the photo, as shown in Figure 12.4.

Figure 12.4: *As you complete each gesture, Windows 8 confirms it by displaying the gesture on the photo.*

 LOOK OUT!

In the same way that you shouldn't choose a blindingly obvious text password, make sure you don't create an obvious picture password. For example, if you're using a photo showing three faces, then an obvious picture password would be a tap on each face. A good picture password not only uses all three available gestures, but also uses them in nonobvious ways.

10. Repeat the gestures to confirm.

11. Click **Finish**.

Now the next time you sign in to Windows 8, you'll be prompted to enter your picture-password gestures. To make sure you've memorized your picture password, you should sign out of your account a few times and then sign back in using the picture password.

Deleting an Account

If you no longer need an account, you may as well delete it to reduce clutter in the Users tab and the sign-on screen. Here's how:

1. Log in using your main administrator account.

2. Press **Windows+W** to return to the Settings search screen.

3. Type **remove user** and then click **Remove user accounts** in the search results. The Manage Accounts window appears on the desktop.

4. Click the user you want to delete.

5. Click **Delete the account**. Windows 8 asks if you want to keep the contents of the user's folders and desktop.

6. If you want to save these things, click **Keep Files** to store them in a new folder named after the user. Otherwise, click **Delete Files**.

7. Click **Delete Account**.

Sharing Documents with (or Hiding Them from) Other Users

Although you'll want to keep most of your documents to yourself, it's conceivable that you'll want other users to be able to see and work with some files. For example, you might scan in some family photos that you want everyone to see or you might store some music that you want other folks to hear.

In Windows 8, no user can access another user's documents directly. However, it's possible to change this and allow other users access to some—or all—of your folders or files, as well as control what they can do with those folders or files. To see how, follow these steps:

1. In the Start screen, click **Desktop** and then click **File Explorer** in the taskbar to open your main user-account folder.

2. Open the folder you want to share. If you want to share a file instead, open its folder and then click the file.

3. Click the **Share** tab, open the **Share with** list, and then click **Specific people.** Windows 8 asks you to choose the user accounts with whom you want to share the item.

4. Type the user name and click **Add**.

5. Repeat step 4 as necessary to share the folder or file with other users.

6. For each user you add, assign a Permission Level by clicking the downward-pointing arrow and selecting one of the following (see Figure 12.5):

   - **Read.** This is the default level. At this level the user can only view the shared file or folder; he or she can't change anything.

   - **Read/Write.** At this level the user can view the shared file or folder, as well as create new items, and make changes to—or delete—any item.

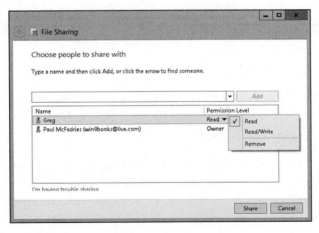

Figure 12.5: *After you add a user, be sure to set the permission level.*

7. Click **Share**. Windows 8 takes a few moments to share the item.

8. If you want to send an email to the users to let them know the folder or file is shared, click **email**; otherwise, click **Done**.

If you no longer want to share a folder or file, you can change sharing using either of the following methods:

- **To remove a user from sharing:** Follow steps 1 through 3 in this section to display the list of shared users. Click the permission level for the user you want to work with, and then click **Remove**.

- **To stop sharing the folder or file entirely.** Follow steps 1 through 2 in this section, click the **Share** tab, and then click **Stop sharing**.

Protecting Your Kids with Family Safety

If you have children who share your computer (how brave of you!), or if you're setting up a computer for their use, it's wise to take precautions regarding the content and programs that they can access. Locally, this might take the form of blocking access to certain programs (such as your financial software), using ratings to control which games they can play, and setting time limits on when the computer is used.

All of this sounds daunting, but never fear: Windows 8's Family Safety feature makes it relatively easy to set all aforementioned options and a lot more.

Before you begin, be sure to create a standard user account for each child who will use the computer. Once that's done, you set up Family Safety by following these steps:

1. Press **Windows+W** to open the Settings search pane.

2. Type **family** and then click **Set Up Family Safety for any user** in the search results.

3. Click the user you want to work with to get to the User Settings page.

4. Activate the option **On, enforce current settings**. This enables the Web Filtering, Time Limits, Windows Store and Game Restriction, and App Restrictions links in the Windows Settings area, as shown in Figure 12.6.

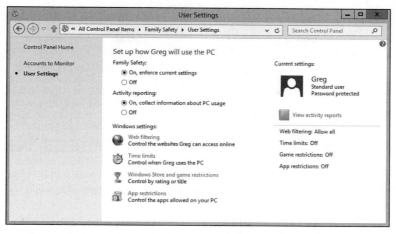

Figure 12.6: *Activate the **On, enforce current settings** option to turn on parental controls.*

5. Use the following links in the Settings area to set up the specific controls for this user (in each case, when you're done, click **User Settings** to return to the User Settings window):

   - **Web filtering.** Click this link to display the Web Filtering window, and then click the *User* **can only use the websites I allow** option (where *User* is the account you chose in Step 3). Now you can allow or block specific websites, set up general site restrictions (such as Child-Friendly websites only), and block file downloads.

   - **Time limits.** Click this link to display the Time Limits page. Click **Curfew,** then click *User* **can only use the PC during the time range I allow** option (where *User* is the account you chose in Step 3). This shows a grid where each square represents an hour during the day for each day of the week. Click the squares to block computer usage during selected times.

   - **Windows Store and game restrictions.** Click this link to display the Game and Windows Store Restrictions page, and then click the *User* **can only use the games and Windows Store apps that I allow** option (where *User* is the account you chose in Step 3). Now you can restrict games and apps based on ratings and contents, and block or allow specific games.

- **App restrictions.** Click this link to display the Application Restrictions page, and then click the *User* **can only use the apps I allow** option (where *User* is the account you chose in Step 3). This displays a list of the programs on your computer. Click the check boxes for the programs you want to allow the person to use.

Setting Up Your Very Own Wireless Network

Sharing what's on your computer with other users of that same machine is a good start. However, in today's radical world of sharing, you need to go beyond your PC and share things with *other* computers.

How on earth are you supposed to do that? The key is Wi-Fi (it rhymes with *hi-fi*), which is short for wireless fidelity—although nobody ever uses the full phrase. The secret sauce is the wireless part, which enables you to share your PC's stuff with other PCs without them being in any way physically connected.

Getting Your Wireless Network Prepared

That sounds like voodoo, I know, but it's the real deal. To set up a wireless network, you need two things:

- Each computer that you want to go wireless must have a wireless network adapter. This component enables the computer to send and receive signals wirelessly. Almost all modern computers have this component built in. How can you tell? Press **Windows+I** to open the Settings pane. If you see the icon pointed out in Figure 12.7, then your computer is wireless-friendly. If not, then you need to purchase a wireless network adapter, which is usually a USB device that you plug into a free USB port on your PC.

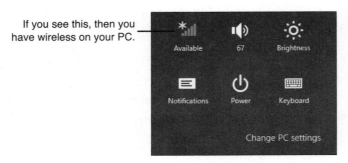

Figure 12.7: *If you see this wireless network icon in the Settings pane, your computer is wireless-ready.*

- You need a device called a wireless router. This device (an example is shown in Figure 12.8) connects to your broadband modem, and it's through the wireless router that your computer connects to the internet.

Figure 12.8: *An example of a wireless router.*

Once you have the wireless router, take out the installation disc, insert it into your computer, and then run the install program. This will take you through some crucial configuration steps, such as giving your network an ironically hip name and setting the router's security options.

Adding the Internet to Your Wireless Network

If you have an internet connection on one computer, you might be wondering a couple of things:

- If you have a second computer, is it possible for that computer to also use the internet connection?

- If your computer is a notebook or similarly portable PC, is it possible to lug the computer to some comfy spot—say, your favorite easy chair or your back patio—and still have access to the internet?

The answer to both questions is a resounding "Yes!" How? By connecting your wireless router to your broadband modem. To do this, first turn off both the broadband modem and the router.

Examine the back of your wireless router and locate the port that it uses for the internet connection. Conveniently, some label this port *internet* (see Figure 12.9), whereas others use *WAN* or *WLAN*. Some annoying routers don't label the internet port at all, but place the port off to the side so it's clearly separate from the router's other ports. Run a network cable from the network port in the back of the modem (which is usually the one labeled *Ethernet* or *LAN*) to the internet port in the back of the wireless router.

Figure 12.9: *Run the network cable from the broadband modem to the internet (or WAN) port in the back of the wireless router.*

Your next step is to configure the wireless router for internet access. Unfortunately, there isn't a single, straightforward way to go about this. There are, in fact, *dozens* of possibilities depending on the type of wireless router you have and the company you're using as your ISP (Internet Service Provider). Obviously, I can't cover all of the possibilities here, but I'll be happy to give you the general steps. For the specifics, see the manual that came with the router and the instructions provided by your ISP.

The first thing you need to do is temporarily connect your computer to the wireless router. Run a network cable from the network port on your computer to a similar port on the back of the router (although not the internet or WAN or WLAN port used by the broadband modem).

Now, follow these steps to access the router's setup pages:

1. On the computer connected to the router, switch to the Start screen and then click **File Explorer**.

2. Click **Network**. Windows displays the devices on your network. You should see an icon for the router. The name of the icon usually is the same as the router's model number. In Figure 12.10, for example, the router is the icon named Alcatel Lucent 7130.

HACKING WINDOWS

What happens if you don't see an icon for your wireless router? All is not lost, fortunately. Get out the router manual and dig through it until you find out the router's IP address, which will be something like 192.168.1.1. Start Internet Explorer, type that address in the Address bar, and press **Enter**.

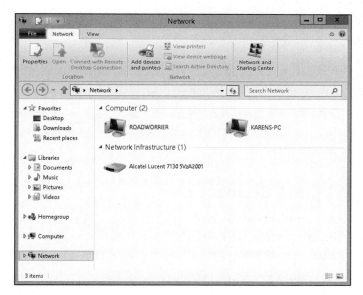

Figure 12.10: *You should see an icon for your router in the Network window.*

3. Double-click the router icon. The router prompts you to log on to the device.

4. Type the default user name and password. (See the router manual for the log-on details.)

5. Click **Log In** (or **OK**, or whatever). The router's setup pages appear.

Now that you're into the setup pages, you can make the necessary modifications. Using your router manual and ISP document as a guide, you should change the following things:

- **The type of internet connection.** This is usually either DHCP (if you have a broadband connection with a cable ISP) or PPPoE (if you have a broadband connection with an ADSL ISP). The latter also requires your connection's user name and password.

- **The network name.** This is a name that you need to think of to uniquely identify your wireless network. This will make it easier for you to make the connection (as I describe in just a bit). The network name is often called the *SSID*.

- **The wireless security options.** To ensure that every nearby Tom, Dick, and Harry can't access your wireless network, you need to configure the security options. For the encryption type, choose WPA2—and then enter a password (which may be called, mysteriously, a *preshared key*).

- **The administration password.** You use this password to access the router's setup pages. All routers come with a default password (usually *admin*), but you should change it so other people can't access the setup pages.

When you've done all that, pat yourself on the back, save your changes, and then disconnect the network cable that's running from the computer to the router. (From now on, you can access the setup pages wirelessly if need be.)

Making the Wireless Connection

With your wireless router now hooked up to the broadband modem and configured with the internet-connection type, the router will automatically create a connection to the internet. Your job now is to wirelessly tap into that connection:

1. Press **Windows+I** to open the Settings pane.

2. Click the wireless network icon, pointed out earlier in Figure 12.7. Windows displays a list of nearby wireless networks.

3. Click your wireless network. That is, click the network name that you created earlier.

4. Activate the **Connect automatically** check box. This tells Windows 8 to connect to your network without your having to repeat these steps.

5. Click **Connect**. Windows prompts you to enter your wireless network password (which it calls a *security key*).

6. Type the password, and then click **Next**. Windows 8 asks if you want to turn on sharing between PCs.

7. Click **Yes, turn on sharing and connect to devices**. Windows connects your wireless network, and you're free to access the other computers and surf the web wirelessly.

Sharing Stuff with a Windows 8 Homegroup

If you have other computers on your network and they're running either Windows 8 or Windows 7, then you can take advantage of network features called the homegroup. A homegroup is a relatively informal link between two or more Windows 8 (or 7) PCs on a home network. By using a single password for every user and every PC, the homegroup lets you easily share libraries and printers with your network neighbors.

Creating a Homegroup

Windows 8 doesn't create a homegroup automatically, so you must cobble one together yourself. Here's how:

1. Press **Windows+W** to open the Settings search pane.

2. Type **homegroup** and then click **HomeGroup** in the search results. Windows 8 launches the PC Settings app and serves up the HomeGroup tab.

3. Click **Create**. Windows 8 coughs up the Libraries and Devices window, shown in Figure 12.11.

4. For each item you want to share, click the switch to the **Shared** position.

5. Scroll down the screen a bit to see the homegroup password. Make a note of the password.

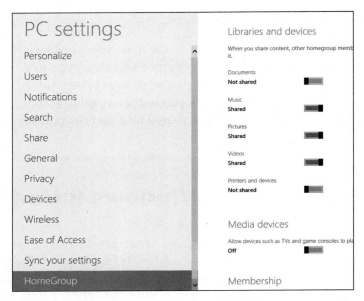

Figure 12.11: *Use this window to specify which libraries and devices you want to share with the folks in your homegroup.*

Joining a Homegroup

Once you've got a homegroup hanging around on your network, other Windows 8 (or 7) PCs can join in the fun by following these steps:

1. Press **Windows+W** to open the Settings search pane.

2. Type **homegroup** and then click **HomeGroup** in the search results. Windows 8 launches the PC Settings app and displays the HomeGroup tab.

3. Type the homegroup password and then click **Join**. Windows 8 joins your computer to the homegroup.

4. For each item you want to share, click the switch to the **Shared** position.

WINDOWS WISDOM

To change the homegroup password, press **Windows+W** to open the Settings search pane, type **homegroup**, and then click **Change homegroup password**. In the Homegroup window, click **Change the password** to open the Change Your Homegroup Password dialog box, click **Change the password**, and then either use the password that Windows 8 generates or type your own.

The Least You Need to Know

- Windows 8 supports two types of user: main administrator and standard user. The main administrator account pretty much allows you to do what you want, including install programs and devices, change system settings, and work with user accounts; the standard user account (every other account) only allows you to view your own files, view shared files, and perform your own Windows customizations.
- The Users tab window is where everything happens; you get there by pressing **Windows+W**, typing **users**, and then clicking **Users**.
- To create a new user account, click **Add a user** in the Users tab.
- To change a user's account settings, log in as that user and then display the Users tab.
- To work with parental controls, press **Windows+W**, type **family**, and then click **Set Up Family Safety for any user**.
- To create or join a homegroup, press **Windows+W**, type **homegroup**, and then click **HomeGroup**.

Wandering the Web

In This Chapter

- Using the Windows 8 app and desktop versions of Internet Explorer to navigate web pages
- Saving web pages to your Favorites list
- Searching for the information you need
- Figuring out these newfangled tabs
- Dealing with file downloads

Whether you're 19 or 90, a world traveler or a channel surfer, I don't think I'm going out on a limb when I say that you've probably never seen anything quite like the World Wide Web. We're talking about an improbably vast conglomeration of the world's wit, wisdom, and weirdness. Arranged in separate pages of information, the web is home to just about every conceivable topic under the sun. If someone's thought of it, chances are someone else has a web page about it.

So the web is definitely worth a look or three. This chapter helps you get those looks by showing you how to use the Windows 8 Internet Explorer programs (the app and the desktop version), which are designed to surf (to use the proper web verb) websites. In this chapter, you learn all the standard page-navigation techniques, and the features that Internet Explorer offers for making your online journeys more efficient and pleasant.

SEE ALSO

If you haven't yet signed up with an internet service provider (ISP), it means you've skipped ahead in this book—and I've caught you! To learn about signing up with an ISP, check out Chapter 7.

Internet Explorer: Two Paths to the Web

As I mentioned in the chapter opening, Windows 8 comes equipped with not one, but *two* versions of Internet Explorer. If you just want to poke around the web a bit, the app version of Internet Explorer is probably your speed. It's easy to use and very secure, so it's about as simple and safe as web surfing gets. For more of a true web experience, you need to use the desktop version of Internet Explorer, which is festooned with bells and whistles to handle just about any web eventuality. The next section looks at the Internet Explorer app, and then the rest of this chapter tackles the desktop version.

Simple Surfing with the Internet Explorer App

You've seen in a few places so far in the book that the Windows 8 apps tend to be scaled-down versions of their desktop cousins. There's nothing wrong with that, of course, since even a scaled-down app can still be useful and fun. That applies in spades to the Internet Explorer app, because even though it's much simpler than the desktop version, it still gets you from web point A to web point B.

Feel free to click the **Internet Explorer** tile on the Start screen. Internet Explorer loads and presents you (most likely) with an almost entirely blank screen. Use the box at the bottom of the screen to type a web address, and then press **Enter**. Internet Explorer loads the page, just like that.

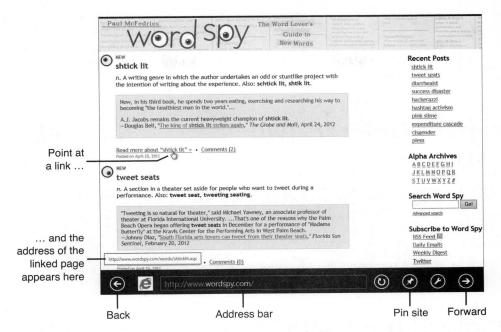

Point at
a link …

… and the
address of the
linked page
appears here

Back   Address bar   Pin site   Forward

Figure 13.1: *The Internet Explorer app with a page displayed.*

To navigate web pages with the Internet Explorer app, you have several choices. Here's the list:

- **Click a link.** A link is a special bit of text or (sometimes) an image that is configured to automatically take you to another web page when you click it. Most link text appears either underlined or in a different color from the rest of the text (sometimes both). As you can see in Figure 13.1, when you point your mouse at a link, Internet Explorer is courteous enough to display the address of the linked page, so you can tell where you going.

- **Type an address.** As you've seen, you can also click inside the Address bar, delete the current address, type the address of the site you want to see, and then press **Enter**.

- **Choose a frequent page.** After you've surfed for a while, the Internet Explorer app keeps track of the sites you frequent most often. When you click inside the Address box, you also see the Frequent list, shown in Figure 13.2. If the page you want is listed there, click it to be instantly transported to your destination.

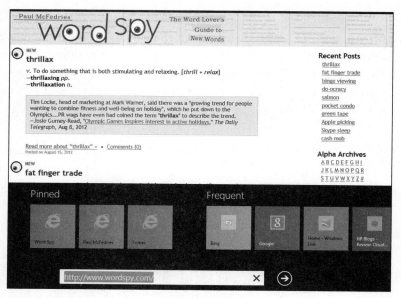

Figure 13.2: *The Internet Explorer app puts your most popular pages on the Frequent list.*

- **Navigate your visited pages.** If you feel like going back to a page you visited recently, you can usually keep clicking the **Back** button (see Figure 13.1) until you get there. To reverse course and traverse your visited pages in the opposite direction, keep clicking the **Forward** button (again handily pointed out in Figure 13.1).

- **Pin a favorite page.** If you have a page you like to visit frequently, you can pin it to your Start screen. This adds a tile for the page to your Start screen, and you can make a beeline for that page at any time by clicking that tile. To make this happen, surf to the page and then click the **Pin site** icon (pointed out, of course, in Figure 13.1). Adjust the page name to taste and click **Pin to Start**.

WINDOWS WISDOM

The Internet Explorer app also adds your pinned page to the Pinned list, which appears to the left of the Frequent list (see Figure 13.2). Click inside the Address bar to display these lists, and then click the page in the Pinned list.

- **Search for a page.** If you don't know *where* you want to go, but you know *what* you want to see, you can search the web for that info. Click inside the Address box, type a word or two that represents the info you seek, and then press **Enter**. The Internet Explorer app hands off your search text to the Bing search engine, which then scours the web for pages that match what you typed. Bing displays a list of matching pages, and then you click any that look promising.

- **Open a page in a new tab.** If you want to keep one page displayed while you go visit a different page, you can load the second page into its own tab, which is like a second window. To give this a whirl, right-click the screen to display the tabs at the top, click **New Tab** (the **+ icon**), and then either enter an address or select a page from either the Frequent or Pinned list. Figure 13.3 shows the Internet Explorer app with two tabs on the go.

Figure 13.3: *Right-click the Internet Explorer app screen to display the current tabs and add more tabs.*

The Nuts and Bolts of Desktop Internet Explorer

Assuming you have your internet connection running, the most straightforward way to get desktop Internet Explorer up and surfing is to launch the Desktop app and then click the Internet Explorer icon in the taskbar (it's the "e" with a swooshy thing around it, usually on the far left of the taskbar).

The first time you launch Internet Explorer, you may have to wrestle with the Set Up Windows Internet Explorer 10 dialog box. You can click the **Ask me later** button if you really don't feel like dealing with this right now, but it'll just keep coming back—believe me—so it's better to get the whole setup rigmarole over with now. Fortunately, all you have to do is click the **Use recommended security and compatibility settings** option, and then click **OK**.

That's it. Now it's on with the web show.

There's a good chance that you are at the Bing website, shown in Figure 13.4. (You may end up at a different site if your version of Windows 8 comes with custom internet settings.) Note that this screen changes constantly, so don't sweat it if the one you see looks different than the one shown in Figure 13.4.

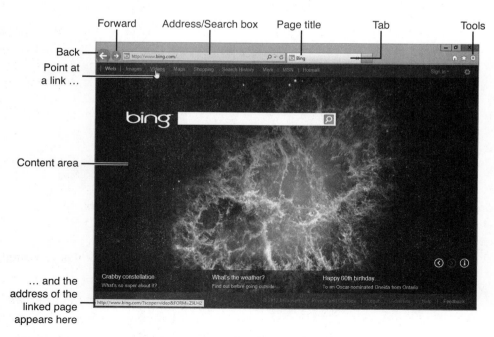

Figure 13.4: *When you launch Internet Explorer, you usually end up at the Bing website.*

Bing is Microsoft's internet starting point. (This kind of site is known as a search engine in the web trade.) With its colorful layout, generous graphics, and loads of links, Bing is a typical example of the professionally designed pages that the big-time sites offer.

HACKING WINDOWS

If you don't like Bing (or whatever you have as Internet Explorer's default start page), it's easy to change it. First, surf to the page that you want to use as the new start page. Click **Tools** (the gear-like icon in the upper-right corner of the window; see Figure 13.4) and then click the **Internet Options** command to lure the Internet Options dialog box out into the open. In the General tab, click **Use current**. If you decide later on that you prefer Internet Explorer's default home page, open the Internet Options dialog box once again, but this time click **Use default**. If you'd rather not see any page at startup (useful if you want to launch Internet Explorer while you're not connected to the internet), open the Internet Options dialog box and click **Use new tab**.

Before I show you how to use this page to see more of the web, let's take a minute or two and get our bearings by checking out the main features of the Internet Explorer window (most of which I've pointed out in Figure 13.4):

- **Page title.** This tells you the name of the current web page.

- **Address/search box.** This area shows you the address of the current page. Web page addresses are strange beasts, indeed. I'll help you figure them out a bit later in this chapter. You also use this text box to search for websites (as explained ever so carefully in this chapter; see Order Out of Chaos: Searching for Sites).

WINDOWS WISDOM

When you surf to another page, Internet Explorer may pause for a while and then display a message that says **This page cannot be displayed**. This often means that the website is kaput or down temporarily. However, I've found that Internet Explorer displays this message for no good reason a lot of the time, and that pressing **F5** to refresh the page will bring the program to its senses.

- **Back** and **Forward.** You use these buttons to return to sites you've visited, as I explain in excruciating detail a bit later.

- **Content area.** This area below the tab takes up the bulk of the Internet Explorer screen. It's where the body of each web page is displayed. You can use the vertical scrollbar to see more of the current page.

- **Links.** The content area for most web pages also boasts a link or two (or ten). These links come in two flavors: images and text (the latter are usually either underlined or in a different color than the rest of the text). When you put the mouse pointer over a link, Internet Explorer does two things (see Figure 13.4): it changes the pointer into a hand with a pointing finger, and it displays the address of the linked page in the status bar.

Web Page Navigation Basics

With that brief introduction out of the way, it's time to start wandering the web. This section runs through a few techniques for getting from one page to another using desktop Internet Explorer.

The most straightforward method is to click any link that strikes your fancy. Click the link, and you're immediately (depending on the speed of your Internet connection) whisked to the other page.

How can I tell what's a link and what isn't?

That, unfortunately, is not as easy as it used to be. Originally, link text appeared underlined and in a different color. That's still the usual case for a link these days, but you can also get links without underlines, as well as images that are links. The only real way to be sure is to park your mouse pointer over some likely looking text or an image, and then watch what happens to the pointer. If it changes into the hand with a pointing finger (see Figure 13.4), then you know for sure that you've got a link on your hands.

> **WINDOWS WISDOM**
>
> Internet Explorer also assumes that most web addresses are of the form *http://www.whatever.com*. Therefore, if you just type **whatever** and press **Ctrl+Enter**, Internet Explorer automatically adds the prefix *http://www.* and the suffix *.com*. For example, you can get to my Word Spy site (http://www.wordspy.com) by typing **wordspy** and pressing **Ctrl+Enter**.

What if I know the address of the page I want to peruse?

Easy money. Here's what you do:

- Click inside the **Address bar**, delete the existing address, type in the address you want to check out, and then press **Enter**.

- If the address is one that you've visited recently, use the Address bar's drop-down list to select it.

Why the heck are web addresses so, well, weird?

Probably because they were created by geeks who never imagined they'd be used by normal people. Still, they're not so bad after you figure out what's going on. Here's a summary of the various bits and pieces of a typical web address (or *URL*, which is short for *Uniform Resource Locator*, another geekism):

http://mcfedries.com/cigwin8/index.asp

http://	This strange combination of letters and symbols tells the browser that you're entering a web address. Note that the browser assumes every address is a web address, so you don't need to include this part if you don't want to do so.
mcfedries.com	This is what's known as the *domain name* of the server computer that hosts the web page. Some sites add "www." to the front of the domain name.
/cigwin8/	This is the web-server directory. Web directories are pretty similar to the folders you have on your hard drive.
index.asp	This is the web page file name.

> **WINDOWS WISDOM**
>
> After you've used Internet Explorer for a while, it will often suggest an address after you've typed in a few characters. If you see the address you want in the list that appears, use the down-arrow key to highlight the address, and then press **Enter**.

Ugh. Is there any easier way to get somewhere?

If you're not sure where you want to go, the MSN.com page has lots of choices. For example, click any of the categories near the top (News, Entertainment, Sports, and so on) to see lots of links related to that topic.

What if I jump to one page and then decide I want to double back to where I was?

That's a pretty common scenario. In fact, you'll often find that you need to leap back several pages, and then leap forward again. Fortunately, Internet Explorer makes this easy, thanks to its Back and Forward toolbar buttons (which I helpfully pointed out back in Figure 13.4). Here's what you can do with them:

- Click **Back** to return to the previous page.
- Click **Forward** to move ahead to the next page.

- To jump directly to any page you've visited recently, drop down the Forward button list (that is, click the **downward-pointing arrow** just to the right of the Forward button) and click the page you want.

- What if you want to go forward or back to a page but you also want to keep the current page at hand? No worries: Press **Ctrl+N** to open up a fresh copy of the Internet Explorer window. You can then use that copy to leap to whatever page you want.

Techniques for Efficient Web Gallivanting

The paradox of the web is that even though it doesn't really exist anywhere—after all, where is the amorphous never-never land of cyberspace?—it's still one of the biggest earthly things you can imagine. There aren't hundreds of thousands of pages, or even millions of them for that matter. No, there are *billions* of web pages. (Of course, if you ignore all the pages that are devoted to vampires and zombies, then, yes, there *are* only a few hundred thousand pages.)

To have even a faint hope of managing just a tiny fraction of such an inconceivably vast array of data and pictures of cute cats, you need to hone your web-browsing skills with a few useful techniques. Fortunately, as you'll see in the next few sections, Internet Explorer has all kinds of features that can help.

Saving Sites for Subsequent Surfs: Managing Your Favorites

One of the most common experiences that folks new to web browsing go through is to stumble upon a really great site, and then not be able to find it again later. They try to retrace their steps, but usually just end up clicking links furiously and winding up in strange web neighborhoods.

If this has happened to you, the solution is to get Internet Explorer to do all the grunt work of remembering sites for you. This is the job of the Favorites feature, which holds shortcuts to web pages and even lets you organize those shortcuts into separate folders.

Here's how you tell Internet Explorer to remember a web page as a favorite:

1. Navigate to the page that has struck your fancy.

2. Click **View Favorites** (the star icon pointed out in Figure 13.5) and then select **Add to Favorites** to get the Add a Favorite dialog box onscreen.

Add to Favorites Bar   Pin the Favorites Center

Favorites
Bar

View
Favorites

Figure 13.5: *Click the Add to Favorites button to get things going.*

> **WINDOWS WISDOM**
>
> You can display the Add a Favorite dialog box in no time at all by pressing
> **Ctrl+D**. If you want to add the site to the Favorites Bar (pointed out in Figure
> 13.5), click the **Add to Favorites Bar** icon (also pointed out in Figure 13.5). By the
> way, to display the Favorites bar, right-click the area above the Address/Search
> box and then click **Favorites bar**.

3. The Name text box shows the name of the page, which is what you'll select
   from a menu later on when you want to view this page again. If you can think
   of a better name, don't hesitate to edit this text.

4. Click **Add** to finish.

After you have some pages lined up as favorites, you can return to any one of them at
any time by clicking the **View Favorites** icon, clicking the **Favorites** tab, and then
clicking the page title.

If you need to make changes to your favorites, you can do a couple of things right
from the Favorites list. Display the list and then right-click the item you want to work
with. In the shortcut menu that slinks in, click **Rename** to change the item name, or
click **Delete** to blow it away. To change the address, click **Properties**, type the new
address in the URL text box, and click **OK**.

If you find yourself constantly reaching for the Favorites Center to get at your favorite pages, you might prefer to have the Favorites Center displayed full time. You can do that by clicking the **Pin the Favorites Center** icon (see Figure 13.5). Internet Explorer then sets aside a chunk of real estate on the left side of the window to display the Favorites list.

For more heavy-duty adjustments, select the **Add to Favorites>Organize Favorites** command. Not surprisingly, this pushes the Organize Favorites dialog box into view. You get four buttons to play with:

- **New Folder.** Click this button to create a new folder. (Tip: If you click an existing folder and then click this button, Internet Explorer creates a subfolder.) Internet Explorer adds the folder and displays New Folder inside a text box. Edit the text and then press **Enter**.

- **Move.** Click this button to move the currently highlighted favorite into another folder. In the Browse For Folder dialog box that saunters by, highlight the destination folder, and then click **OK**.

- **Rename.** Click this button to rename the currently highlighted favorite. Edit the name accordingly and then press **Enter**.

- **Delete.** Click this button to nuke the currently highlighted favorite. When Windows 8 asks whether you're sure about this, click **Yes**.

When you're done, click **Close** to return to Internet Explorer.

Order Out of Chaos: Searching for Sites

Clicking willy-nilly in the hope of finding something interesting can be fun if you've got a few hours to kill. But if you need a specific tidbit of information *now*, then a click-click here and click-click there just won't cut the research mustard. To save time, you need to knock the web down to a more manageable size, and the Internet Explorer Search feature can help you do just that.

The idea is straightforward: you supply a search engine (as they're called) with a word or two that describes the topic you want to find. The search engine then rummages around the web for pages that contain those words, and presents you with a list of matches. Does it work? Well, it depends on which search engine you use. There are quite a few available, and some are better than others at certain kinds of searches. The biggest problem is that, depending on the topic you're searching, the search engine might return hundreds or even thousands of matching sites! You can usually get a more targeted search by adding more search terms and by avoiding common words. For example, suppose you want to know the airspeed velocity of an unladen swallow. If you search "swallow," you'll hit a wall of tens of millions of results. However, a search for "airspeed unladen swallow" will get you some pretty good results right off the bat.

A basic site search couldn't be easier: use the Address/Search box to type the word or phrase you want to find and then press **Enter**. Internet Explorer passes the search buck over to the Bing search site, which then displays the results a few seconds later. You get a series of links and descriptions. (Generally speaking, the higher the link is in the list, the more likely the linked page matches your search text.) Clicking a link displays the page.

One-Window Browsing: Surfing with Tabs

Earlier in this chapter I mentioned that you can keep the current site in Internet Explorer and surf to a different site by pressing **Ctrl+N** to open a new Internet Explorer window. That's a neat trick, but it's not unusual to use it *too* often and end up with six or more Internet Explorer windows crowding the desktop. That's a lot of windows to wield.

Fortunately, the Time of Many Windows may soon be a thing of the past. That's because Internet Explorer comes with a nifty feature called *tabs* that lets you browse multiple sites in a *single* window. Sweet!

The way it works is that you create a new tab in the current window, and you then use that tab to display a different web page. How do you create a new tab? Press **Ctrl+T** or click the **New Tab** button, pointed out in Figure 13.6. You then type the address you want and press **Enter** to load the page into the new tab.

Figure 13.6: *Internet Explorer lets you surf sites using tabs.*

Here are a few tab techniques you can use to impress your friends:

- If you see a link that you want to load into a separate tab, right-click the link and then select **Open in New Tab**.

- To view a page that you have loaded in another tab, click the tab.

- To get rid of a tab, move the mouse pointer over the tab and then click the **X** that appears on the right side of the tab.

Dealing with Files in Internet Explorer

As you click your way around the web, you may find some links don't take you to other pages but are, instead, tied directly to a file. In this case, Internet Explorer makes you jump through some or all of the following hoops:

1. In most cases, after you click the link to the file, you see the Information bar, which asks whether you want to run or save the file. It's much safer to save the file, so click **Save**.

2. Once the download is complete, you see another Information bar, which offers three buttons:

   - **Open.** Click this button to launch the downloaded file.

   - **Open folder.** Click this button to open a window that displays the contents of the folder into which you saved the file. This is a good choice if you want to do something other than launch the file (such as rename it or sic your antivirus program on it).

   - **View downloads.** Click this button to eyeball all your downloaded files.

LOOK OUT!

Be careful about downloading files; they can contain viruses that wreck your system. To be safe, you should only download from reputable sites, or from sites that you trust explicitly. If you plan on living dangerously and downloading files willy-nilly, at least get yourself a good antivirus program—such as Microsoft Security Essentials (microsoft.com/security/pc-security/mse.aspx), McAfee (mcafee.com), or Norton (symantec.com)—and use it to check each file you download.

The Least You Need to Know

- To run the Internet Explorer app, click the **Internet Explorer** tile in the Start screen.
- To start desktop Internet Explorer, click the **Desktop** tile and then click the **Internet Explorer** icon in the taskbar.
- To surf to another page, either click a link or type an address in the Address box and then press **Enter**.
- To scour the web for a particular topic, type a word or two in the Address/Search box and press **Enter**.
- Click the **View Favorites** button and then click the **Add to Favorites** command (or press **Ctrl+D**) to save a page to the Favorites list.
- To create a new tab, press **Ctrl+T** or click the **New Tab** button. You can also right-click a link and then click **Open in New Tab**.

Sending and Receiving Email

In This Chapter

- Getting to know the Mail app
- Giving Windows 8 your email account particulars
- How to compose and send an email message
- Handling file attachments
- How to get and read incoming messages

The world passed a milestone of sorts a few years ago when it was reported that, in North America at least, more email messages were sent each day than postal messages. Now, email volume is several times that of "snail mail" (as regular mail is derisively called by the wired set), and the number of emails shipped out each day is counted in the *hundreds of billions*.

The really good news is that email has become extremely easy to use because email programs have become much better over the years. As you see in this chapter, shipping out messages and reading incoming messages is a painless affair thanks to the admirable email capabilities of both the Mail app and the Windows Live Mail desktop program.

Email Made Easy: Using the Mail App

If you're new to the email thing and you really just want to get up to speed as quickly and as painlessly as possible, look no further than Mail, the app that resides on the Windows 8 Start screen. If you're an email old-timer and you're sick and tired of wrestling with complex and arcane email programs, you should look no further than the Mail app. How can an app appeal to rookies and veterans alike? The main reason is that Mail strips away anything and everything that's superfluous and obscure. You can scour every nook and cranny of the Mail app and you won't find a bell to ring or a whistle to blow. Instead, you just get a simple program that can handle all basic email chores.

To use the Mail app, you need to have a Microsoft account, which I talked about way back in Chapter 7. If you've done that, go ahead and click the **Mail** tile on the Start screen. If Mail asks you to log in to your Microsoft account, type your email address and password and then press **Enter**.

SEE ALSO

For the details on procuring your very own Microsoft account for use with Mail (and other Windows 8 apps), see the section Setting Up a Microsoft Account in Chapter 7 (Getting Onto the Internet).

In your initial look at the Mail screen, you see two columns: Inbox on the left and the reading pane on the right (see Figure 14.1).

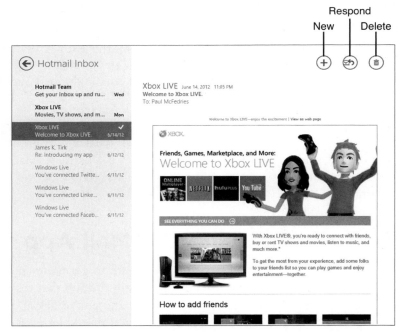

Figure 14.1: *Launch Mail to see your Inbox and the reading pane.*

Checking for Messages

What if you don't have any messages? The Mail app does check for messages frequently, but if you'd like to make sure you're not missing anything, right-click the screen to slide up the application bar, and then click **Sync**.

Sending a Message

When you're ready to ship out a message of your own using the Mail app, follow these steps:

1. Click **New** (the + icon pointed out in Figure 14.1). Mail offers up a brand-new message.

2. Use the To box to type the address of your recipient and then press **Enter**. You can add more than one address, if need be.

3. If you want someone else to receive a copy of the message, type that person's address in the CC (Courtesy Copy) box and then press **Enter**. Again, Mail has no problem if you want to add multiple addresses here.

4. Use the Subject field to type a short description of the message (a few words).

5. Use the big box below that to type your message. With the cursor inside the message area, right-click the screen to bring up the application bar, which is brimming with buttons for formatting your text.

6. If you want to ship a file along for the ride, click **Attachments**, locate and select the file you want to send, and then click **Attach**.

7. When your message is complete, take a deep breath and click **Send** (the icon pointed out in Figure 14.2). Mail ships out your message.

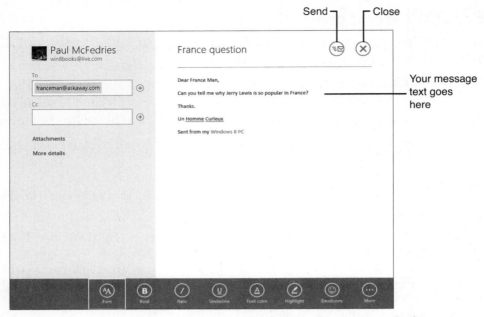

Figure 14.2: *Click inside the message area and then right-click the screen to see the formatting options.*

Responding to a Message

If you receive a message that asks a question, solicits an opinion, or otherwise requires feedback from you, you can send a response. Click the message in the Inbox pane, click the **Respond** icon (see Figure 14.1), and then click one of the following commands:

- **Reply.** Select this command to send a response back to the sender of the message. Mail automatically addresses the message to the sender, includes the original subject line preceded by *RE:* (regarding), and adds the original messages text.

- **Reply all.** If the note was foisted on several people, select this command to send your response to everyone who received the original. Mail automatically addresses the message to the sender and all the recipients of the original message, includes the original subject line preceded by *RE:*, and adds the original messages text.

- **Forward.** Select this command to have someone else take a gander at the message you received. Mail automatically includes the original subject line preceded by *FW:* and adds the original messages text. Note that you'll need to supply a recipient address.

Add your own text to the message and then click **Send** to fire off the response.

Dealing with Your Messages

You probably don't want your messages gumming up your Inbox forever, so Mail gives you two ways to deal with the clutter:

- **Move a message to another folder.** Click the message, right-click the screen, and then click **Move** in the application bar. When the Folders list shows up, click the folder you want to use as the new home for the message.

- **Delete a message.** Click the message and then click the **Delete** icon (pointed out in Figure 14.1).

It may come as a bit of a surprise to learn that Mail has other folders, since they're quite well hidden. In fact, Mail comes with a full half-dozen folders: Inbox, Drafts (saved messages you haven't sent yet), Sent Items (messages you've sent), Outbox (messages waiting to be sent), Junk (unsolicited commercial messages), and Deleted Items (messages you've deleted). To switch to another folder, click the **Back** button (the left-pointing arrow in the upper-left corner) to open the Folders list, and then click the folder.

HACKING WINDOWS

If you're composing a message and decide you want to finish it later, you can save your work as a draft. To save a draft of a message, click the **Close** icon (see Figure 14.2) and then click **Save draft**.

Sharing Files with Friends and Family

In these days of ubiquitous social networking, we're immersed in a world of sharing: happenings, links, information, and much more. Windows 8 gets into the spirit by offering the Share feature, which lets you use the Mail app or the People app to share data with other people. For example, you can send a photo, alert a person about a web page, or let someone know about some cool music. Here's how it works:

1. Using an app, open or select the data you want to share.

2. Press **Windows+C** to open the Charms menu. If you're using a tablet, swipe in from the right edge to display the Charms menu.

3. Click **Share.** The Share pane appears.

4. Select the app you want to use to share:

    • **Mail.** Use Mail to email the data as an attachment. Windows 8 creates a new Mail message and attaches the data you opened in step 1.

    • **People.** Use People to send the data as a post to your Facebook or Twitter account (see Chapter 15).

5. Fill in any data that is required to send the item, and then click **Send**.

> **WINDOWS WISDOM**
>
> When you open an app, select an item, and then click **Share** in the Charms menu, Windows 8 might tell you "*App* can't share," where *App* is the name of the app. What's up with that? Unfortunately, the Windows 8 Share feature is only supported by certain apps. In a default Windows 8 installation, for example, Share only works for items that can be sent via email using the Mail app. However, you may be able to share a wider variety of items by installing third-party apps that extend the Share feature.

Getting Started with Windows Live Mail

As you might have guessed from the "Live" portion of its name, Windows Live Mail is part of Windows Live Essentials, which is the collection of desktop programs that Microsoft decided to leave out of Windows 8. To learn how to install it, hike back to Chapter 6 and read the section titled Installing Windows Live Essentials.

Once that's done, you fire up the program by clicking the **Windows Live Mail** tile on the Start screen.

Setting Up Your Internet Email Account

Before Windows Live Mail loads for the first time, it calls in the Add an Email Account Wizard to handle the various steps required to divulge the details of the email account you have with your ISP (Internet Service Provider). There are two possible routes here: the high (easy) road, and the low (hard) road.

The High Road: Quick Account Setup

Windows Live Mail understands that many (perhaps even most) email accounts are really straightforward; with just a bit of information it can glean the underlying details of the account. This process is relatively foolproof with well-known email providers such as Microsoft's Hotmail, and it seems to work okay with other providers, too.

In this scenario, all you need to know is your email address and your password. You enter that data in the Add an Email Account wizard initial dialog box, plus the display name you want to use (this is the name people see when you send them a message). Click **Next**, read the instructions (if any) that the wizard tells you to follow to complete the setup, and then click **Finish**.

The Low Road: Configuring an Account by Hand

If the wizard can't configure your email account automatically, then you've got to roll up your sleeves and do it yourself. Here's a rundown of the information you should have at your fingertips:

- Your email address.

- The type of server the ISP uses for incoming email: POP or IMAP.

- The internet name used by the ISP's incoming *mail server* (this often takes the form mail.*provider*.com or pop.*provider*.com, where *provider* is the name of the ISP). Note that your ISP might call this its *POP server*.

> **DEFINITION**
>
> A **mail server** is a computer that your ISP uses to store and send your email messages.

- The internet name used by the ISP's outgoing mail server (this often takes the form smtp.*provider*.com, where *provider* is the name of the ISP, but in some cases it's the same as the incoming email server). Some ISPs call this their *SMTP server*.

> **WINDOWS WISDOM**
>
> The acronyms and abbreviations are thick on the ground in this section. You don't have to understand them to send and receive email, but here's what they mean just in case you're interested: **POP3** stands for Post Office Protocol version 3; **IMAP** stands for Internet Message Access Protocol; and **SMTP** stands for Simple Mail Transfer Protocol.

- Whether your ISP's outgoing mail server requires authentication (most do, nowadays).

- Whether your ISP requires you to use special port numbers. You can think of ports as communications channels, and Windows Live Mail and your ISP must be tuned to the same channel for things to work. If you don't have any info on this, then your ISP probably uses the standard port numbers, and you don't have to sweat this part.

- The user name and password for your email account. (If your email provider is your ISP, then these are almost always the same as your internet log-on name and password.)

Here's what to do with your information:

1. In the initial wizard dialog box, enter your address in the Email address text box and your password in the Password text box.

2. Use the Display Name text box to type the name you want other folks to see when you send them a message (most people just use their real name) and then click **Next**.

3. In the Incoming Server Information section, use the Server type list to specify the type of email server your ISP uses; most are POP.

4. Use the Server address text box to enter the name of the server that your ISP uses for incoming mail. Also, change the Port value if your ISP uses a port other than the one shown.

5. Use the Log-on user name text box to enter your email user name (this should already be filled in for you) or address (whichever one you're supposed to use to log on).

6. In the Outgoing Server Information section, use the Server address text box to enter the name of the server that your ISP uses for outgoing mail. Also, change the Port value if your ISP uses a port other than the one shown.

7. Activate the Requires authentication check box if your ISP's outgoing mail server does the authentication thing.

8. Click **Next** to get your account set up.

9. Click **Finish**.

The Lay of the Windows Live Mail Land

By default, Windows Live Mail is set up to go online and grab your waiting messages when you launch the program. We'll get there eventually, so for now just close the Connect dialog box if it shows up.

At long last, the Windows Live Mail window shows itself, and it looks much like the one in Figure 14.3.

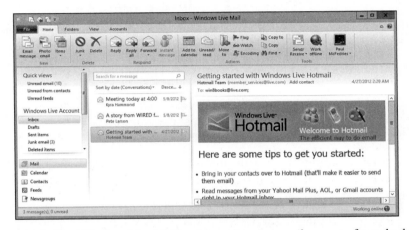

Figure 14.3: *Use Windows Live Mail to ship and receive email messages from the desktop.*

The Folder pane on the left lists the various storage areas that come with Windows Live Mail. I talk about folders in more detail later in this chapter. For now, here's a quick summary of the default folders:

- **Quick views.** This section offers special views of your messages, such as Unread Email, which shows you all the messages you haven't read.

- **Inbox.** This folder is where Windows Live Mail stores the email messages that you receive.

- **Drafts.** This folder stores messages you're in the middle of composing and have saved.

- **Sent items.** This folder stores a copy of the messages you've sent.

- **Junk email.** This folder is the Siberia to which Windows Live Mail exiles suspected spam messages. See the section in Chapter 21 titled Using the Junk Mail Filter to Can Spam.

- **Deleted items.** This folder stores the messages you delete.

The Outbox: Sending an Email Message

Let's begin the tour of Windows Live Mail with a look at how to foist your "e-prose" on unsuspecting colleagues, friends, family, and *Brady Bunch*–cast members. This section shows you the basic technique to use, and then gets a bit fancier in discussing the Contacts list, attachments, and other Windows Live Mail sending features.

The Basics: Composing and Sending a Message

Without further ado (not that there's been much ado to this point, mind you), here are the basic steps to follow to fire off an email message to some lucky recipient:

1. In the Home tab, click the **Email message** button. (Keyboard fans will be pleased to note that pressing **Ctrl+N** also does the job.) You end up with the New Message window onscreen, as shown in Figure 14.4.

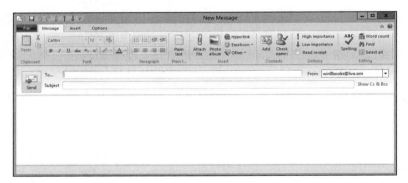

Figure 14.4: *You cobble together an email message in the New Message window.*

2. In the To text box, type in the email address of the recipient. (It's perfectly acceptable to enter multiple addresses in this text box. Use a semicolon [;] or a comma [,] to separate each address.)

3. The address you put in the To box is the main recipient of the message. However, it's common to shoot off a copy of the message to a secondary recipient. To do that, click **Show CC and BCC** and then enter their email address in the CC text box. (Again, you can enter multiple addresses, if you're so inclined.)

   Alternatively, there's also a blind courtesy (or carbon) copy (BCC), which also delivers a copy of the message to a specified recipient; however, none of the other recipients see that person's address anywhere. Click **Show CC and BCC** (if you didn't do that already) and type the address in the **BCC** text box.

4. Use the Subject line to enter a subject for the message. (The subject acts as a kind of title for your message. It's the first thing the recipient sees, so it should accurately reflect the content of your message, but it shouldn't be too long. Think *pithy*.)

5. Decide what type of message you want to send. You have two choices:

   - **Rich Text (HTML).** This is the default message format, and it enables you to make your message look its best because you can format your message text. However, your recipient might have problems if his or her email program doesn't support this formatting—although most do these days. (Just so you know, HTML stands for Hypertext Markup Language. It's a series of codes used to format characters and things, and it's used to create web pages. Don't worry, you don't have to know anything about HTML to use this feature.)

   - **Plain Text.** This is the route to take if you prefer to send the message without any formatting. This makes life easier for your recipient if he or she doesn't have an email program that supports formatting—although, again, this is very rare these days. To switch to plain text, select the **Message** tab and then click the **Plain text** button.

6. Use the large, empty area below the Subject line to type in the message text (also known as the message body).

7. If you chose the Rich Text (HTML) format, after you're inside the message text area, notice that many of the items in the Message tab suddenly come alive. Use these buttons and commands to change the font, format paragraphs, add a background image, apply stationery, and more.

8. When your message is fit for human consumption, click **Send**.

WINDOWS WISDOM

Windows Live Mail has a Spelling command in the Message tab. It's a good idea to run this command before sending your message to the recipient. It just takes a sec, and if the spell checker finds an error or two, you'll save yourself a bit of embarrassment.

Note that after your message is 'net-bound, Windows Live Mail also is kind enough to save a copy of it in the Sent Items folder. This is handy because it gives you a record of all the missives you launch into cyberspace.

Easier Addressing: Using the Contacts List

If you find yourself with a bunch of recipients to whom you send stuff regularly (and it's a rare emailer who doesn't), you soon grow tired of entering their addresses by hand. The solution is to toss those regulars into the Contacts list. That way, you can fire them into the To or CC lines with just a few mouse clicks.

Here's how you add someone to the Contacts list:

1. In Windows Live Mail, click the **Contacts** button.

2. In the Contacts window that reports for duty, click the Home tab's **Contact** button. (Alternatively, press **Ctrl+Shift+C**.) The Contacts window conjures up the Add a Contact dialog box.

3. In the **Quick add** tab, enter the person's first and last names.

4. Use the **Personal email** text box to enter the recipient's address.

5. Fill in the person's phone number and company name, as well as the fields in the other tabs, if you feel like it.

6. When you're done, click **Add contact** to add the new recipient.

After you have some folks in your Contacts list, Windows Live Mail gives you a ton of ways to get them a message. Here's my favorite method:

1. In the New Message window, click **To**. Windows Live Mail displays the Send an Email dialog box.

2. Click the contact name.

3. Click **To** (or **CC** or **BCC**).

4. Repeat steps 2 and 3 as required.

5. Click **OK**.

WINDOWS WISDOM

If you want to send a message to a particular set of recipients, you can organize them into a category and then specify the category name in the To line. To create a category, open the Contacts window and then click the Home tab's **Category** button (or press **Ctrl+Shift+G**). Enter a category name, click each contact you want in the category, and then click **Save**.

Inserting Attachments and Other Hangers-On

Most of your messages will be text-only creations (perhaps with a bit of formatting tossed in to keep things interesting). However, it's also possible to send entire files along for the ride. Such files are called, naturally enough, *attachments*. They're very common in the business world, and it's useful to know how they work. Here goes:

DEFINITION

An **attachment** is a separate file that accompanies an email message.

1. In the New Message window, click the Home tab's **Attach file** button. The Open dialog box rears its head.

2. Find the file you want to attach and then select it.

3. Click **Open**. Windows Live Mail returns you to the New Message window where you see a new Attach box that includes the name of the file.

As you can see, adding attachments isn't that hard. However, that doesn't mean you should bolt an attachment or two onto every message you send. Adding attachments can greatly increase the size of your message, so it may take the recipient quite a while to download your message—which won't be appreciated, I can tell you. Some ISPs put an upper limit on the size of a message, so it's also possible that your recipient may never see your note. Use common sense and only attach files when it's necessary.

The Inbox: Getting and Reading Email Messages

Some people like to think of email as a return to the days of *belles lettres* and *billets-doux* (these people tend to be a bit pretentious). Yes, it's true that email has people writing again, but this isn't like the letter writing of old. The major difference is that the turnaround time for email is usually much quicker. Instead of waiting weeks or even months to get a return letter, a return email might take as little as a few minutes or a few hours.

So if you send a message with a question or comment, chances are you will get a reply before too long. Any messages sent to your email address are stored in your account at your ISP. Your job is to use Windows Live Mail to access your account and grab any waiting messages. This section shows you how to do that and what to do with those messages after they're safely stowed on your computer.

Getting Your Messages

Here are the steps to stride through to get your email messages:

1. Click the **Home** tab.

2. Click the top half of the **Send/Receive** button (or press **F5**). Windows Live Mail accesses your mail account, absconds with any waiting messages, and then stuffs them into the Windows Live Mail–Inbox folder.

3. If it's not already displayed, click the **Inbox** folder so you can see what the "e-postman" delivered.

When you're working online, Windows Live Mail automatically checks for new messages every 10 minutes. You can change that by selecting **File>Options>Mail**. In the General tab, use the spin box that's part of the **Check for new messages every X minute(s)** option to set the checking interval.

Reading Your Messages

Figure 14.5 shows the Inbox folder with a few messages displayed in the aptly named Messages list. The first thing to notice is that Windows Live Mail uses a bold font for all messages you haven't read yet. For each message you also see the Subject line, the name of the sender, and the delivery time (if it was delivered today) or date (if it was delivered before today).

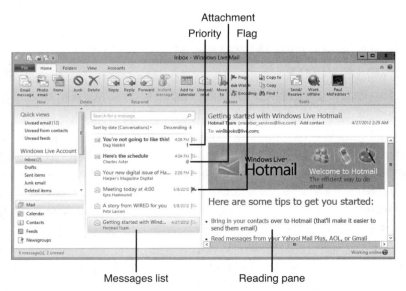

Figure 14.5: *After you've pilfered your incoming messages from your ISP, they get stored in your Inbox folder.*

You also get the following info about each message:

- **Priority.** This column tells you whether the sender set up the message with a priority ranking. If you see a red exclamation mark, it means the message was sent with high priority ("Handle this pronto, buster!"); if you see a blue, downward-pointing arrow, it means the note was sent with low priority ("Handle this whenever, man").

- **Attachment.** If you see a paper-clip icon in this column, it means the message is accompanied by a file attachment. See the section Attending to Attachments later in this chapter.

- **Flag.** If you want to remind yourself to deal with a message, you can flag it for future follow-up (a sort of digital string-tied-to-the-finger thing). You do this by clicking the Flag icon beside the message.

Windows Live Mail offers two methods for seeing what a message has to say:

- Select the message in the Inbox folder. Windows Live Mail displays the text of the note in the Reading pane. After a couple of seconds, Windows Live Mail removes the bolding from the message to indicate that it has been read.

- Double-click the message in the Inbox folder. (For the heck of it, you also can select the message and press **Enter**.) This method opens the message in its own window.

Attending to Attachments

As I mentioned earlier, if you get a message that has one or more files tied to it, you see a paper clip icon beside the message in the Messages list. You also see an icon for the file in the reading pane. Windows Live Mail gives you a few ways to handle any attachments in the current message:

- **Save the file.** Select **File>Save>Save attachments** to convince the Save Attachments dialog box to drop by. If there are multiple files, use the Attachments To Be Saved list to highlight the ones you want to save. Use the Save To text box to specify where you want the files to be stored (click **Browse** to choose the folder from a dialog box). Then click **Save** to dump the file (or files) onto your hard disk.

LOOK OUT!

Although Windows Live Mail makes it easy to deal with attachments, you should never just blithely open an attached file because you might end up infecting your computer with a virus. (To learn more about this and how to protect your computer from virus attachments, see Chapter 21.)

- **Save the file from the reading pane.** Right-click the file icon in the reading pane, click **Save as**, and follow the steps I just took you through in the step above.

- **Open the file.** If you just want to see what's in the file, you can open it. To do that, right-click the file icon in the reading pane, and then click **Open**.

What to Do with a Message After You've Read It

This section gives you a rundown of all the things you can do with a message after you've read it. In each case, you either need to have a message highlighted in the Inbox folder, or you need to have the message open. Here's the list:

- **Ship out a reply.** If you think of a witty retort, you can email it back to the sender by clicking the Home tab's **Reply** button. (The keyboard route is **Ctrl+R**.)

- **Ship out a reply to every recipient.** If the note was foisted on several people, you might prefer to send your response to everyone who received the original. To do that, click the Home tab's **Reply all** button. (The keyboard shortcut is **Ctrl+Shift+R**.)

- **Forward the message to someone else.** To have someone else take a look at a message you received, you can forward it by clicking the top half of the Home tab's **Forward** button. (Keyboarders can press **Ctrl+F**.) In some cases, you should ask permission from the original sender before forwarding that person's message. Use your best judgment.

WINDOWS WISDOM

A forwarded message contains the original message text preceded by a header reading *Original Message* and some of the message particulars (who sent it, when they sent it, and so on). If you want your recipient to see the message exactly as you received it, click the bottom half of the Home tab's **Forward** button, then click **Forward as attachment**.

- **Move the message to some other folder.** If you find your Inbox folder getting seriously overcrowded, you should think about moving some messages to other folders. The easiest way to go about this is to drag the message from its current folder and drop it on another folder in the Folders list.

- **Delete the message.** If you don't think you have cause to read a message again, you might as well delete it to keep the Inbox clutter to a minimum. To delete a message, click the Home tab's **Delete** button. (A message also can be vaporized by pressing **Ctrl+D** or by dragging it to the Deleted Items folder.) Note that Windows Live Mail doesn't get rid of a deleted message completely. Instead, it just dumps it in the Deleted Items folder. If you later realize that you deleted the message accidentally (insert forehead slap here), you can open the Deleted Items folder and then move the message back to the Inbox.

Manufacturing New Message Folders

Right out of the box, Windows Live Mail comes with the six prefab folders that I described earlier in this chapter. Surely that's enough folders for anyone, right?

Maybe not. Even if you're good at deleting the detritus from your Inbox folder, it still won't take long before it becomes bloated with messages and finding the note you need becomes a real needle-in-a-haystack exercise. What you really need is a way to organize your mail. For example, suppose you and your boss exchange a lot of email. Rather than storing all her messages in your Inbox folder, you could create a separate folder just for her messages. You could also create folders for each internet mailing list to which you subscribe, for current projects, or for each of your regular email correspondents. In short, there are 1,001 uses for folders, and this section tells you how to create your own.

 WINDOWS WISDOM

You can save yourself a step or two by heading for the Folder pane and right-clicking the folder in which you want the new folder to appear. Then click **New folder**, enter the folder name, and click **OK**.

To create a new folder, follow these steps:

1. Select the **Folders** tab.

2. Click **New folder** to display the Create Folder dialog box.

3. In the Select the folder… list, click the folder within which you want the new folder to appear. For example, if you want your new folder to be inside your inbox, click the Inbox folder.

4. Use the Folder name text box to enter the name of the new folder.

5. Click **OK**.

The Least You Need to Know

- For simplified emailing, use the Mail app, which you get off the ground by clicking the **Mail** tile in the Start screen.

- To share data with someone special (or even someone merely semi-special), open the data, press **Windows+C** to open the Charms menu, click **Share**, and then click **Mail**.

- To start Windows Live Mail, click the Start screen's **Windows Live Mail** tile.

- To compose a message, click the Home tab's **Email message** button, enter the address and a Subject line, fill in the message body, and then click **Send**.

- To receive messages, click the top half of the Home tab's **Send/Receive** button.

- Make liberal use of folders to organize your messages. You create new folders by selecting the Folders tab's **New folder** button.

Places to Go, People to See: Getting Social with Windows 8

In This Chapter

- Seeing what the People app can do
- Making a date with the Calendar app
- Checking out Windows Live Mail's Calendar
- Scheduling appointments
- Keeping on top of your things-to-do-places-to-go-have-your-people-call-my-people life

It seems almost redundant to describe modern life as busy. Everyone is working harder, cramming more appointments and meetings into already-packed schedules, and somehow finding the time to get their regular work done between crises. As many a management consultant has advised over the years (charging exorbitant fees to do so), the key to surviving this helter-skelter, pell-mell pace is time management. And although there are as many theories about time management as there are consultants, one of the keys is that you should always try to make the best use of the time available. Although that often comes down to self-discipline and prioritizing your tasks, an efficient scheduling system can certainly help.

That's where Windows 8 comes in, because it offers two ways to manage your bee-busy schedule: the Calendar app and Windows Live Mail Calendar feature. It also offers the People app, which can keep you up to date with your social network. This chapter gives you the deal on these three programs.

Using the People App

The People app is your Windows 8 address book where you can store all kinds of useful (and even useless) information about your family, friends, colleagues, acquaintances, old high school classmates, and anyone else who falls within the borders of your social circle. And when I say "social circle," I mean *social* circle. That's because the People app was built from the ground up with social networking in mind, so you can use it to connect with your friends on Facebook, Twitter, LinkedIn, and Google.

To get the fun started, click the **People** tile on the Start screen.

Adding Contacts

Let's keep it simple to start and see how you go about adding contacts to the People app. When you first launch People, you either see a more or less blank screen, or if you're using a Microsoft account, you see your contacts from that account (if any).

Either way, here are the steps to follow to add a contact:

1. Right-click the screen and then click **New**. This brings you into contact with the New Contact screen, shown in Figure 15.1.

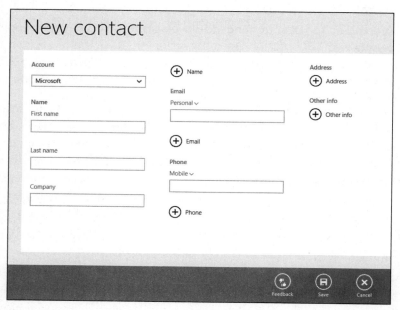

Figure 15.1: *Use the New Contact screen to spell out the particulars of your contact.*

2. Use the First name, Last name, and Company text boxes to fill in the person's name and company name.

3. If you want to add other name-related data today, such as the person's middle name, nickname, or title, click the + icon beside **Name**, click the field you want to use, and then enter the data.

4. Use the Email field to type the person's email address. Note, too, that you can click the **Personal** label and then click either **Work** or **Other** to properly label the address. If the person has another email address you want to include, click the + icon beside **Email**, click a label, and then type the address in the new text box that pops up.

5. Use the Phone field to type the person's phone number. Be sure to click the **Mobile** label and then click an appropriate label for the number. If the person has another number you want to include, click the + icon beside **Phone**, click a label, and then type the number in the new text box that appears.

6. If you want to make note of the person's physical address, click the + icon beside **Address**, click a label, and then use the text boxes that slide in to enter the street address, city, state or province, zip or postal code, and country.

7. If you've got all kinds of time on your hands and want to keep entering information about your contact, click the + icon beside **Other info**, click the field you want to use (Job Title, Significant Other, Website, or Notes), and then enter the data in the text box provided.

8. Click **Save**. The People app adds your new contact.

Connecting Your Social Networks

Adding contacts one by one with your bare hands is one way to populate your contacts list, but it's a bit on the slow side. Fortunately, if you're on a social networking site such as Facebook, Twitter, or LinkedIn, you can save yourself all kinds of time by bringing your friends into the People app. You do that by connecting your social networks to your Microsoft account, and the People app takes care of the rest.

SEE ALSO

As you may have surmised, getting your social networks into the People app requires that you use a Microsoft account in Windows 8. I tell you what that's all about in Chapter 7, Getting Onto the Internet.

Assuming you're using a Microsoft account to sign in to Windows 8, follow these painless steps to connect a social network to that account using the People app:

1. In the People app, click the **Connected to** message that appears in the upper-right corner of the screen. This convinces the People app to display the Accounts pane.

2. Click **Add an account**. The People app displays a list of social networks you can add, which includes Facebook, Twitter, LinkedIn, and Google.

3. Click the social network you want. The People app displays an overview of what's about to happen.

4. Click **Connect**. The People app contacts the social network and sends the connection request. Note that at this point if you are not already logged in to the social network, the People app prompts you for your log-in info. In response, the social network asks for your permission to connect. Figure 15.2 shows the response you see from Facebook.

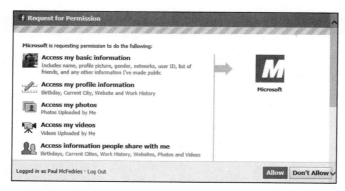

Figure 15.2: *Before the People app can connect to a social network, you must give your permission.*

5. Allow the connection. How you do this depends on the social network. For example, with Facebook you click **Allow** and with Twitter you click **Authorize app.**

6. Click **Done**.

With that done, you can use the tabs at the top of the People app to peruse your social domain:

- **All.** Click this tab to see the complete list of your friends (or, in the case of Twitter, the people you follow). Click a contact to see more info about that person, send the person a message, and more.

- **What's new.** Click this tab to see the latest news from your social networks, including your Facebook news feed and posts by the people you follow on Twitter.

- **Me.** Click this tab to see your own info, including your contact data, your most recent Facebook status updates and notifications, your social network photos, and more.

Using the Calendar App

If your goal is to keep your affairs in order, I salute you. I also recommend the Calendar app, which can help you keep track of each appointment, meeting, event, and rendezvous in your social schedule. To arrange a meeting with your new digital personal assistant, click the **Calendar** tile on the Start screen.

Navigating the Calendar

Let's take a second to get to know the Calendar screen so that you can find your way around. First, you should know that Calendar offers three different views. To see them, right-click the screen to display the application bar, which holds the following icons:

- **Day.** Click this icon to change the calendar to show just a single day. This is useful for getting a detailed look at that day's events.

- **Week.** Click this icon to display Sunday through Saturday for the current week. This is a great way to get a good idea of what you're up against schedulewise for that week.

- **Month.** Click this icon to see the current month. This is the view to use to get an overview of your schedule.

I should mention that you can also click the **Today** icon in the application bar to be whisked to today's date on the calendar.

To navigate the calendar, move the mouse to display the Next and Previous arrows, pointed out in Figure 15.3. Click **Next** to jump to the next day, week, or month (depending on the current view), and click **Previous** to go back a day, week, or month.

Figure 15.3: *Use the Calendar app to keep track of your appointments.*

Adding an Event

Now that you've got a feel for the Calendar app, you're ready to start adding events. Here's what you do:

1. Navigate to the date on which the appointment occurs.

2. Click the date. If you're in Day or Month view, click the time when the event begins. Calendar creates a new appointment.

> **WINDOWS WISDOM**
>
> What if you want to enter an event that has no set start time, such as a birthday or a vacation? No worries. Switch to Day or Week view, then click the slot that appears just below the date. This tells Calendar to create an all-day event.

3. Type a title that describes your appointment.

4. Use the **Where** text box to specify the location (such as a room number or address) for the appointment.

5. If necessary, use the **Start** controls to adjust the date and time that the appointment starts.

6. Use the **How long** list to select a length for the appointment. If you don't see a time that works for you, click **Custom** and then enter the date and time the appointment ends.

7. If you want Calendar to enter multiple versions of the appointment, use the **How often** list to select a repeat interval (such as Every Day or Every Week).

8. If you want Calendar to alert you when the appointment is getting near (always a good idea), use the **Reminder** list to select when you want to see the alert.

9. Use the large text box on the right of the screen (see Figure 15.4) to type anything else you can think regarding the appointment: a longer description, talking points, a few good jokes, and so on.

10. Click **Save**. Calendar adds your appointment.

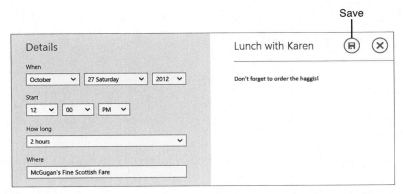

Figure 15.4: *Use the Details screen to specify the particulars of your appointment.*

Using Windows Live Mail's Calendar

If you're more of a desktop person, then consider using Windows Live Mail Calendar feature to handle your appointments. It's a sort of electronic secretary that, while it won't get coffee for you, will at least help you keep your schedule on track. Calendar is a simple electronic day planner you can use to keep track of appointments, meetings, tasks, and other commitments. So whether you have a date and you can't be late, or you have a rendezvous you need to remember, Calendar can handle it.

SEE ALSO

Since Calendar is part of Windows Live Mail, it goes without saying (but apparently I'm going to say it anyway) that you need to download and install Windows Live Mail before you traipse through the rest of this chapter. In Chapter 6, Installing and Removing Programs and Devices, see Installing Windows Live Essentials Programs.

Navigating the Calendar Window

To open Calendar, first start Windows Live Mail by clicking the Start screen's **Windows Live Mail** tile, then click **Calendar** in the lower-left corner of the window. (Pressing the shortcut key combo **Ctrl+Shift+X** will also get you where you want to go.) You see a window similar to the one shown in Figure 15.5.

Figure 15.5: *Use the Calendar section of Windows Live Mail to keep track of appointments, all-day events, and tasks.*

As you can see, Calendar is laid out more or less like a day planner or desk calendar. Here's a quick tour of the three main sections:

- **Date Navigator.** This area shows one month at a time (usually the current month). You use the Date Navigator to change the date displayed in the Events area. Note that today's date always has a red square around it.

- **Events.** The appointments and meetings you schedule will appear in this area.

- **Calendars.** This area displays a list of your calendars. Most people use just a single calendar, but you might want separate calendars for, say, business use and personal use. Your Microsoft account also comes with a Birthday calendar (based on the birthdays you enter in the Contacts list) and a U.S. Holidays calendar.

Changing the Calendar View

By default, Calendar uses the Month view in the Events area, which shows a month's worth of appointments and meetings. However, Calendar is quite flexible and has several other views you can use. Here's the complete list:

- **Day.** In the Home tab, click **Day** (or press **Ctrl+Alt+1**).

- **Week.** Displays Sunday through Saturday for the current week. In the Home tab, click **Week** (or press **Ctrl+Alt+2**).

- **Month.** Displays the current month. In the Home tab, click **Month** (or press **Ctrl+Alt+3**).

Time Traveling: Changing the Date

Calendar usually opens with the current month displayed and today's date selected. However, if you want to work with a different day, the Date Navigator makes it easy. All you have to do is click a date in the Events area. If the month you need isn't displayed in the Date Navigator, use either of the following techniques to pick a different month:

- Click the **Previous Month** arrow beside the month to move backward one month at a time. Similarly, click the **Next Month** arrow to move forward one month at a time.

- Move the mouse pointer over the month name and then click to display a list of the months in the current year. Click the month you want.

Setting Your Social Schedule: Entering Events

Got a party to plan, a meeting to make, or a lunch to linger over? The gadabouts, hobnobbers, and other social butterflies in the crowd will like how easy Calendar makes it to schedule these and other get-togethers.

Before getting down to brass Calendar tacks, you should know that Calendar lets you create two kinds of events:

- **Appointment.** An appointment is the most general Calendar item. It refers to any activity for which you set aside a block of time. Typical appointments include a lunch date, a trip to the dentist or doctor, or a back waxing. You can also create recurring appointments that are scheduled at regular intervals (such as weekly or monthly).

- **All-day event.** An all-day event is any activity that consumes one or more entire days. Examples include conferences, trade shows, vacations, and mental-health days. In Calendar, all-day events don't occupy blocks of time. Instead, they appear as banners above the affected days. You can also schedule recurring all-day events.

> **LOOK OUT!**
>
> Calendar insists on using the term *event* to apply to both appointments and all-day events. Nothing wrong with that, I guess, but I'll keep using the terms *appointment* and *all-day event* throughout the rest of this chapter so you always know exactly what kind of Calendar item I'm yammering on about.

The next few sections show you how to create appointments and all-day events.

Adding an Appointment

Here are the steps you need to trudge through to set up an appointment:

1. Navigate to the date on which the appointment occurs.

2. Make sure you're in the Day view by clicking **Day**.

3. Select the time you want to set aside for the appointment:

   - If the appointment is a half hour, click the half-hour block in the Events area.

   - For all other appointments, click and drag your mouse in the Events area to select the appointment time you want to use. (Don't worry too much if you don't get the time exactly right; you'll get a chance to fix it in a sec.)

4. In the Home tab, click **Event**. Calendar opens the New Event window.

5. Use the **Subject** text box to type a title that describes your appointment. Note that Calendar changes the name of the window from New Event to your Subject text.

6. Use the **Location** text box to specify the location (such as a room number or address) for the appointment.

7. If necessary, use the two **Start** controls to set the date and time that the appointment starts. Use the left control to change the date, and the right control to change the time.

8. If necessary, use the two **End** controls to set the date and time that the appointment ends. Use the left control to change the date, and the right control to change the time.

9. If you happen to have multiple calendars going, click the **Calendar** list and then click the calendar you want to use for this appointment.

WINDOWS WISDOM

To create another calendar, use the Calendar window to click the Home tab's **Calendars** button (slamming **Ctrl+Shift+D** also does the job). Type a name for the calendar, pick out a suitable color, and then click **Save**.

10. Use the large text box at the bottom of the window (see Figure 15.6) to type anything else regarding the appointment: details to note, things to remember, tales to tell, and so on.

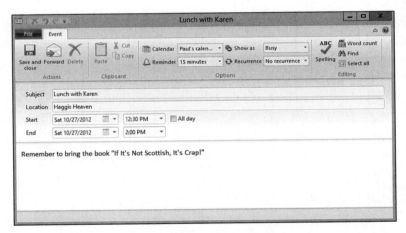

Figure 15.6: *Use this window to specify the details of your new appointment.*

11. Click **Save & close** (or press **Ctrl+S**). Calendar adds your appointment to the Events area.

WINDOWS WISDOM

If the start and end times change for your appointment, you can use your mouse to make the adjustments right in the Events area. To change the start time, click and drag the top edge of the appointment in the Events area; to change the end time, click and drag the bottom edge of the appointment.

Creating a Recurring Appointment

If you have an appointment that occurs at a regular interval (say, weekly or monthly), Calendar lets you schedule a recurring appointment. For example, if you create a weekly appointment, Calendar will fill in that appointment automatically on the same day of the week at the same time for the duration you specify. It's both handy *and* dandy!

To schedule a recurring appointment, follow the steps from the previous section. (If you want to add the recurrence to an existing appointment, double-click it.) In the event window, use the **Recurrence** list to select one of the recurrence patterns, including **Daily, Weekly, Monthly,** or **Yearly.** You can also select **Custom** to pop up the Event Recurrence dialog box and use it to set the recurrence pattern to a specific number of days, weeks, months, or years.

Scheduling an All-Day Event

As I mentioned earlier, an all-day event is an activity that consumes one or more days (or, at least, the working part of those days; you do have a life outside of work, right?). Some activities are obvious all-day events: trade shows, sales meetings, corporate retreats, and so on. But what about, say, a training session that lasts from 9 A.M. to 4 P.M.? Is that an all-day event or just a really long appointment?

From Calendar's point of view, the main difference between an appointment and an all-day event is that an appointment is entered as a time block in the Events area, but an all-day event is displayed as a banner at the top of the Events area (see Figure 15.7). This means that you can also schedule appointments on days that you have all-day events.

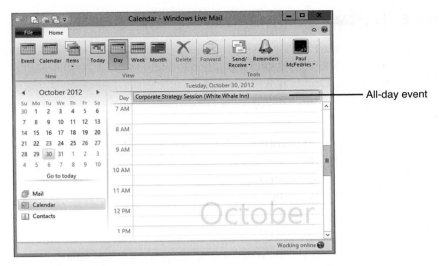

Figure 15.7: *All-day events appear at the top of the Events area.*

A good example that illustrates these differences is a trade show. Suppose the show lasts an entire day and you're a sales rep who will be attending the show. You could schedule the show as a day-long appointment. However, what if you also want to visit with customers who are attending the show? It's possible to schedule conflicting appointments, but having that day-long appointment in there just clutters the Events area. In this case, it makes more sense to schedule the show as an all-day event. This leaves the Events area open for you to schedule appointments with your customers.

Scheduling an all-day event is exactly the same as setting up an appointment. In fact, there are just two differences:

- You need to activate the **All day** check box.
- You can only specify dates for the **Start** and **End** of the event.

HACKING WINDOWS

An even easier way to crank out an all-day event is to navigate to the date, switch to Day or Week view, and then double-click the **Day** area.

The Least You Need to Know

- To create a new contact in the People app, right-click the screen and then click **New**.

- To create a new event in the Calendar app, navigate to the date and then either click the date or, if you're in Day or Month view, click the time when the event begins.

- To use Calendar, you need to download and install Windows Live Mail, as described in Chapter 6.

- To change dates in Windows Live Mail Calendar, use the **Date Navigator** to click the date you want; use the arrows to the left and right of the month to move backward or forward one month at a time.

- To create an appointment in Windows Live Mail Calendar, navigate to the date, click and drag to select the block or time, and then click **Event**.

- To create an all-day event, navigate to the date and then either double-click the **Day** area, or start a new appointment and activate the **All day** check box.

Fax-It-Yourself: Using Windows 8's Faxing Features

In This Chapter

- Getting Windows 8 ready for faxing
- Sending a fax message
- Creating custom fax cover pages
- Receiving incoming faxes

If you're of a certain age, you can probably remember when faxing was one of the wonders of the modern world. Imagine being able to send a facsimile of a document anywhere in the world over a phone line! Nowadays, faxing is a humdrum, even faintly anachronistic, part of the workaday world, and that miracle machine of the 1980s—the fax machine—is practically obsolete.

Now hang on a sec, Jack. How can I fax without a fax machine!?

I'm glad you asked. The secret is a little device inside your computer called a *fax modem*—a modem that has the capability to send and receive faxes in addition to its regular communications duties. (Almost all modern modems can fax, so if you're not sure what type of modem you have, assume you have a fax modem.) Not only does this make faxing affordable for small businesses and individuals, but it also adds a new level of convenience to the whole faxing experience, because you can send faxes right from your computer without having to print the document—and if you have hard copy anyway? Not a problem, because Windows 8 can send a fax right from a document scanner.

If you want to enjoy the fax fast lane from the comfort of your computer, look no further than the Windows Fax and Scan program that comes with Windows 8. This chapter introduces you to Fax and Scan and shows you how to use it to send and receive faxes.

SEE ALSO

Before you can send or receive faxes, you must connect your computer's fax modem to a phone line. For the details, see the section Doing It with Dial-Up in Chapter 7.

Running Windows Fax and Scan

To get the faxing show on the road, switch to the Start screen, type **fax**, and then click **Windows Fax and Scan**. Windows 8 displays the Windows Fax and Scan window, as shown in Figure 16.1. Fax and Scan is where you'll do your fax work in Windows 8.

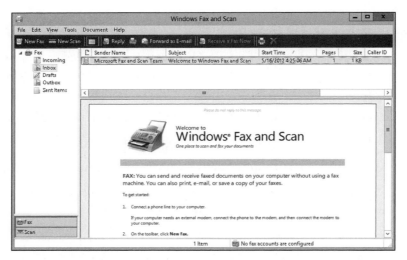

Figure 16.1: *Windows Fax and Scan is your home base for Windows 8 faxing.*

Fax and Scan includes five folders that store fax-related things:

- **Incoming.** This folder displays information about the fax that is currently being received. For example, during fax reception the Status column displays *In progress* and the Extended Status column displays *Answered* and then *Receiving.*

- **Inbox.** This folder stores the incoming faxes that were received successfully. Note that the *Sender Name* column shows the name or phone number of the sender.

- **Drafts.** This folder stores copies of saved faxes that you're composing but haven't sent.

- **Outbox.** This folder stores data about the fax that's currently being sent. For example, during the send the Status column displays *In progress*, and the Extended Status column displays ***Transmitting***.

- **Sent Items.** This folder stores a copy of the faxes that were sent successfully.

After you first start Windows Fax and Scan, there are two chores you need to perform before going on to more useful pursuits: create a fax account and tell the program a bit about yourself. The next two sections take you through these mundane but necessary tasks.

Creating a Fax Account

Before you can do anything useful with Windows Fax and Scan, you have to create a fax account, which the program uses to store your incoming and outgoing faxes. Here's what you have to do to create an account:

1. Select **Tools>Fax Accounts** to get the Fax Accounts dialog box in your face.

2. Click **Add** to launch the wizard that will help you get through this.

3. Select **Connect to a fax modem** to move on to the next wizard dialog box.

4. Use the **Name** text box to type a name for your account, and then click **Next**. The Choose How to Receive Faxes dialog box shows up.

5. Click one of the following options:

   - **Answer automatically.** Click this option to have Windows Fax and Scan automatically answer the line after five rings. This is the way to go if you have separate voice and fax lines.

   - **Notify me.** Click this option to answer incoming calls manually. This is the route to take if you have a single phone line that you use for both voice and fax calls.

   - **I'll choose later; I want to create a fax now.** Click this option if you can't make up your mind and would rather just move on with your life. Fortunately, you can configure this stuff down the road; see Setting Up Fax Receiving, later in this chapter.

6. If at this point you see a Windows Security Alert dialog box, try to stay calm. Take a deep breath and then click the **Allow access** button, which tells Windows Firewall that Windows Fax and Scan can talk to the internet. The wizard returns you to the Fax Accounts dialog box, where you see your freshly minted account in the list.

7. Click **Close**.

Entering Some Personal Data

When you send a fax with a cover page, Windows Fax and Scan includes fields for your name, fax number, business phone number, and home phone number. (You can customize these fields; see the section Covering Your Fax: Creating a Fax Cover Page, later in this chapter.) If you don't want your recipients to see blanks in these fields, follow these steps to add this personal data to your fax account:

1. Select **Tools>Sender Information** to see the Sender Information dialog box.

2. Type your full name.

3. Type your fax number.

4. Type your home phone.

5. Type your work phone.

6. Fill in the other fields if you feel like it.

7. Click **OK**.

With your account up and running and your personal data safely stored, you're ready to start faxing stuff left and right.

Using *Fax* as a Verb: Sending a Fax

To fax something to a friend or colleague (or, heck, even a total stranger), Windows Fax and Scan gives you three ways to proceed:

- You can fax a simple note by sending just a cover page.

- You can fax a more complex document by sending it to the Windows 8 fax printer.

- You can fax a document right from your scanner.

The next three sections take you through the specifics of each method.

Faxing a Simple Note

Let's start with the simple cover-page route, which requires the following steps:

1. Select **File>New>Fax** (or click the **New Fax** button). The New Fax window shows up (see Figure 16.2).

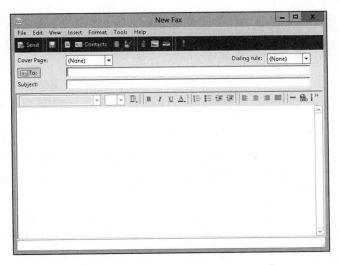

Figure 16.2: *Use the New Fax window to send a simple cover-page fax.*

2. The top part of the New Fax window defines your cover page. Fill in the following fields:

   - **Cover page.** Select the cover page you want to use. (See Covering Your Fax: Creating a Fax Cover Page later in this chapter to find out about these predefined cover pages.)

   - **To.** Enter the recipient's fax number. If you need to add details such as the recipient's company name, address, and phone number, click **To**, click **New Contact**, and then use the tabs in the Properties dialog box to fill in all the information about the recipient. (Be sure to fill in the **Fax** field in either the Work tab or the Home tab.) Click **OK** when you're done. When you return to the Select Recipients dialog box, make sure the new contact name is highlighted, click **To**, and then click **OK**.

   - **Subject.** Enter the subject of the fax.

   - **Cover page notes.** Enter your message.

3. Select **File>Send Fax**. (You can also press **Alt+S** or click the **Send** toolbar button.) Windows Fax and Scan dials the number and sends the fax. The Fax Monitor window shows up to enable you to follow the progress of the send.

Faxing a Document

Simple notes on a cover page are fine, but if you want to go beyond this, you have to take a different tack. Specifically, you have to use WordPad or some other program to create a document, and then you fax that document to the recipient. Here's how it works:

1. Create the document that you want to ship.

2. Select the program's **File>Print** command to get to the Print dialog box.

3. Select the **Fax** printer and then click **Print**. Your old friend, the New Fax window, reappears. Notice that your document has been converted to an attachment.

4. Follow the steps in the previous section to set the fax options and send the fax. (Note that with this method you don't have to bother with a cover page.)

Faxing a Hard Copy from a Scanner

If you already have a document hard copy that you want to fax, that's no problem for Windows Fax and Scan because the program is happy to grab a copy from your document scanner and then fax the copy. It'll even grab multiple-page scans if your scanner supports that kind of thing. Here's how it works:

1. Place the document (or documents) on your scanner.

2. Select **File>New>Fax From Scanner**. Windows 8 scans the document and the New Fax window appears with the scanned document converted to an attachment.

3. Follow the previously outlined steps to set the fax options and send the fax. (Again, note that with this method you don't have to bother with a cover page.)

"Incoming!" Receiving a Fax

The ability to broadcast a fax from your computer to the far corners of the planet is handy, to say the least. However, my favorite part of computer-based faxing is the opposite chore: receiving incoming faxes.

Setting Up Fax Receiving

You probably need to configure Windows Fax and Scan to answer incoming faxes. Here are the steps to follow:

1. Select **Tools>Fax Settings**. The Fax Properties dialog box appears.

2. In the General tab, activate the **Allow the device to receive fax calls** check box.

3. Select one of the following options:

   - **Manually answer.** Activate this option to answer incoming calls manually. This is the best option if you have a single phone line that you use for both voice and fax calls.

   - **Automatically answer after *X* rings.** Activate this option and set the number of rings you want the program to wait before answering. This is the best option if you have a second phone line that you only use for data (faxing, internet, and so on).

4. Click **OK**.

Handling Incoming Calls

When a fax call comes in, what happens next depends on whether you set up Windows Fax and Scan to answer calls automatically or manually. If it's the latter, you hear a ringing tone and the taskbar's notification area pops up a message that says *Fax ID is calling* (where *Fax ID* is the fax identification or phone number of the faxer). Click that message to receive the fax. (If you happen to have the Fax Monitor open already, click the **Answer now** button.)

WINDOWS WISDOM

If you find fax-service sounds (such as the ringing associated with an incoming call) annoying, you can disable them. Select **Tools>Fax Settings** and then display the **Tracking** tab. Click **Sound Options** and then deactivate the check boxes for each sound you want to silence.

When the fax service answers a call, the Fax Monitor dialog box elbows its way to the fore and shows you the progress of receiving the fax (see Figure 16.3). When it's done, you see a **New fax received** message in the notification area. Click that message to open the Fax and Scan window, where you then see the new fax in the Inbox folder.

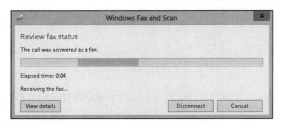

Figure 16.3: *The Fax Monitor appears when the fax service answers the incoming call.*

Getting the fax service to answer incoming calls is great if you have a dedicated fax line, but what if you share voice and fax calls on the *same* line? In this case, the first thing you need to do is make sure that the fax service is set up so that you can handle incoming calls manually. Then the next time the phone rings, pick up the telephone handset. If you hear a series of tones, then you know it's a fax, so click the taskbar's *Fax ID* **is calling** message and then hang up the handset. (Don't replace the handset before clicking the message or you'll disconnect the call.)

From the Fax and Scan window, you can perform the following chores:

- **Read the fax.** Double-click the fax in the Inbox folder (or highlight the fax and select **File>Open**).

- **Print the fax.** Highlight the fax and then select **File>Print**.

- **Save the fax as an image of a file.** Highlight the fax and then select **File>Save As**. Use the Save As dialog box to choose a name and location for the file and then click **Save**. Note that the fax is saved as a TIFF image.

- **Email the fax as an attachment.** Highlight the fax and then select **Document>Forward as Email** (or click the **Forward as Email** button). Use the New Message window to set up the email message and then click **Send**.

- **Delete the fax.** Highlight the fax and then select **Edit>Delete** (or just press the **Delete** key).

LOOK OUT!

Windows Live Mail sets up the fax as an online photo album, which is weird. To convert the fax to a plain file attachment, click the fax, and then under Photo Album Tools, click **Format**. In the Album Style gallery, click **Attach photos to this message** (the paper-clip icon).

The Least You Need to Know

- Start Windows Fax and Send by typing **fax** in the Start screen and then clicking **Windows Fax and Send**.
- To fax a simple note on a cover page, select the Fax and Send **File>New>Fax** command.
- To fax a document from a program, select **File>Print**, choose the **Fax** printer, and then click **Print**.
- To fax a document hard copy from a scanner, select the Fax and Send **File>New>Fax from Scanner** command.
- To answer a call manually and then have the computer intercept the fax, click the taskbar's *Fax ID* **is calling** message.
- To view a received fax, click the taskbar message **New fax received** and then double-click the fax in Fax and Scan's Inbox folder.

Windows 8 and Your Portable PC

Chapter

17

In This Chapter

- Becoming friends with the Mobility Center
- Keeping an eye peeled on your battery status
- Using power management to extend the life of your portable PC battery
- Setting up your portable PC for making presentations
- Checking out Windows 8's portable device doodads

If you have a notebook, tablet, or some other portable PC, then you know full well these machines are fundamentally different from their desktop cousins and that the difference goes well beyond mere luggability. There are batteries to monitor, presentations to set up, and on and on.

The Windows 8 programmers must have had to wrestle with portable PCs a time or two themselves, because they've put together a passel of portable PC perks. Windows 8 offers power management for sensitive portable batteries, an easy way to configure your device to make a presentation, and powerful tools for bringing it all together. I discuss all of these capabilities in this chapter.

Your One-Stop Portable Shop: The Mobility Center

Windows 8 is chock-full of portable PC knickknacks, most of which seem to have been designed with a single purpose in mind: to give us portable PC toters easier access to those features we use most. Thanks!

This makes sense (oh, such a rare phrase when talking about computers) because when you're using a PC on the go, you may have a limited amount of juice in your battery, and you don't want to waste precious power trying to locate some configuration option. And sadly, it's still the case that most portable PC keyboards and pointing devices are harder to use than their full-size desktop cousins, so the fewer keystrokes and mouse clicks required to perform Windows tasks the better.

Your first indication that Windows 8 wants to make your mobile computing life easier is the Windows Mobility Center, shown in Figure 17.1. Fire it up yourself by pressing **Windows+W** to launch the Settings search pane, typing **mobility**, and then clicking **Windows Mobility Center**.

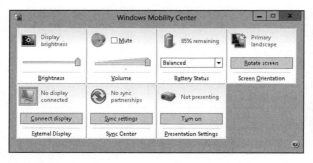

Figure 17.1: *Mobility Center offers a smorgasbord of information and controls for portable-related features.*

The idea behind Mobility Center is simple but surprisingly useful: Bring together in a single spot all the Windows 8 configuration options that are directly or indirectly related to portable PCs. Whether you want to change the screen orientation on your tablet, adjust settings before a presentation, or change power options, it's all just mere mouse clicks away.

Mobility Center is loaded with information on seven key notebook areas, as well as controls that let you adjust these features when the mood strikes you:

- **Brightness.** The current brightness setting of your portable PC screen—if your machine supports this feature, that is. Use the slider to adjust the brightness.

- **Volume.** The current speaker volume. Use the slider to adjust the volume to your liking, or click **Mute** to knock off the portable PC's racket entirely.

- **Battery Status.** The current charge level of the portable PC battery. Use the drop-down list to select one of three power plans: **Balanced**, **Power saver**, or **High** performance (see Better Battery Life Through Power Management following for the details on these plans).

- **Screen Orientation.** The current orientation of the tablet PC screen. Click **Rotate screen** to rotate the screen by 90 degrees in the counterclockwise direction.

- **External Display.** The current status of the external monitor connected to your portable PC or docking station.

- **Sync Center.** The current synchronization status of your offline files. Click the **Sync settings** button to synchronize your portable PC's offline files.

- **Presentation Settings.** The current presentation status. Click **Turn on** to activate Windows 8's portable PC presentation settings. (Want to know more? Of course you do, so check out Setting Up Your Portable PC for a Presentation, later in this chapter.)

Note, too, that Microsoft is letting PC manufacturers get their not-all-that-grubby hands on the Mobility Center, so your version of the Mobility Center window may be tricked out with features specific to your device.

Better Battery Life Through Power Management

When using batteries to run your portable PC on an airplane or some other no-power-outlet-in-sight location, it's natural to worry. That's because the battery can last only so long, so you have a limited amount of time to work or play before your electronic world goes dark. Windows 8 can help relieve some of that worry thanks to its *power management* features. For example, one of these features enables the system to shut down idle components (such as the hard disk and monitor) to prevent them from gobbling up battery power unnecessarily. Another feature lets you monitor how much power is left in the battery. This section takes you on a tour of these and other Windows 8 power-management landmarks.

DEFINITION

Power management refers to those Windows 8 features that enable you to monitor and manage the power consumption of components, particularly portable PC batteries and your hard disk and monitor.

Keeping an Eye on Battery Life

Keeping watch over your remaining battery life is crucial, and that's probably why Windows 8 gives you not one, not two, but *three* ways to do it:

- **Use the Mobility Center.** You saw earlier that the Mobility Center doohickey includes a Battery Status section (flip back to Figure 17.1 if you don't believe me) that gives you estimates on both the time and percentage remaining on the battery.

- **Eyeball the taskbar's Power icon.** When you're running under battery power, you see the Power icon shown in Figure 17.2. When the battery is fully charged, the icon is white from top to bottom; as the battery gradually loses its steam, the level of white in the icon falls. For example, when there is 50 percent of battery life remaining, the icon shows as half white and half gray.

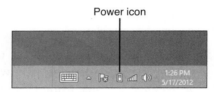

Figure 17.2: *The Power icon tells you how much juice is left in your battery.*

- **Point at the Power icon.** If deciphering the amount of white in the Power icon is just a bit too vague for you, you can get a less hieroglyphic reading by moving your mouse pointer over the Power icon. As you can see in Figure 17.3, Windows 8 raises a small banner that shows the time and percentage of power remaining.

Figure 17.3: *Point the mouse at the Power icon to get a more detailed readout of the battery status.*

Power to the People: Specifying a Power Plan

As I mentioned earlier, Windows 8 cheerfully shuts down some system components in an effort to keep your battery on its feet longer. This is controlled by your current power plan, a power management configuration that specifies which bits and pieces get shut down and when Windows 8 shuts them down. Windows 8 has three power plans to choose from:

- **Power saver.** Components such as the screen and hard disk are powered down after a short idle interval. For example, on battery power, Windows 8 turns off the display after 2 minutes.

- **High performance.** Components are powered down after a longer idle interval, which improves performance because you're less likely to have to wait for them to start up again. For example, on battery power, Windows 8 turns off the display after 10 minutes.

- **Balanced.** This is the middle road (more or less) between the Power saver and High performance plans. For example, on battery power, Windows 8 turns off the display after 5 minutes.

The default power plan is Balanced, but Windows 8 again gives you three methods to change it:

- **Via the Mobility Center.** In the Battery Status section, use the drop-down list to select a power plan.

- **Via the Power icon.** Click the **Power** icon to see the banner shown in Figure 17.4, and then click either **Balanced** or **Power saver**. (Sadly, the High performance power plan isn't available using this method.)

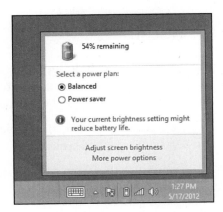

Figure 17.4: *Click the Power icon and then click a power plan.*

- **Via the Power Options window.** Click the **Power** icon and then click **More power options** to display the Power Options window shown in Figure 17.5, then click a power plan option. (If you're looking for that elusive High performance plan, you have to click **Show additional plans** to make it come out of hiding.)

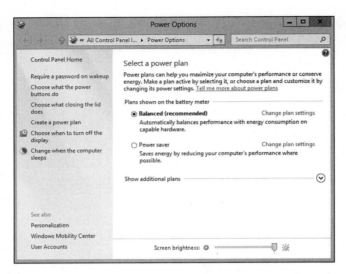

Figure 17.5: *Double-click the Power icon to display the Power Options window.*

Cobbling Together Your Own Power Plan

If you're feeling different drummerish, you don't have to accept the default configuration for any of the power plans. Windows 8 offers a few different options for each plan, and you're free to play around with them to concoct a plan that suits the way you work. Here's how:

1. In the Power Options window, click **Change plan settings** beside the plan you want to mess with. The Edit Plan Settings window shows up. Figure 17.6 shows the Edit Plan Settings window for the Balanced power plan.

2. In the **On battery** column, use the **Dim the display** list to select when you want Windows 8 to reduce screen brightness.

3. In the **On battery** column, use the **Turn off the display** list to select when you want Windows 8 to shut down the display.

4. In the **On battery** column, use the **Put the computer to sleep** list to select when you want Windows 8 to put your portable PC into sleep mode.

5. In the **On battery** column, use the **Adjust plan brightness** slider to set the standard screen brightness.

6. Repeat steps 2 to 5 to configure the same options in the **Plugged in** column.

7. Click **Save changes**.

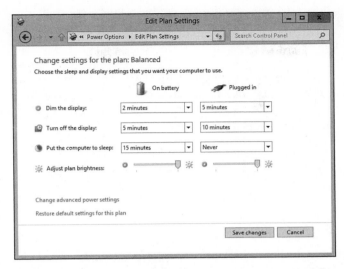

Figure 17.6: *Use the Edit Plan Settings window to customize your own personal power plan.*

Configuring Your Portable PC's Power Buttons

Most newer portable PCs enable you to configure three power buttons: closing the lid, the on/off button, and the sleep button. (On some portables, there isn't a separate sleep button. Instead, you tap the on/off button quickly.) When you activate these buttons, they put your system into sleep or hibernate mode, or turn it off altogether.

Follow these steps to configure these buttons for power management:

1. In the Power Options window, click **Choose what the power buttons do**. The System Settings window shows up.

2. In each of the following three sections, select a power management option for running **On battery** and **Plugged in**:

    • **When I press the power button.** Choose Do nothing, Sleep, Hibernate, or Shut down.

    • **When I press the sleep button.** Choose Do nothing, Sleep, or Hibernate.

    • **When I close the lid.** Choose Do nothing, Sleep, Hibernate, or Shut down.

3. Click **Save changes**.

Setting Up Your Portable PC for a Presentation

The portability of a mobile computer means that these machines are now the first choice as the source of content for presentations from the boardroom to the conference room. That's the good news. The bad news is that there are always a few chores you need to (or should) tend to before starting your presentation:

- Turn off your screen saver. The last thing you want is your screen saver kicking in while you're spending some extra time explaining a point.

- Turn off system notifications, including alerts for incoming email messages and instant messaging posts. Your viewers don't want to be interrupted by these distractions.

- Adjust the speaker volume to an acceptable level.

- Select an appropriate desktop wallpaper image. Your desktop may be visible before or after the presentation, if only briefly. Even so, you probably want a wallpaper that invokes a professional image, or you may prefer a blank desktop.

If you're a regular presenter, changing all these settings before each presentation and reversing them afterwards is a time-consuming chore. However, Windows 8 comes with a feature called Presentation Settings that promises to take most of the drudgery out of this part of presenting. The Presentation Settings feature is a collection of configuration options, including screen blanking, system notifications, speaker volume, and desktop wallpaper. You use Presentation Settings to specify the configuration options you want to use during a presentation. Once you've done that, you can then use Presentation Settings to turn those options on (and off) with just a few mouse clicks.

To configure the Presentation Settings, follow these steps:

1. Press **Windows+W** to open the Settings search pane.

2. Type **present** and then click **Adjust settings before giving a presentation**. Windows 8 displays the Presentation Settings dialog box shown in Figure 17.7.

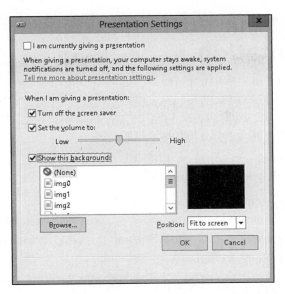

Figure 17.7: *Use the Presentation Settings dialog box to set up a computer configuration to use when you're giving a presentation.*

WINDOWS WISDOM

If you happen to have the Mobility Center onscreen, a quicker way to open the Presentation Settings dialog box is to click the projector icon in the Presentation Settings section.

3. Use the following controls to set up your portable PC for presentations:

- **Turn off the screen saver.** Activate this check box to prevent the screen saver from kicking in.

- **Set the volume to.** Activate this check box and then use this slider to set the volume level you want.

- **Show this background.** Activate this check box and then click **Browse** to select a background (or click **None**).

4. Click **OK** to save the settings.

When it's time to take center stage and make your presentation, you have two ways to switch over to your saved settings:

- Open Mobility Center and select **Turn on** in the Presentation Settings section. (Select **Turn off** when you're done.)

- Open the Presentation Settings dialog box, activate the **I am currently giving a presentation** check box, and click **OK**. (Deactivate this check box after the applause has subsided and you're ready to leave.)

The Least You Need to Know

- Press **Windows+W**, type **mobility**, and then click **Windows Mobility Center** to try out Windows 8's Mobility Center feature.
- When running your portable PC on batteries, be sure you use the taskbar's Power icon to keep a close eye on the battery level.
- Click the **Power** icon to select a different power plan.
- Double-click the **Power** icon to open up the Power Options window.
- To configure your preferred presentation settings, press **Windows+W**, type **present**, and then click **Adjust settings before giving a presentation**.

Customizing, Maintaining, and Troubleshooting

In these media-saturated times, quoting media guru Marshall McLuhan has become the ultimate badge of the so-hip-it-hurts set. Always happy to jump on a passing bandwagon, I hereby offer this book's token McLuhanism: "The mark of our time is its revulsion against imposed patterns." This shameless name- and quote-dropping is not meant to impress, but to introduce the main theme of Part 4: customizing Windows 8. The out-of-the-shrink-wrap look and feel of Windows 8 certainly qualifies as an "imposed pattern." Microsoft designed Windows 8 to be suitable for someone whom they consider a typical user. However, if the notion of being typical fills you with fear and loathing, then you've come to the right place because the chapters coming up will show you how to refurbish Windows 8 to suit your tastes and the way you work. This part of the book also proffers a few pointers on keeping Windows 8 running smoothly and fixing problems that may crop up.

Customizing the Desktop

In This Chapter

- Messing with the desktop background
- Redoing the desktop colors
- Adding and changing desktop icons
- Monkeying around with the display screen resolution

For most of its history, the PC has maintained a staid—nay—dull exterior. Fortunately, the Nuthin'-but-Beige school has given way in recent years to some almost-stylish machines cavorting in gunmetal gray or shiny black exteriors. And with PCs set to invade our living rooms and family rooms in the coming computer-as-the-center-of-the-media-universe revolution, it's likely that colorful and truly stylish machines will become the norm before too long.

That's a good thing because lots of people don't like the same old same old. These rugged individualists want to express themselves, and that's hard to do with beige (unless you call it *ecru* instead). The same goes for the Windows 8 desktop. Yes, when you were installing Windows 8 or setting up your new computer, you probably had the chance to pick out a nifty desktop background, but maybe now you prefer a different scene or even a solid color. If so, you'll see in this chapter that Windows 8 offers plenty of ways to make your mark with a custom desktop color or background.

Why Customize?

Yo, Geek Boy! Changing the desktop sounds great and everything, but most of the time I can't even see it. Isn't all this just a waste of time?

Hey, who're you calling a geek? It's actually not a waste of time because many of the changes you make to the desktop apply to the Desktop app as a whole. For example, you can change the colors of window titles and borders, and change the overall size of the screen area. You'll learn all about these customization options—and many more—in this chapter.

You launch most of these customizations from the friendly confines of the Personalization window. To get this window on the desktop, use either of the following techniques:

- Press **Windows+W** to open the Settings search pane, type **personalization**, and then click **Personalization**.

- If you're already using the Desktop app, right-click an empty section of the desktop and then click **Personalize**.

Changing the Desktop Background

It's true that the desktop is usually hidden, particularly if you spend a lot of time using Windows 8 apps or, like me, you prefer to run your desktop programs maximized. Still, there are plenty of times when the desktop is visible, such as when you first launch the Desktop app and when you close your programs. And on many Windows 8 systems, you can get a quick peek at the desktop by using your mouse to hover over the **Show Desktop** button that's hunkered down on the far right of the taskbar.

If that's enough of an excuse for you to tweak the look of the desktop, then you'll enjoy this section where I show you how to change the desktop background or color.

You can choose one of the prefab backgrounds that come with Windows 8, one of your own pictures, or a solid color. Here's how it works:

1. In the Personalization window, select **Desktop Background** to arrange a rendezvous with the Desktop Background window.

2. Use the **Picture location** list to select the collection of background images you want to view, such as **Windows Desktop Backgrounds**; select **Pictures Library** to see the contents of your Pictures library; or select **Solid Colors** to apply a simple color to the desktop.

3. Click the image or color you want to use.

WINDOWS WISDOM

If you want to use multiple images and create a desktop slide show, activate the check box for each image you want to use, and then use the **Change picture every** list to set how often you want to see a new picture.

4. If you choose an image, select one of the following **Picture position** options:

- **Fill**. Displays a single copy of the image extended on all sides so it fills the entire desktop. As it extends the picture, Windows keeps the ratio of width to height the same, so this usually means part of the image gets cut off.

- **Fit**. Displays a single copy of the image extended until either the width of the picture fits the width of the screen, or the height of the picture fits the height of the screen. Use this position if you want to display the entire image without distortion and without cutting off any of the image.

- **Stretch**. Displays a single copy of the image extended on all sides so it fills the entire desktop. In this case, Windows doesn't keep the ratio of the width to height, so your picture may end up a bit distorted.

- **Tile**. Displays multiple copies of the image repeated so they fill the entire desktop. Choose this option for small images.

- **Center**. Displays a single copy of the image centered in the screen. This is a good choice for large images.

5. Click **Save changes** to confirm your new desktop background.

WINDOWS WISDOM

The Windows 8 list of approved images isn't the only background game in town. There's no problem using some other image if that's what you prefer. To do this, click the **Browse** button to promote the Browse For Folder dialog box, find and select the folder that contains the image file, and then click **OK**. When Windows 8 displays the images from that folder, click the one you want to use.

Populating the Desktop

On most systems, the Windows 8 desktop is a rather Spartan affair with just one measly icon: the Recycle Bin. If you hate seeing all that desktop real estate going to waste, there's nothing to stop you from tossing as many knickknacks on there as can fit. You can fill out the desktop with Windows 8 desktop icons and your own program shortcuts. The next few sections take you through these desktop shenanigans.

Adding Desktop Icons

To get your desktop repopulation program underway, click the **Change desktop icons** link in the Personalization window. The Desktop Icon Settings dialog box that jumps aboard is where you deal with the Windows 8 built-in desktop icons.

In the Desktop icons section, use the check boxes to add icons such as User's Files and Computer to the desktop. If you want to change the icon displayed by Windows 8, select it in the list and then click **Change Icon** (see the following section, Changing an Icon, for the details).

Adding Program Shortcuts

Windows 8's paltry half-dozen-minus-one ready-made desktop icons aren't going to do much to solve your desktop underpopulation problem. If you really want to have icons cheek-by-jowl on the desktop, you need to roll up your sleeves and toss a bunch of them on there yourself. You can create shortcuts for your favorite programs or documents, and double-clicking any shortcut will launch the associated program or document, without any further fuss or fanfare. Creating these shortcuts isn't quite as easy as pie, but it's pretty darn close:

1. You have two ways to get the shortcut-creation party started:

    * If you want to create a shortcut for a program, press **Windows+R** to open the Run dialog box, type **C:\ProgramData\Microsoft\ Windows\Start Menu\Programs**, and then click **OK**.

    * If you want to create a shortcut for a document, open File Explorer and then open the library that contains the file.

2. Find the icon for which you want to create the shortcut.

3. Right-click the icon and then click **Send To>Desktop (create shortcut)**. Windows 8 plops a new shortcut icon on the desktop.

Note if the default icon Windows 8 uses isn't to your liking, you can change it. To get started, right-click the shortcut, click **Properties**, and then click **Change Icon**. The next section takes you on the rest of the journey.

> **WINDOWS WISDOM**
>
> Windows 8 also enables you to sort your desktop icons. Right-click the desktop, click **Sort By**, and then click a sort order: **Name**, **Size**, **Item type** (that is, by type of file), or **Date modified** (that is, by date). Felix Unger types can keep things in apple-pie order all the time by clicking **View**, and then activating the **Auto Arrange icons** command and the **Align icons to grid** command.

Changing an Icon

In several places throughout this book (including the previous two sections), you learn how to customize an object by changing its icon. How you get started depends on the object with which you're working. However, in all cases you eventually end up at the Change Icon dialog box shown in Figure 18.1.

Figure 18.1: *The Change Icon dialog box lists the icons that are available in an executable or icon file.*

Here are some notes about working with this dialog box:

- In Windows 8, icons are usually stored in groups within executable files, particularly .exe and .dll files. Files with the .ico extension are pure icon files.

- If the icon you want isn't displayed in the Change Icon dialog box, use the Look for Icons in This File text box to enter the name of an icon file and then press **Tab**. Here are a few suggestions:

  - %SystemRoot%\system32\shell32.dll

  - %SystemRoot%\system32\Pifmgr.dll

  - %SystemRoot%\explorer.exe

- If you're not sure about which file to try, click the **Browse** button and choose a file in the dialog box that appears.

- Click the icon you want to use, then click **OK**.

Screen Saver Silliness

In olden times (say, 20 years ago), monitors weren't as good as they are today, and most of us struggled along using ugly DOS screens. One of the problems people faced was leaving their monitors on too long and ending up with some DOS hieroglyphics permanently burned into the screen (this is usually referred to, not surprisingly, as burn-in). To prevent this from happening, some genius came up with the idea of a screen saver: a program that automatically kicks in after the computer is idle for a few minutes. The screen saver displays some kind of moving pattern on the screen that helps prevent burn-in. However, with a simple touch of a key or jiggle of a mouse, the normal screen returns, unharmed and none the worse for wear.

Nowadays, it's pretty tough to burn an image into your screen. Improvements in monitor quality and the graphical nature of Windows have made such a fate much more difficult (although not impossible). Curiously, though, screen savers are still around and are, in fact, flourishing. The reason: most of them are just plain cool. Who cares about preventing burn-in when you can watch wild, psychedelic patterns or your favorite cartoon every few minutes?

WINDOWS WISDOM

Most folks use screen savers for the fun factor, but they have a practical side as well. For example, if you set up the screen saver to kick in quickly (say, after just one minute), then it's useful for hiding your screen when you're not at your desk. Also, as you'll see in this section, you can secure your computer by configuring it to display the sign-in screen when you leave the screen saver.

There are scads of commercial screen savers on the market, and Windows 8 comes equipped with some of its own. To try them out, first select **Screen Saver** in the Personalization window to open the Screen Saver Settings dialog box. Now drop down the Screen saver list, and select a screen saver.

You can also choose the following options:

- **Wait.** This spin box controls the amount of time your computer must be inactive before the screen saver starts doing its thing. You can enter a number between 1 and 9,999 minutes.

- **On resume, display log-on screen.** Activate this check box to have Windows 8 display the log-on screen when you stop the screen saver. This means you have to sign in to Windows again.

WINDOWS WISDOM

Having to sign in each time your screen saver kicks in sounds like a hassle, but it's actually an effective security feature. If you leave your desk for a while, any snoop who tries to gain access to your computer will run smack dab into the log-on screen and be foiled. Of course, you must set up your Windows 8 user account with a password (see Chapter 12) for this tactic to stop anyone with the IQ of a trained monkey or better.

- **Preview.** Click this button to give the screen saver a trial run. To return to the dialog box, move your mouse or press any key.

- **Settings.** Click this button to set various options for the screen saver (note, however, that some screen savers don't have any options). The Settings dialog box that appears depends on which screen saver you choose. Choose the options you want, and then click **OK** to return to the Personalization window.

Changing the Desktop Colors

Systems with decent graphics hardware get to eyeball one of Windows 8's most striking features: the "glass" interface that makes the taskbar, and the borders and title bars of windows and dialog boxes, semitransparent. Why does the world need such an effect, I hear you ask? Windows 8 flacks will tell you that it helps people (like you and me) focus better on the content of a window rather than the window itself. That might be true, but the effect sure is striking, so what the heck?

If the default blue that Windows 8 applies to the taskbar and window borders just doesn't do it for you, or if the glass effect is just too weird, these settings are easily changed. You begin by clicking **Window Color** in the Personalization window. This gets you an appointment with the Window Color and Appearance window, which is simplicity itself, as you can see in Figure 18.2. Just click the color you prefer. If you don't like the glass effect, you can nix it by deactivating the **Enable transparency** check box. If you select one of the nonautomatic colors (that is, any swatch that doesn't have the paint chip–cards icon), you can also use the Color intensity slider to change the amount of transparency. (The further to the right you drag the slider, the less transparent your windows become.) When you're done, click **Save changes**.

HACKING WINDOWS

If Windows 8 built-in colors don't do it for you, create your own. Choose a nonautomatic color and then click **Show color mixer** to display three sliders: Hue, Saturation, and Brightness. Play with these sliders to come up with a color you like.

This is the automatic color

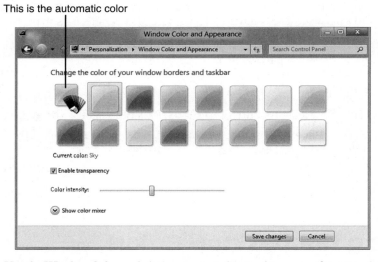

Figure 18.2: *Use the Window Color and Appearance window to choose your favorite color and turn the "glass" effect on or off.*

After you make changes to the Windows 8 theme, you might want to save those changes so you can apply them easily later on. Good idea! Here's how:

1. In the Personalization window's My Themes area, click **Unsaved Theme**.

2. Click **Save theme**, to open the Save Theme As dialog box.

3. Enter a cute or witty name for your theme.

4. Click **Save** to return to the Personalization window. You've now saved your custom theme, which means you can return to it (by selecting it in the My Theme lists) anytime you like if you change the color scheme later on.

Changing the Screen Resolution

The next bit of desktop decoration I'll put you through relates to screen resolution. Again, these are options that apply not just to the desktop, but to everything you see on your screen. To see these settings, you've got a couple of ways to go:

- Press **Windows+W** to open the Settings pane, type **resolution**, and then click **Adjust screen resolution**.

- Right-click the desktop and then click **Screen resolution**.

Either way, the Screen Resolution window that fades in is shown in Figure 18.3.

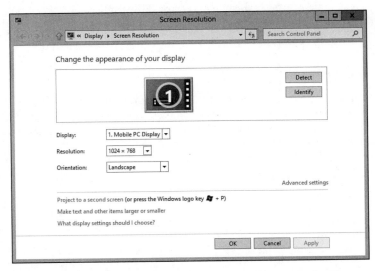

Figure 18.3: *The Screen Resolution window lets you muck around with your display.*

The **Resolution** list contains a slider that determines the number of pixels used to display stuff on the screen. I've mentioned pixels before, but it's worth repeating here: a pixel is an individual pinpoint of light. All the colors you see on your screen are the result of thousands of pixels getting turned on and set to display a specific hue.

The lowest screen-area value is 1024×768. This means that Windows 8 uses pixels arranged in a grid that has 1024 columns and 768 rows. That's more than 786,000 pixels for your viewing pleasure! The number of higher resolution values you can pick depends on your monitor and on your video adapter. Here are some notes:

- The more pixels you use (that is, the higher you go on the Resolution slider), the smaller things will look on the screen.

- In general, you should tailor the screen-area value with the size of your monitor. If you have a 17- or 19-inch monitor, 1,024×768 is fine; for a 21- or 24-inch monitor, give 1,280×800 a try; if you're lucky enough to have a 27-inch behemoth, go for 1,600×1,200 or even 1,920×1,080 (if your video adapter will let you).

- If you have an older game or other program that has to be run at 640×480, you might think you're out of luck, but perhaps not. Locate and right-click the program icon and then click **Properties**. In the Compatibility tab, activate the **Run in 640×480 screen resolution** check box.

When you've made your changes, click **OK**. If you choose a different resolution, Windows 8 changes the setting and then asks whether you want to keep it. Click **Yes**. If things don't look right for some reason, click **No** to return to your normally scheduled display settings.

LOOK OUT!

If your display goes haywire when Windows 8 applies the new settings, it probably means that you tried some combo that was beyond the capabilities of your adapter/monitor team. Your screen may be unreadable, but don't panic. Windows 8 will automatically reset the display after 15 seconds.

The Least You Need to Know

- To create a desktop shortcut for a program or document, locate the program or document, right-click its icon, and then click **Send To>Desktop (create shortcut)**.
- To open the Personalization window, either press **Windows+W**, type **personalization**, and then click **Personalization**, or right-click the desktop and then click **Personalize**.
- Most background images are small, so you need to use the Tile option to get the fill effect. For larger images, use either Center or Fit to Screen.
- Try to use a screen resolution value that matches your monitor. For most monitors, 1,280×800 is ideal.

Revamping the Start Screen and Taskbar

In This Chapter

- Organizing the Start screen to suit the way you work
- Adding your own tiles to the Start screen
- Some useful taskbar tweaks
- Customizing the notification area

You probably deal with the Start screen dozens of times a day, clicking this, dragging that. And if you've still got a foot or two in the desktop world, then no doubt you spend plenty of time performing taskbar duties. If you could just figure out some ways to perform these chores more quickly and efficiently, you'd probably save yourself lots of time for more interesting pursuits.

Well then, you've come to the right chapter! Here's where you'll stumble upon all kinds of useful settings, options, tips, and techniques that not only let you work with the Start screen and taskbar, but let you customize these Windows bits to make yourself more productive.

A Smart Start: Reconstructing the Start Screen

The Start screen is your royal road to Windows 8 riches, as well as many of the programs installed on your machine—particularly your Windows 8 apps. Because you use this road a lot during the course of a day, you'll probably want to make it as short and straight as possible. Fortunately, Windows 8 gives you lots of ways to customize the Start screen to do that and to suit the way you work.

Rearranging Start Screen Tiles

Most new users just assume the arrangement of icons on the Start screen is a permanent part of the Windows 8 landscape. Nope. The Start screen is completely open for customization business—as you see in the next few sections. Perhaps the easiest way to rework the Start screen in your own image is to move the tiles around. Why would you want to do that? Here are some (mostly) good reasons:

- Tiles on the left side of the Start screen are usually easier to find and click, so you might want to move the apps you use most frequently to the left flank of the screen.

- You might want to place related tiles near each other on the screen for easier access. For example, you could bring all the game-related tiles together.

- Arrange the tiles by color to make the Start screen easier on the eyes.

Whatever the reason, use one of the following techniques to move a tile to a different position on the Start screen:

- **Mouse method.** Click and drag the tile. As you drag the tile, Windows 8 automatically shifts the other tiles to make room for the interloper. When the tile is in the position you prefer, release the mouse.

- **Touch method.** Tap and hold the tile and then drag your finger (or stylus) up or down until a border appears around the tile. Now drag the tile to the position you want and then release the tile.

HACKING WINDOWS

The tiles come in two sizes—large and small—and this means you might end up with unsightly gaps after moving tiles around a bit. You should be able to get rid of those gaps by resizing tiles strategically. To resize a tile, right-click it (or swipe down on it if you're using a tablet PC) and then click either **Smaller** or **Larger**. Note that this doesn't work for every tile.

Grouping Start Screen Tiles

In the previous section I mentioned that moving tiles hither and thither enables you to arrange related tiles near each other for easier access. If that's what you're all about, then I've got an even better way to go about it: grouping tiles. A tile group is a collection of tiles separated from the others on the Start screen. You can even give a group a name if you feel like it; and who doesn't?

Here are the steps to follow to make all this happen:

1. Click and drag (or tap and drag) the first tile you want to include in your group.

2. Drag the tile to the left side of the Start screen until you see a vertical bar appear, as shown in Figure 19.1.

Figure 19.1: *Drag the first of your group tiles to the left side of the screen until the vertical bar magically appears.*

3. Drop the tile. Windows 8 creates a new group on the left side of the Start screen.

4. For each tile you want to include in the group, drag it to the left side of the screen and then drop it within the new group.

5. Press **Ctrl+-** (hyphen) to zoom out.

6. If you want your group to appear elsewhere in the Start screen, drag the group to the position you prefer.

7. Right-click the group and then click **Name group**. Windows 8 offers up a dialog box for naming the group, as shown in Figure 19.2.

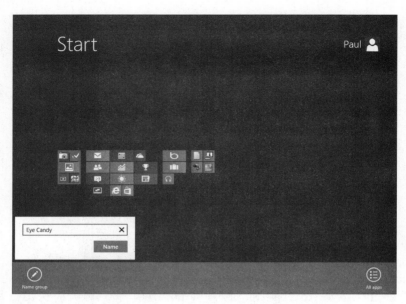

Figure 19.2: *Zoom out, right-click the group, and then click* **Name group** *to give your new group a wise or witty name.*

8. Type the name you want to use and then click **Name**.

9. Click the screen. Windows 8 zooms back in and your newly minted and named group is ready for action.

Turning Off Live Tiles

One of the goals of the Start screen is to give you an overview of what's happening on your computer (and so, to a certain extent, what's happening in your life). Windows 8 accomplishes this by making some of the Start screen tiles *live*, meaning they display the latest information. For example, the Weather app is happy to provide you with the current weather conditions, and the Finance app tells you what's going on in the markets. On a more personal level, the Mail app lets you know when you have new messages, the Calendar app alerts you to upcoming appointments, and the People app gives you the latest from your social networks.

This is all great in theory but in practice, well, it tends to get a bit busy. After a while, the Start screen gives off a positively Times Squareish vibe with the constant movement, the barrage of visual signals, and the endless tourists.

Okay, there are no tourists, but what's a body to do when the Start screen becomes the Start *scream*? Turn down the visual volume by turning off a few of the less useful live tiles. You do that by right-clicking a tile (or swiping down on the tile if you're a tablet user) and then clicking **Turn live tile off**.

Pinning a Program to the Start Screen

The items on the main Start screen—including Photos, Calendar, Mail, and Internet Explorer—are oh-so handy because they require a mere click to launch. On the other hand, to start up all your other programs, you must right-click the Start screen (or swipe up from the bottom edge on a tablet), click **All apps**, scroll through the Apps screen to find the program you want to run, and *then* click it. I'm tired just writing about it.

For those programs you use most often, you can avoid all this exercise by pinning them to the main Start screen. All pinned programs appear to the right of the main Start screen tiles. So once you've pinned a program to your Start screen, you can always launch that program by scrolling right and then clicking the program tile. (Or, of course, you can move the pinned program to the left side of the Start screen for even easier access.)

Here's how to pin a program to the Start screen:

1. In the Windows 8 Start screen, begin typing the name of the program you want to pin. (On a tablet, swipe left from the right edge of the screen to display the Charms menu, tap **Search**, tap inside the search box, and then begin typing the program name.) Windows 8 starts displaying the programs with names that match your typing.

2. When the program appears in the Apps screen, right-click the program; on a tablet, swipe down on the program. The application bar appears.

3. Click **Pin to start**. Windows 8 adds a tile for the program to the Start screen.

WINDOWS WISDOM

Do you have a folder that you open constantly? If so, you can pin that folder to the Start screen. No, really. Launch File Explorer and then open the location that contains the folder you want to pin. Click the folder, click the **Home** tab, click **Easy access**, and then click **Pin to Start**. See? I told you.

Pinning a Website to the Start Screen

If you have a website that you haunt frequently, wouldn't it be nice to have some way to surf to that site quickly and easily? Why yes, yes it would. Fortunately, you're reading this section, which is going to tell you exactly how to do that. Specifically, you use the Internet Explorer app to pin the website to the Start screen, where an effortless click of the mouse (or tap of the screen) is all it takes to bring the site into view.

Here's what's required of you:

1. On the Start screen, click **Internet Explorer**.

2. Navigate to the website you want to pin.

3. Click the **Pin site** icon, which is the pushpin that appears to the right of the address bar, as shown in Figure 19.3.

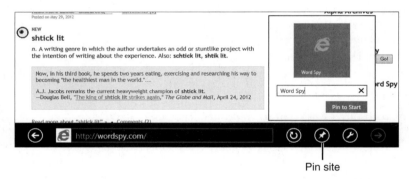

Pin site

Figure 19.3: *Navigate to your website and then click **Pin site** and click **Pin to Start**.*

4. Edit the website name, if you feel like it.

5. Click **Pin to Start**. Windows 8 adds a tile for the website to the Start screen.

HACKING WINDOWS

When you click the pinned website, it always opens in Internet Explorer app. If you're a dedicated user of desktop Internet Explorer, are you doomed? Nope. Open desktop Internet Explorer, click **Tools** (the gear icon) and click **Internet options** to display the Internet Options dialog box. Click the **Programs** tab, activate the **Open Internet Explorer tiles on the desktop** check box, and then click **OK**.

Removing a Tile from the Start Screen

Adding stuff to the Start screen is all well and good, but what about the opposite procedure, when you need to get rid of something on the Start screen? I'm glad you asked. To remove a tile, right-click it (on a tablet, swipe down on the tile) and then click **Unpin from start**. Windows 8 does what you ask and removes the tile from the Start screen.

Renovating the Taskbar

Like the Start screen, the taskbar also seems to be a nonmalleable feature of the Windows 8 countryside. If that were true, however, then this chapter would end right about here. The fact that you still have a few pages left tells you that, indeed, the taskbar is readily malleable. Not only that, but most of the taskbar customizations you'll see over the next few sections are practical timesavers and not mere Hey-Ma-look-what-I-can-do! tricks. (Although feel free to show off these techniques to any handy family member.)

Pinning a Program to the Taskbar

A bit earlier in this chapter you learned how to pin a program to the Start screen. However, that is only helpful if you use the Start screen regularly. If you're more of a desktop person and you have a program that you use frequently, is it possible to get the same one-click convenience? You bet. You can do this by pinning that program to the Windows 8 taskbar.

As with previous versions of Windows, the Windows 8 taskbar displays an icon for each running program. However, you can also use the taskbar to store program icons. Once you have a shortcut icon for a program pinned to the taskbar, you can then launch that program just by clicking the icon—easy peasy, as they say.

Here's how to pin a program to the taskbar:

1. In the Windows 8 Start screen, start typing the name of the program you want to pin. (On a tablet, swipe left from the right edge of the screen to display the Charms menu, tap **Search**, tap inside the search box, and then start typing the name.) Windows 8 displays a list of the programs with names that match your typing.

2. When the program shows up in the search results, right-click it. (On a tablet, swipe down on the program.) Windows 8 displays the application bar.

3. Click **Pin to taskbar**. Windows 8 adds an icon for the program to the taskbar.

> **WINDOWS WISDOM**
>
> As you pin program icons to the taskbar, Windows 8 displays the icons left to right in the order you added them. If you prefer a different order, click and drag a taskbar icon to the left or right and then drop it in the new position. Note that this technique applies not only to the icons pinned to the taskbar, but also to the icons for any running programs.

Unlocking the Taskbar

When Microsoft was testing Windows with new users, they found that people often ended up with inadvertently customized taskbars they didn't know how to fix. For example, it's quite easy to accidentally resize the taskbar while trying to resize a window. To prevent this kind of faux customization (and the confusion it creates), Windows 8 comes with its taskbar locked so that it can't be moved or sized.

To unlock the taskbar so you can manhandle it on purpose: right-click an empty section of the taskbar and then use the shortcut menu that appears to look for the **Lock the Taskbar** command. If there's a check mark beside it, click the command to remove the check mark and unlock the taskbar.

Taskbar Travels: Moving and Sizing the Taskbar

The taskbar, recumbent on the bottom of the screen, seems quite comfy. However, that position might not be comfy for *you*, depending on the ergonomics of your desk and chair. Similarly, you might have a program where you need to maximize the available vertical-screen space, so you might not appreciate having the taskbar usurp space at the bottom of the screen. These are mere molehills that can be easily leapt by moving the taskbar to a new location:

1. Right-click an empty section of the taskbar and then click **Properties**. The Taskbar Properties dialog box appears.

2. Click the **Taskbar location on screen** list, and then click the location you prefer: **Left**, **Right**, **Top**, or **Bottom**.

3. Click **OK**. Windows 8 tosses the taskbar to the new location.

What if you're not so much interested in moving the taskbar as in resizing it? For example, if you're feeling particularly frisky, you might end up with a truckload of programs running. However, each of those programs claims a bit of taskbar turf. Eventually, the taskbar reaches its maximum capacity and it sprouts little up and down arrows to the right of the icons, as pointed out in Figure 19.4. Click the **down arrow** to see the icons for your other running programs, and then click the **up arrow** to return to the original batch of icons.

Click these arrows to see your other taskbar icons

Figure 19.4: *Once you've got a bunch of programs running, extra clicks are required to see the rest of the taskbar icons. Boo!*

That extra click to get to the icon you need is a real hassle and flies in the face of the taskbar's one-click convenience. The way you fix that is by expanding the taskbar from its single-row setup to a setup that has two or more rows. Here's how:

1. Move the mouse pointer so that it rests on the top edge of the taskbar. The pointer changes into a vertical two-headed arrow.

2. Click and drag the edge of the taskbar up slightly. After you travel a short distance, a second taskbar row springs into view, as shown in Figure 19.5.

Figure 19.5: *To see all taskbar buttons, stretch the taskbar into this two-row configuration.*

3. Keep dragging the taskbar up until the taskbar is the size you want, and then release the mouse button.

I should mention here that if you've moved the taskbar to the left or right side of the screen, dragging the outer edge only increases the width of the taskbar—it doesn't create new rows.

Some Useful Taskbar Options

The next round of taskbar touchups involves a small but useful set of properties, which can be displayed by using either of the following techniques:

- Press **Windows+W** to open the Settings search pane, type **taskbar**, and then click **Taskbar**.

- Right-click an empty section of the taskbar and then click **Properties**.

This reunites you with the Taskbar Properties dialog box. The controls in the Taskbar tab control the look and feel of the taskbar. Here's a summary of the available controls:

- **Lock the taskbar.** This check box toggles the taskbar lock on and off.

- **Auto-hide the taskbar.** If you activate this check box, Windows 8 shrinks the taskbar to a teensy blue strip that's barely visible along the bottom of the screen. This gives a maximized window more room to stretch its legs. When you need the taskbar for something, just move the mouse pointer to the bottom of the screen. Lo and behold, the full taskbar slides into view. When you move the mouse above the taskbar, the taskbar sinks back whence it came.

- **Use small taskbar icons.** When this option is activated, the taskbar icons convert into smaller versions, which is a great way to get more icons crammed into a single taskbar row.

- **Taskbar location on screen.** As I described in the previous section, you use this list to move the taskbar to a different location.

- **Taskbar buttons.** The items in this list determine how and whether Windows 8 combines taskbar icons. As you know, when you run a program, Windows 8 adds a button for the program to the taskbar. The default value is **Always combine, hide labels**, which means that Windows 8 reduces clutter by combining similar taskbar buttons into a single button. For example, if you have two or three instances of File Explorer on the go, they'll get grouped into a single button. If you choose **Combine when taskbar is full** instead, then Windows 8 only does the combining thing once the taskbar becomes completely filled with buttons. To forego all this combining malarkey, choose **Never combine**.

- **Notification area.** I talk about this in the next section, so please be patient.

- **Use Peek to preview the desktop.** When this long-winded check box is activated, you get a sneak peek of what's on the desktop by maneuvering the mouse pointer to the far right edge of the taskbar. This causes the current desktop windows to disappear temporarily. Move the mouse pointer elsewhere to reinstate the windows.

Click **OK** to put your settings into effect.

Getting Control of the Notification Area

The notification area on the right side of the taskbar is blissfully low on icons in Windows 8. (If you've used previous versions of Windows, you might have ended up with a notification area festooned with a ridiculous number of icons.) In Windows 8, no matter how many of your installed programs try to run roughshod over the notification area, you always see *only* the following icons: Volume, Network, Action Center, and—if you have a portable PC—Power. Sweet!

That doesn't mean all your other notification area icons are gone for good, they're just permanently hidden, although in two different ways:

- Some icons are visible, but to see them you have to click the **upward-pointing arrow** on the left side of the notification area (see Figure 19.6).

- Some icons are completely hidden, but you do see any notification messages displayed by those icons.

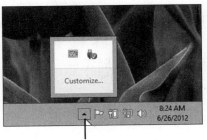

Click here to see more notification area icons

Figure 19.6: *In Windows 8, you have to click the arrow to see your other notification area icons.*

This new setup simplifies things considerably and gives you more taskbar breathing room, but there are times when it's not so convenient. For example, if you frequently control a program by right-clicking its notification area icon, you either have that extra click to get to the icon, or you can't get to it at all. Fortunately, you can customize the notification area to show an icon right in the notification area, hide it in the extra menu, or remove it completely and just see its notifications. Here's how:

1. Click the **notification area arrow** and then click **Customize**. (You can also right-click the taskbar, click **Properties**, and then click **Customize**.) The Notification Area Icons window appears, as shown in Figure 19.7.

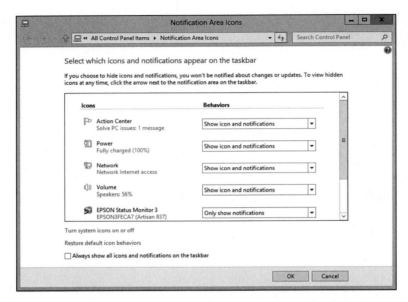

Figure 19.7: *Use the Notification Area Icons window to set up the notifications area to suit your style.*

2. For each icon, click the **Behaviors** list to choose one of the following options:

   • **Show icon and notifications.** Choose this option to add the icon to the main notification area.

   • **Hide icon and notifications.** Choose this option to shuffle the icon off to the notification area extra menu.

   • **Only show notifications.** Choose this option to completely remove the icon from the main notification area. Windows 8 will still display the icon notifications, however.

WINDOWS WISDOM

If you find you *miss* having a boatful of icons in the notification area, you can return to days of yore by activating the **Always show all icons and notifications on the taskbar** check box.

3. Click the **Turn system icons on or off** link. The System Icons window appears. The system icons are the four icons I mentioned earlier: Volume, Network, Action Center, and Power, plus a fifth icon, Clock (and a sixth icon called *Input Indicator* that you can safely ignore).

4. Select **Off** in the Behaviors list for each system icon you don't use.

5. Click **OK** to return to the Notification Area Icons window.

6. Click **OK**.

The Least You Need to Know

- You can rearrange the Start screen tiles by dragging them to new locations. Drag a tile all the way to the left edge of the screen to create a tile group.

- To pin a program to the Start screen, locate it in the Apps screen, right-click it, and then click **Pin to Start**.

- To pin a program to the taskbar, locate it in the Apps screen, right-click it, and then click **Pin to taskbar**.

- Before embarking on any taskbar modifications, be sure to unlock it first. The quickest route is to right-click an empty part of the taskbar and then deactivate the **Lock the Taskbar** command.

- To eyeball the taskbar options, right-click an empty stretch of the taskbar and then click **Properties**.

- To mess around with the notification area, click the **notification area arrow** and then click **Customize**.

Maintaining Your System in 10 Easy Steps

In This Chapter

- Maintain your hard disk by checking for errors, monitoring free space, deleting unnecessary files, and defragmenting files
- Set up your system for easier recovery by creating restore points, backing up your files, creating a full system backup, and creating a recovery drive
- Keep your system up to date by checking for solutions to problems
- Set up a maintenance schedule to keep your system running in peak form without burdening your schedule

We tend to forget that computers are mechanical devices that can fail at any time, or can simply wear out over time. In other words, the data you've stored on your computer is at risk *right now*. Not months or years from now. *Now*. This doesn't mean you should just sit around and wait for your computer to start sucking mud. ("Sucking mud" is a colorful phrase used by programmers to refer to a crashed machine. Legend has it that the phrase comes from the oil-field lament, "Shut 'er down, Ma, she's a-suckin' mud!")

No, what you *should* be doing is a little proactive system maintenance to help prolong your machine's life and to help propel your system to new heights of efficiency and speed. This chapter can help by showing you the Windows 8 tools that can get you in what I like to call ounce-of-prevention mode—and, down the road, to avoid what I call pound-of-cure mode. In particular, I give you a step-by-step plan for maintaining your system and checking for the first signs of problems.

Step 1: Check Your Hard Disk for Errors

You see later in this chapter that you should back up your files frequently because all hard disks eventually go to the Great Computer in the Sky. However, it's possible to avoid premature hard disk death (as well as lost files and otherwise-inexplicable system crashes) by regularly checking your disk for errors. (By regularly, I mean about once a week or so.) Here's how you do it:

1. Shut down any programs that are running.

2. Open File Explorer and click **Computer** to open the Computer window.

3. Click your hard disk, click the **Computer** tab, and then click **Properties**.

4. In the dialog box that appears, display the **Tools** tab.

5. Click the **Check** button.

6. If Windows 8 tells you that you don't need to scan the drive, yell "Woo hoo!" and click **Cancel**; otherwise (or if you want to scan the drive anyway), click **Scan drive** (or, in some cases, **Scan and repair drive**).

7. If any errors are found, you'll see a dialog box alerting you to the bad news. Follow the instructions provided.

8. When the check is done, a dialog box lets you know. Click **Close**.

Remember that Check Disk can take quite a while under some circumstances, so only run the program at the end of the day or when you know you won't be needing your computer for a while.

Step 2: Check Free Disk Space

Ever wonder how much free space you have left on your hard disk? It's easy enough to find out:

1. Open File Explorer.

2. Click **Computer** to get reunited with the Computer folder.

3. Select the **View** tab.

4. Click **Tiles**. (This is the default Computer folder view, so it might already be selected.)

As you can see in Figure 20.1, in Tiles view Windows 8 tells you how much free space is left on each drive.

This is the drive where Windows is stored

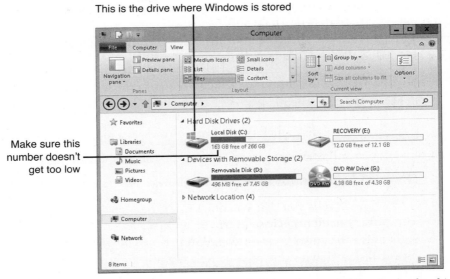

Make sure this number doesn't get too low

Figure 20.1: *Open the Computer folder to see how much disk real estate is left to be developed in each of your drives.*

WINDOWS WISDOM

How do you know when your hard disk is getting low on disk space? First, use the Computer folder to see if Windows shows the amount of used space on the drive in red, which is an indication that it's nearly full. As a general rule, on the disk where Windows 8 is stored (see Figure 20.1) you should never let that disk get much below a gigabyte (GB) or two.

Step 3: Delete Unnecessary Files

If you find your hard disk is getting low on free space, you should delete any unneeded files and programs. Here are a few methods you can use to perform a spring cleaning on your hard disk by hand:

- **Uninstall programs you don't use.** If you have an internet connection, you know it's easier than ever to download new software for a trial run. Unfortunately, that also means it's easier than ever to clutter your hard disk with unused programs. You should uninstall these and other rejected applications (see Chapter 6).

- **Delete downloaded program archives.** Speaking of program downloads, your hard disk is probably also littered with zip files or other downloaded archives. For those programs you use, you should consider moving the archive files to a removable medium for storage. For programs you don't use, consider deleting the archive files.

- **Delete or move personal files you don't need.** If you've got lots of old files that you no longer use—particularly digital media files, which can take up lots of space—consider moving them to another drive (such as a USB flash drive) or deleting them.

Once you've completed these tasks, you next should run the Disk Cleanup utility, which can automatically remove several other types of files, including the following:

- **Downloaded program files.** Small web page programs downloaded onto your hard drive.

- **Temporary internet files.** Copies of web pages that Internet Explorer keeps on hand so the pages view faster the next time you visit them. Deleting these files will slow down some of your web surfing slightly, but will also rescue lots of disk space.

- **Offline web pages.** Web page copies stored on your hard drive for offline viewing.

- **Recycle Bin.** These are the files that you've deleted recently. Windows 8 stores them in the Recycle Bin for a while just in case you delete a file accidentally. If you're sure you don't need to recover a file, you can clean out the Recycle Bin and recover the disk space.

- **Temporary files.** "Scratch pad" files that some programs use to doodle on while they're up and running. Most programs toss out these files, but a program or computer crash can prevent that from happening; delete these files at will.

- **Thumbnails.** Copies of picture files used by Windows 8 to quickly display thumbnail versions of those files. If deleted, Windows 8 will recreate them as needed.

Note that you may not have all of these types of files on your system, so if you don't see some of them when you run Disk Cleanup, don't sweat it.

Follow these steps to use Disk Cleanup to trash any or all of these kinds of files:

1. Windows 8 offers you two different routes to get started:

    - In the Computer folder, select the hard disk, select the **Computer** tab, and then click **Properties**. In the dialog box that beams up, click the **Disk Cleanup** button.

    - Press **Windows+W** to open the Settings search pane, type **cleanup**, and then click **Free up disk space by deleting unnecessary files**.

2. If you used the second of these paths and you have multiple hard disks, the Select Drive dialog box will ask you which one you want to work with. Use the Drives list to pick out the drive and then click **OK**.

3. Either way, you end up at the Disk Cleanup window shown in Figure 20.2. Activate the check box beside each type of file you want to blow to kingdom come.

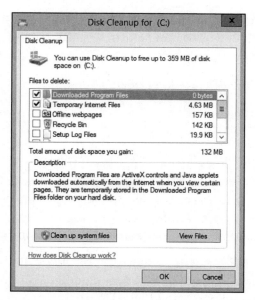

Figure 20.2: *Use Disk Cleanup to obliterate all kinds of more or less useless files from your hard disk.*

4. Click **OK**. Disk Cleanup asks whether you're sure.

5. Click **Yes**.

Step 4: Defragment Your Hard Disk

With its fancy-shmancy Start screen and newfangled apps, Windows 8 surely presents a polished surface to the world. However, when it's just kicking around at home, Windows 8 is a bit of a slob. I'm thinking, in particular, about how Windows 8 stores files on your hard disk. It's actually remarkably casual about the whole thing, and tosses bits and pieces of each file wherever it can find room. This doesn't matter much at first, but after a while you end up with files that are scattered willy-nilly all over your hard disk. This is a problem because it means that to open a file, Windows 8 has to make lots of little, time-consuming trips to the far corners of the hard disk in order to gather up all those disparate chunks.

This is why computers feel nice and zippy when you first take them out of the box but seem to get more sluggish over time. In geek terms, the problem is that the files on your hard disk have become *fragmented*. The solution is to run the Windows 8 Disk Defragmenter program, which will rearrange the contents of your hard disk so that each file's chunks are arranged consecutively (or contiguously, as the geeks like to say). Don't worry, though: your documents and programs don't get changed in any way and your disk contents will look exactly the same when you view them in My Computer.

DEFINITION

A hard disk is **fragmented** when pieces of its files are scattered in various places throughout the disk.

The good news about all this defragmentation stuff is that Windows 8 is set up to automatically defragment your hard disk every week. (The default time is 3 A.M., so that may be why you haven't noticed, insomniacs excluded.) Therefore, you probably won't ever have to worry about it. However, it's a good idea to check that the automatic defragmenter is on the job, which you do by following these steps:

1. You can get underway by using any of the following techniques:

   - In the Computer window, click the hard disk, select the **Computer** tab, and then click **Properties**. In the dialog box that gets piped in, display the **Tools** tab and click the **Optimize** button.

   - Press **Windows+W** to open the Settings search pane, type **defrag**, and then click **Defragment and optimize your hard drives**.

2. In the Optimize Drives window that results, click **Change settings**. The Optimization Schedule dialog box shows up.

3. Make sure the **Run on a schedule** check box is activated, as shown in Figure 20.3.

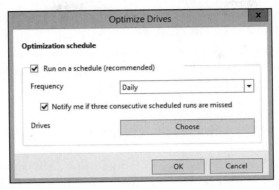

Figure 20.3: *Make sure the automatic defragmenter is doing its defragmentation duty while you're asleep.*

4. To change how often the automatic defragmenter does its thing, click the **Frequency** list and then select **Daily**, **Weekly**, or **Monthly**. (Weekly is probably best for most people.)

5. Click **OK**.

On the other hand, maybe you *want* to run a defragment anyway—just because you can. Hey, it's a free country. Before getting to the Disk Defragmenter details, here's a bit of prep work you need to do:

- Shut down all running programs.

- Run the Check Disk program to be sure there are no errors on your hard disk.

- Use the methods I outlined in the previous section to get rid of any files you don't need.

With that done, click **Optimize** in the Optimize Drives window. The defragmenting process might take some time, depending on the size of your disk and how severely fragmented it is. Because it's not unusual for a defragment job to take a couple of hours or more, consider running Disk Defragmenter just before you leave the office or go to bed.

Step 5: Set System Restore Points

One of the most frustrating Windows experiences is to have your system sailing along without so much as an electronic hiccup, and then have everything crash or become unstable after installing a program or piece of hardware. This all-too-common scenario means that some program component or device driver simply doesn't get along with Windows 8, and that the two are now at loggerheads. Uninstalling the program or device can often help, but that's not a foolproof solution.

To help guard against software or hardware installations that bring down the system, Windows 8 has a feature called System Protection. Its job is straightforward, yet clever: to take periodic snapshots—called *restore points*—of your system, each of which includes the current Windows 8 configuration. The idea is that if a program or device installation causes problems on your system, you use a related feature called *System Restore* to revert your system to the most recent restore point before the installation. Voilà; you're back in business.

System Protection automatically creates restore points at the following times:

- Every week; this is called a *system checkpoint*.

- Before installing an update via the Automatic Updates feature (discussed later in this chapter).

SEE ALSO

I show you how to use System Restore to recover from a problem in Chapter 22. See the section titled Recovering Using System Restore.

- Before installing certain applications. Some newer applications—notably Office 2000 and later—are aware of System Protection and ask it to create a restore point prior to installation.

- When you attempt to install a device driver that is unsigned (meaning it can't be verified that the driver will work properly with Windows 8).

You can also create a restore point manually using the System Protection feature. Follow these steps:

1. Press **Windows+W** to open the Settings search pane, type **protection**, and then click **Create a restore point**. The System Properties dialog box appears and kindly displays the System Protection tab for you.

2. In the Protection Settings table, make sure you see On in the Protection column of your hard disk. If it says Off instead, say "What the ...?", click **Configure**, activate the **Turn on system protection** option, and then click **OK**.

3. Click **Create**. The System Protection dialog box appears.

4. Use the text box to enter a description for the new restore point and then click **Create**. System Protection creates the restore point and displays a dialog box letting you know when the task is done.

5. Click **Close** to return to the System Protection tab.

6. Click **OK**.

> **WINDOWS WISDOM**
>
> Don't worry about creating too many restore points. Windows 8 restricts the amount of disk space restore points use, and if you bump against that ceiling, Windows 8 automatically deletes the oldest restore points. If you want to give your system more room for restore points, click **Configure** and then drag the **Max Usage** slider.

Step 6: Back Up Your Files

Other than a few people who insist on living in It-Can't-Happen-to-Me Land, I think most folks get the *why* of backing up. They know computers crash all the time and they can lose irreplaceable data if they don't have backups kicking around. However, many of those people just don't get the *how* part. That is, they'd like to run backups, but it's such a time-consuming chore that it just doesn't seem worth the hassle. For many people, backing up ranks just above root canal on the Top 10 Most Unpleasant Chores list. "Sorry, I'd like to do a backup, but I have to call the IRS to schedule an audit."

If backing up has always seemed like too much of a bother, wait until you get a load of File History, the backup feature that comes with Windows 8.

You might be used to thinking of a file backup as something akin to just copying the file to another drive. True that, but there may be times when it's simply not good enough just to store a copy of a file. For example, if you make frequent changes to a file, you might want to copy not only the current version, but also the versions from an hour ago, a day ago, a week ago, and so on. In Windows 8, these previous versions of a file are called its file history, and you can save this data for all your documents by activating the File History feature.

When you turn on File History and specify an external drive to store the data, Windows 8 begins monitoring your libraries, your desktop, your contacts, and your Internet Explorer favorites. Once an hour, Windows 8 checks to see if any of this data has changed since the last check. If it has, Windows 8 saves copies of the changed files to the external drive. Once you have some data saved, you can then use it to restore a previous version of a file, as described in Chapter 22 (see the section titled Restoring a Previous Version of a File).

Even better, File History makes backing up your precious files about as painless and hassle-free as this stuff gets. You run through a relatively short and comprehensible procedure to activate and configure File History, and then Windows 8 handles everything for you behind the scenes. In fact, after the initial setup, you may never have to do anything with File History again, unless a system glitch forces you to restore a file. How sweet does that sound (the File History feature, that is, not the system glitch)?

As a final bit of prep, note that File History is happy to store the history in one of two ways:

- **On an external hard drive.** This is the easiest solution because you can buy behemoth hard drives with hundreds or even thousands of gigabytes of storage that plug into a USB port on your computer and are ready to go in seconds flat. These external hard drives are big enough to hold all your file history and are fast enough you won't even notice Windows 8 protecting your files.

- **In a network folder.** If you've got your computers talking to each other over a network, then you might have one machine with lots of extra hard disk space. If so, you could share a folder on that hard disk with the network and then use that shared folder as a backup spot. This is the way to go if you don't have an external hard drive.

Now that we've knocked the whole backup process down to size, let's whip out the brass tacks and get down to business:

1. Connect an external drive to your PC.

2. In the Windows 8 Start screen, press **Windows+W** to open the Settings search pane.

3. Type **history** and then click **File History**. The File History window appears. Windows 8 should detect your external hard drive and display it in the File History window. If this is the correct drive, feel free to skip to step 6.

4. Otherwise, click **Select drive**. The Select Drive window appears.

5. Click the drive you want to use and then click **OK**.

WINDOWS WISDOM

If you don't have an external drive, or if your drives don't have enough capacity (Windows 8 will let you know), you can use a network folder to store your file history. In the Change Drive window click **Add network location**, use the Select Folder dialog box to open a computer on your network, select a shared folder to which you have permission to add files, and then click **Select Folder**.

6. Click **Turn on**. Windows 8 turns on File History and starts saving copies of your files, as shown in Figure 20.4.

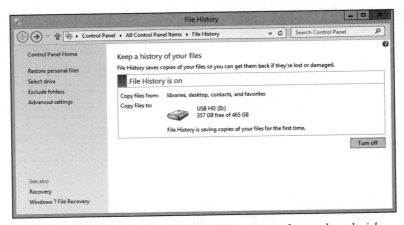

Figure 20.4: *Windows 8 with File History turned on and on the job.*

Step 7: Create a System Image Backup

If a system goes kaput, one of the most common reasons is a corrupted system file that Windows 8 requires to get itself out of bed in the morning. Therefore, you can often resurrect a seemingly dead system by repairing those mucked-up files. This may sound difficult, but Windows 8 has a feature that makes it relatively easy. The safety net I'm talking about here is actually a complete backup of your Windows 8 installation; this is called a system image backup, and it's part of the System Recovery Options I discuss in Chapter 22.

It takes a long time to create a system image (at least several hours, depending on how much stuff you have), but it's worth it for the peace of mind.

Here are the steps to follow to create the system image:

1. Press **Windows+W**. The Settings search pane appears.

2. Type **file recovery** and then click **Windows 7 File Recovery**. The Windows 7 File Recovery window appears on the desktop.

3. Click **Create a system image**. The Create a System Image Wizard drops by.

4. The wizard asks you to specify a backup destination. You have three choices (click **Next** when you're ready to continue):

    - **On a hard disk.** Select this option if you want to use a disk drive on your computer. If you have multiple drives, use the list to select the one you want to use.

    - **On one or more DVDs.** Select this option if you want to use DVDs to hold the backup.

    - **On a network location.** Activate this option and then click **Select** to choose a shared folder on your network.

5. If you see the Which Drives Do You Want to Include in the Backup? dialog box (which only reports for duty if your PC has two or more hard drives), activate the check box beside each extra drive you want to add to the backup, and then click **Next**. Windows 8 asks you to confirm your backup settings.

6. Click **Start backup**. Windows 8 does just that.

Step 8: Create a Recovery Drive

We all keep our fingers crossed that our computers operate trouble-free over their lifetimes but, alas, we know from bitter experience that this is rarely the case. Computers are incredibly complex beasts, so there's a certain inevitability to system glitches. If your hard drive is still on its feet, you can boot to Windows 8 and access the recovery tools, as I describe in Chapter 22.

If your hard drive is kaput or flaky enough to make regular Windows 8 boots problematic, then you must boot using some other drive. If you have your Windows 8 installation media, you can boot using that drive, but if you don't, all is not lost.

You can still recover if you had the foresight to create a USB recovery drive. This is a USB flash drive that contains the Windows 8 recovery environment, which enables you to refresh or reset your PC, use System Restore, recover a system image, and more. (Again, see Chapter 22 to learn what on earth I'm talking about.)

Here are the instructions for creating a USB recovery drive:

1. Insert the USB flash drive you want to use.

LOOK OUT!

To use a USB flash drive as a recovery drive, the drive must have a capacity of at least 256 MB. Also, Windows 8 will erase all data on the drive, so make sure the flash drive does not contain any files you want to keep. If it does, be sure to move those files to a different drive before you begin this procedure.

2. Press **Windows+W** to open the Settings search pane.

3. Type **recovery drive** and then click **Create a recovery drive**. Ever vigilant, User Account Control asks you to confirm.

4. Click **Yes**. (If you're using a standard account, enter your PC administrator credentials to continue instead.) The Recovery Drive wizard makes an appearance.

5. The initial dialog box just offers a not-all-that-helpful introduction, so click **Next** to move on to more productive pursuits. The Recovery Drive wizard prompts you to choose the USB flash drive.

6. Click the drive (if it isn't selected already) and then click **Next**. The Recovery Drive wizard warns you that all data on the drive will be deleted.

7. Say "No problem, bro" and confidently click **Create**. The wizard formats the drive and copies the recovery tools and data.

8. Click **Finish**.

WINDOWS WISDOM

To make sure your recovery drive works properly, you should test it by booting your PC to the drive. Insert the recovery drive and then restart your PC. How you boot to the drive depends on your system. Some PCs display a menu of boot devices and you select the USB drive from that menu. In other cases, you see a message telling you to press a key.

Step 9: Check for Solutions to Problems

Microsoft, bless their nerdy hearts, are constantly collecting information about Windows 8 from folks just like you. When a problem occurs, Windows 8 usually asks whether you want to report the problem to Microsoft and, if you do, they store these tidbits in a massive database. Engineers then tackle the issues (as they euphemistically call them) and hopefully come up with solutions.

The great news is that they make these solutions available to anyone who goes looking for them. Windows 8 keeps a list of problems your computer might be having, so you can tell it to go online and see if a solution is available. If there's a solution waiting, Windows 8 will grab it, install it, and fix your system. Nice!

Here are the steps to follow to check for solutions to problems:

1. Press **Windows+W** to meet up with your new best friend, the Settings search pane.

2. Type **solutions** and then click **View solutions to problems**. Windows 8 displays the Actions Center.

3. Under the Maintenance heading, look for information on a problem your computer is having.

4. If a solution exists for your problem, click the solution to install it.

Step 10: Set Up a Maintenance Schedule

Maintenance is effective only if it's done regularly, but there's a fine line to be navigated here. If maintenance is performed too often, it can become a burden and interfere with more interesting tasks; if it's performed too seldom, it becomes ineffective. So how often should you perform the maintenance steps listed in this chapter? Here are some guidelines:

- **Checking your hard disk for errors.** If you use your computer daily, check your main hard drive (that is, the one that holds Windows) about once a week, and any other hard drives about once every couple of weeks. If you use your PC only occasionally, check your hard drive for errors every month or so.

- **Checking free disk space.** Do this about once a month. If you have a drive in which the free space is getting low, check it about once a week.

- **Deleting unnecessary files.** If free disk space isn't a problem, run this chore about once every two or three months.

- **Defragmenting your hard disk.** How often you defragment your hard disk depends on how often you use your computer. If you use it every day, then the Disk Defragmenter default daily schedule is just right for you. If your computer doesn't get heavy use, you probably need to run Disk Defragmenter only weekly or even monthly.

- **Setting restore points.** Windows 8 already sets regular system restore points, so you need only create your own restore points when you're installing a program or device or making some other major change to your system.

- **Backing up your files.** Once you turn on File History, backing up your file versions is automatic, so there's nothing more for you to do here.

- **Creating system image backups.** These take a very long time, so either do them once every month or two, or just wait until you've made major changes to your system.

- **Creating a recovery drive.** This is a one-time-only chore, so once you've created the recovery drive, you're done. However, it's probably a good idea to test the recovery drive once a month or so to make sure it still works.

- **Checking for solutions to problems.** You probably only need to check for solutions once every couple of months, but if your system is behaving erratically check more frequently.

The Least You Need to Know

- To run Disk Cleanup, select a hard disk in the Computer folder, click **Properties** to open the drive's Properties dialog box, click the **General** tab, and click **Disk Cleanup**.

- To run Check Disk or Disk Defragmenter, select a hard disk in the Computer folder, click **Properties** to open the Properties dialog box for that drive, click the **Tools** tab, and then click **Check** or **Optimize**.

- You should run Disk Cleanup every couple of weeks and Check Disk every week.

- If you want to be completely prepared for any eventuality, no matter how dire, set system restore points when you install programs and devices, leave File History turned on, and create both a system image backup and a USB recovery drive.

Keeping You and Your Computer Safe

In This Chapter

- Keeping hackers and other miscreants out of your system
- Guarding against nasty email viruses, spam, and other useless messages
- Maintaining email privacy
- Foiling phishing
- Blocking those annoying pop-up windows

The internet is a more cosmopolitan place now than in its relatively lawless beginnings. However, although the internet is no longer the digital equivalent of the Wild West, we've progressed only to about the level of Al Capone's Chicago of the 1930s. In other words, although most of your internet dealings will be safe and pleasant, there are plenty of cyberhoodlums and e-gangsters roaming the net's dark streets and alleyways. You need to exercise some caution to avoid the internet version of mugging and extortion.

Fortunately, the situation is not so grim that you can't easily protect yourself. As you'll see in this chapter, avoiding viruses, spam scams, system intruders, and other internet bad guys is a relatively simple combination of common sense and the prudent tweaking of a few settings.

Squashing Spyware with Windows Defender

If you access the net using a broadband—cable modem or digital subscriber line (DSL)—service, chances are you have an always-on connection, so you might think there's a much greater chance that a malicious hacker could find your computer and have his or her way with it. Fortunately, that's not the case. True, black-hat hackers might stumble upon your broadband modem while out looking for trouble, but that's as far as they'll get because all broadband modems have built-in security features that hide your computer and so prevent nefarious users from going any further.

And even if a cracker (a malicious hacker) was somehow able to get past your modem's defenses, he or she still couldn't get into your system thanks to a second line of defense called Windows Firewall, which blocks unauthorized access to your computer and which is (thankfully) activated by default in Windows 8.

WINDOWS WISDOM

It pays to take a second and check that Windows Firewall is actually on the job. Press **Windows+W** to open the Settings search pane, type **firewall**, and then click **Check firewall status**. In the Windows Firewall window, make sure the Windows Firewall state shows On. If it doesn't, click **Turn Windows Firewall on or off** and then select **Turn on Windows Firewall**.

However, in recent years, a new threat to our PCs has emerged. It's called spyware, and it's a nasty bit of digital business that threatens to deprive a significant portion of the online world of their sanity. Spyware refers to a program that surreptitiously monitors your computer activities—particularly the typing of passwords, PINs, and credit card numbers—or harvests sensitive data on your computer, and then sends that information to an individual or a company via your internet connection.

You might think that having Windows Firewall between you and the bad guys would make spyware a problem of the past. Unfortunately, that's not true. These programs piggyback on other legitimate programs that you actually *want* to download, such as file-sharing programs, download managers, and screen savers. To make matters even worse, most spyware embeds itself deep into a system and removing it is a delicate and time-consuming operation beyond the abilities of even most experienced users. Some programs actually come with an uninstall option, but it's nothing but a ruse, of course. The program appears to remove itself from the system, but what it actually does is reinstall a fresh version of itself when the computer is idle. A pox on all their houses!

All this means that you need to buttress Windows Firewall with an antispyware program that can watch out for these unwanted programs and prevent them from getting their hooks into your system. Happily, Windows 8 comes with just such a program, and it has an appropriate (and hopefully accurate!) name: Windows Defender.

Out of the box, Windows 8 sets up Windows Defender to protect your system from spyware nastiness in two ways:

- Windows Defender scans your system for spyware infestations every day at 3 A.M.

- Windows Defender runs in the background full-time to watch out for spywarelike activity. If it detects a spyware fiend trying to sneak in the back door, Windows Defender terminates the brute with extreme prejudice.

As with Windows Firewall, what you need to do is check to make sure that both of these protection features are turned on. Here's how:

1. In the Start screen, type **defend** and then click **Windows Defender** in the search results.

2. Select the **Settings** tab.

3. Select **Real-time protection** and then activate the **Turn on real-time protection** check box.

4. Select **Administrator** and then activate the **Turn on Windows Defender** check box.

5. Click **Save changes**.

WINDOWS WISDOM

Feel free to run a scan on your computer right now, if you like. Launch Windows Defender and then click the Home tab's **Scan** button to do a quick scan. If you want a more thorough check, select the **Full** option and then click **Scan**.

Working with Email Safely and Securely

Email is by far the most popular online activity, but it can also be the most frustrating in terms of security and privacy. Email viruses are legion, spam gets worse every day, and bozos who send out dumb or offensive messages are a dime a dozen (if that). Fortunately, it doesn't take much to remedy these and other email problems, as you see over the next few sections.

Protecting Yourself Against Email Viruses

Until just a few years ago, the primary method that computer viruses used to propagate themselves was the floppy disk. A user with an infected machine would copy some files to a floppy, and the virus would surreptitiously add itself to the disk. When the recipient inserted the disk, the virus copy would come to life and infect yet another computer.

When the internet became a big deal, viruses adapted (as viruses are wont to do) and began propagating either via malicious websites or via infected program files downloaded to users' machines.

Over the past couple of years, however, by far the most productive method for viruses to replicate has been the humble email message. Melissa, ILOVEYOU, BadTrans, Sircam, Klez ... the list of email viruses is a long one, but they all operate more or less the same way—they arrive as a message attachment, usually from someone you know. When you open the attachment, the virus infects your computer and then, without your knowledge, uses your email program and your address book to ship out messages with more copies of itself attached. The nastier versions will also mess with your computer; the soulless beasts might delete data or corrupt files, for example.

You can avoid getting infected by one of these viruses by implementing a few commonsense procedures:

- Never open an attachment that comes from someone you don't know.

- Even if you know the sender, if the attachment isn't something you're expecting, assume the sender's system is infected. Write back and confirm that he or she sent the message.

- Some viruses come packaged as "scripts"—miniature computer programs—that are hidden within messages using Rich Text (HTML) format. This means that the virus can run just by you viewing the message! If a message looks suspicious, don't open it—just delete it. (Note that you'll need to turn off the Windows Live Mail reading pane before deleting the message. Otherwise, when you highlight the message, it will appear in the preview pane and set off the virus. Click the **View** tab, click **Reading pane**, and then click **Off**.)

- Install a top-of-the-line antivirus program, particularly one that checks incoming email. Also, be sure to keep your antivirus program's virus list up to date. As you read this, there are probably dozens, maybe even hundreds, of morally challenged scum-nerds designing even nastier viruses. Regular updates will help you keep up. Here are some security suites to check out:

Microsoft Security Essentials (microsoft.com/security/pc-security/mse.aspx)

Norton Internet Security (symantec.com/index.jsp)

McAfee Internet Security Suite (mcafee.com/us)

Avast! Antivirus (avast.com)

AVG Internet Security (free.grisoft.com/)

Besides these general procedures, Windows Live Mail also comes with its own set of virus protection features. Here's how to use them:

1. In Windows Live Mail, select **File>Options>Safety options**. The Safety Options dialog box appears.

2. Display the **Security** tab.

3. In the **Virus Protection** section of the dialog box, you have the following options:

   - **Select the security zone to use.** You use the security zones to determine whether scripts inside HTML-format messages are allowed to run. If you choose Internet Zone, scripts are allowed to run; if you choose Restricted Sites Zone, scripts are disabled. Restricted Sites Zone is the default setting, and it's the one I highly recommend.

   - **Warn me when other applications try to send mail as me.** As I mentioned earlier, it's possible for programs and scripts to send email messages without your knowledge. When you activate this check box, Windows Live Mail displays a warning dialog box when a program or script attempts to send a message behind the scenes.

   - **Do not allow attachments to be saved or opened that could potentially be a virus.** When you activate this check box, Windows Live Mail monitors attachments to look for file types that could contain viruses or destructive code. If it detects such a file, it halts the ability to open or save that file, and it displays a note at the top of the message to let you know about the unsafe attachment.

4. Click **OK**.

5. Select **File>Options>Mail** to switch to the Options dialog box.

6. In the Read tab, activate the **Read all messages in plain text** check box.

7. Click **OK**.

Using the Junk Mail Filter to Can Spam

Spam—unsolicited commercial messages—has become a plague upon the earth. Unless you've done a masterful job at keeping your address secret, you probably receive at least a few spam emails every day, and it's more likely that you receive a few dozen. The bad news is most experts agree that it's only going to get worse. And why not? Spam is one of the few advertising mediums where the costs are substantially borne by the users, not the advertisers.

The best way to avoid spam is to not get on a spammer's list of addresses in the first place. That's hard to do these days, but there are some steps you can take:

- Never use your actual email address in a newsgroup account. The most common method that spammers use to gather addresses is to harvest them from newsgroup posts. One common tactic is to alter your email address by adding text that invalidates the address but is still obvious for other people to figure out. For example:

      user@myisp.remove_this_to_email_me.com

- When you sign up for something online, use a fake address if possible. If you need or want to receive email from the company and so must use your real address, make sure you deselect any options that ask if you want to receive promotional offers. Alternatively, enter the address from a free web-based account (such as a Hotmail account), so that any spam you receive will go there instead of to your main address.

- Never open suspected spam messages, because doing so can sometimes notify the spammer that you've opened the message, thus confirming your address is legit. For the same reason, you should never display a spam message in the Windows Live Mail preview pane. As described earlier, shut off the preview pane before highlighting any spam messages that you want to delete.

- Never, I repeat, *never*, respond to spam, even to an address within the spam that claims to be a removal address. By responding to spam all you do is prove that your address is legitimate, so you just end up getting *more* spam.

If you do get spam despite these precautions, the good news is that Windows Live Mail comes with a Junk Email feature that can help you cope. Junk Email is a spam filter, which means that it examines each incoming message and applies sophisticated tests to determine whether the message is spam. If the tests determine that the message is probably spam, the email is exiled to a separate Junk Email folder. It's not perfect—no spam filter is—but with a bit of fine-tuning as described in the next few sections, it can be a very useful antispam weapon.

Setting the Junk Email Protection Level

Filtering spam is always a trade-off between protection and convenience. That is, the stronger the protection you use, the less convenient the filter becomes, and vice versa. This inverse relationship is caused by a filter phenomenon called the *false positive*. This is a legitimate message that the filter has pegged as spam and, in the case of Windows Live Mail, moved to the Junk Email folder. The stronger the protection level, the more likely it is that false positives will occur, so the more time you must spend checking the Junk Email folder for legitimate messages that need to be rescued. Fortunately, Windows Live Mail gives you several Junk Email levels to choose from, so you can choose a level that gives the blend of protection and convenience that suits you.

To set the Junk Email level, select **File>Options>Safety options**. Windows Live Mail displays the Safety Options dialog box. The Options tab gives you four choices for the Junk Email protection level:

- **No Automatic Filtering.** This option turns off the Junk Email filter. Choose this option only if you use a third-party spam filter or if you handle spam using your own message rules.

- **Low.** This level is designed to move only messages with obvious spam content to the Junk Email folder. This is a good level to start with—particularly if you get only a few spams a day—because it catches most spam and has only a minimal risk of false positives.

- **High.** This is the default protection level. It handles spam aggressively, so only rarely misses a junk message. On the downside, the High level also catches the occasional legitimate message in its net, so you need to check the Junk Email folder regularly to look for false positives. Use this level if you get a lot of spam—a few dozen messages or more each day.

WINDOWS WISDOM

If you get a false positive in your Junk Email folder, click the message, select the **Home** tab, and then click the top half of the **Not junk** button.

- **Safe List Only.** This level treats all incoming messages as spam, except for those messages that come from people or domains in your Safe Senders list (see Specifying Safe Senders, following). Use this level if your spam problem is out of control (a hundred or more spams each day) and if most of your non-spam email comes from people you know or from subscribed mailing lists.

If you hate spam so much that you never want to even *see* it, much less deal with it, activate the **Permanently delete suspected junk email instead of moving it to the Junk Email folder** check box.

> **LOOK OUT!**
>
> Spam is so hair-pullingly frustrating that you may be tempted to activate the **Permanently delete suspected junk email instead of moving it to the Junk Email folder** check box out of sheer spite. I don't recommend this, however. The danger of false positives is just too great, even with the Low level, and it's not worth missing a crucial message.

Specifying Safe Senders

If you use the Low or High Junk Email protection level, you can reduce the number of false positives by letting Windows Live Mail know about the people or institutions that regularly send you mail. By designating these addresses as Safe Senders, you tell Windows Live Mail to automatically leave their incoming messages in your Inbox and never to redirect them to the Junk Email folder. And certainly if you use the Safe Lists Only protection level, you must specify some Safe Senders because Windows Live Mail treats everyone else as a spammer!

Your Safe Senders list can consist of three types of addresses:

- Individual email addresses of the form *someone@somewhere.com*. All messages from these individual addresses will not be treated as spam.

- Domain names of the form *@somewhere.com*. All messages from any address within that domain will not be treated as spam.

- Your Contacts list. You can tell Windows Live Mail to treat everyone in your Contacts list as a Safe Sender, which makes sense because you're unlikely to be spammed by someone you know.

You can specify a Safe Sender either by entering the address by hand (using the Safe Senders tab in the Safety Options dialog box) or by using an existing message from the sender (right-click the message, select **Junk email**, and then select either **Add sender to safe sender list** or **Add sender's domain to safe sender list**).

Blocking Senders

If you notice that a particular address is the source of much spam or other annoying email, the easiest way to block the spam is to block all incoming messages from that address. You can do this using the Blocked Senders list, which watches for messages from a specific address and relegates them to the Junk Email folder.

As with Safe Senders, you can specify a Blocked Sender either by entering the address by hand (using the Blocked Senders tab in the Safety Options dialog box) or by using an existing message from the sender (right-click the message you want to work with, select **Junk email,** and then select either **Add sender to blocked sender list** or **Add sender's domain to blocked sender list**).

Caveat Surfer: Internet Explorer and Security

Tons of people are flocking to the web, and tons of content providers are waiting for them there. Still, many people view the web as an essentially scary and untrustworthy place. There are many reasons for this, but one of the biggest is the security issue.

Internet Explorer offers quite a number of features that tackle this issue directly. The Internet Explorer window gives you visual cues that tell you whether a particular document is secure. For example, Figure 21.1 shows Internet Explorer displaying a secure web page. Notice how a lock icon appears to the right of the address, and that the address of a secure page uses *https* up front rather than *http*. Both of these features tell you that the web page has a security certificate that passed muster with Internet Explorer.

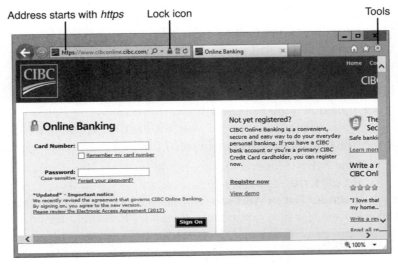

Figure 21.1: *An example of a secure web page.*

Avoiding the Lures of Scammers with the SmartScreen Filter

Phishing refers to creating a replica of an existing web page to fool you into submitting personal info, financial data, or a password. It's a whimsical word for a serious bit of business, but the term comes from the fact that internet scammers are using increasingly sophisticated lures as they "fish" for your sensitive data.

The most common ploy is to copy the web-page code from a major site—such as AOL or eBay—and use that code to set up a replica page that appears to be part of the company's site. You receive a fake email with a link to this page, which solicits your credit card data or password. When you submit the form, it sends the data to the scammer while leaving you on an actual page from the company's site so you don't suspect a thing.

A phishing page looks identical to a legitimate page from the company because the phisher has simply copied the underlying source code from the original page. However, no spoof page can be a perfect replica of the original. Here are four things to look for:

- **Weirdness in the address.** A legitimate page will have the correct domain—such as aol.com or ebay.com—while a spoofed page will have only something similar—such as aol.whatever.com or blah.com/ebay.

- **Weirdness in the addresses associated with page links.** Most links on the page probably point to legitimate pages on the original site. However, there may be some links that point to pages on the phisher's site.

- **Text or images that aren't associated with the trustworthy site.** Many phishing sites are housed on free web-hosting services. However, many of these services place an advertisement on each page, so look for an ad or other content from the hosting provider.

- **No lock icon.** A legitimate site would only transmit sensitive financial data using a secure connection, which Internet Explorer indicates by placing a lock icon in the Address box, as described earlier. If you don't see the lock icon with a page that asks for financial data, then the page is almost certainly a spoof.

If you watch for these things, you'll probably never be fooled into giving up sensitive data to a phisher. However, phishing attacks are becoming legion, so we need all the help we can get. To that end, Internet Explorer comes with a tool called the SmartScreen Filter. This filter alerts you to potential phishing scams by doing two things each time you visit a site:

- Analyzing the site content to look for known phishing techniques (that is, to see if the site is "phishy").

- Checking to see if the site is listed in a global database of known phishing sites.

Phishing has become such a problem that Internet Explorer doesn't even bother to ask you whether you want to use the SmartScreen Filter; it just turns it on by default. To make sure the SmartScreen Filter is on, click **Tools** (the gear icon in the upper right corner; see Figure 21.1) and then click **Safety**. If you see the **Turn on SmartScreen Filter** command, click it. In the Microsoft SmartScreen Filter dialog box that shows up, make sure the **Turn on SmartScreen Filter** option is activated, and then click **OK**.

WINDOWS WISDOM

If you turn off the automatic SmartScreen Filter checks, you can still check for phishing site by site. After you navigate to a site that you want to check, select **Tools>Safety>Check this website**.

Here's how the SmartScreen Filter works:

- If you come upon a site that Internet Explorer knows is a phishing scam (see Figure 21.2), it changes the background color of the Address bar to red and displays an Unsafe Website message in the Security Report area (just to the right of the address). It also blocks navigation to the site by displaying a separate page that tells you the site is a known phishing scam.

The Security Report area

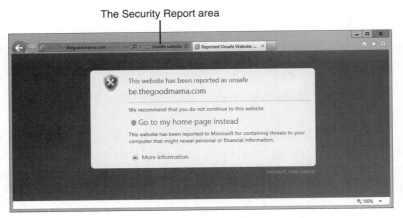

Figure 21.2: *Run right back to where you started from: the SmartScreen Filter lets you know about known phishing sites.*

- If you come upon a site that Internet Explorer thinks is a potential phishing scam, it changes the background color of the Address bar to yellow and displays a Suspicious Website message in the Security Report area.

Click the Suspicious Website text and Internet Explorer displays a security report with a link that enables you to report the site. If you're sure this is a scam site, be sure to report it to help improve the database of phishing sites and prevent others from giving up sensitive data.

Covering Your Tracks: Deleting Your Browsing History

As you roam around the web, Internet Explorer stores information about the sites you visit. For example, it saves copies of page text, images, and other content so that sites load faster the next time you view them. Here's a list of all the types of stuff Internet Explorer squirrels away:

- **Temporary Internet files.** These are copies of text, images, media, and other content from pages you've visited recently. Internet Explorer stores all this data so that the next time you view one of those pages, it can retrieve data from the cache and display the site much more quickly. This is clearly a big-time privacy problem because it means that anyone can examine the cache to learn where you've been surfing.

- **Cookies and website data.** These are small text files that sites store on your computer. Most cookies are benign, but they can be used to track your activities online.

- **History.** This is a list of addresses of the sites you've visited in the past 20 days, as well as each of the pages you visited within those sites. Again, this is a major privacy accident just waiting to happen, because anyone sitting at your computer can see exactly where you've been online over the past 20 days.

- **Download history.** This is a list of the files you've downloaded, and it's ridiculously easy for a snoop to find: just select **Tools>View downloads** (or press **Ctrl+J**).

- **Form data.** This refers to the AutoComplete feature, which stores the data you type in forms and then uses that saved data to suggest possible matches when you use a similar form in the future. This is definitely handy, but it also means that anyone else who uses your computer can see your previously entered form text.

- **Passwords.** This is another aspect of AutoComplete, and Internet Explorer uses it to save form passwords. Sure, it's nice and convenient, but it's really just asking for trouble because it means that someone sitting down at your computer can log on to a site, a job made all the easier if you activated the site option to save your user name!

- **ActiveX Filtering and Tracking Protection data.** This is information that Internet Explorer gathers to detect when third-party providers are supplying data to the sites you visit.

Taken together, all this is called your *browsing history*, and it's certainly useful because it generally makes your web surfing expeditions quicker and easier. However, it is also dangerous because other people who use your computer can just as easily visit or view information about those sites. This can be a problem if you visit financial sites, private corporate sites, or some other page that you would not want another person to visit. You reduce this risk by deleting some or all of your browsing history.

DEFINITION

Your **browsing history** is the collection of temporary page files, cookies, addresses, downloads, form data, and passwords that Internet Explorer saves as you surf the web.

Follow these steps to delete bits of your browsing history:

1. Select **Tools>Safety>Delete browsing history** (or press **Ctrl+Shift+Delete**) to display the Delete Browsing History dialog box, shown in Figure 21.3.

2. If you don't want to save the files associated with sites on your Favorites list, deactivate the **Preserve Favorites Website Data** check box.

3. Activate the check box beside each type of data you want to smite.

4. Click **Delete**. Internet Explorer does its deletion duty.

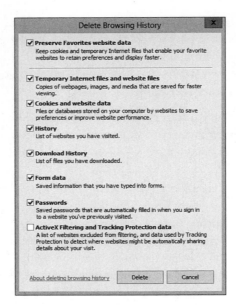

Figure 21.3: *Use the Delete Browsing History dialog box to choose what web stuff you want to blow away.*

Your Own Private Web: InPrivate Browsing

Deleting your browsing history is a handy technique, for sure, but you have to remember to do it, and it's a distressingly all-or-nothing affair. That is, when you delete form data, passwords, history, cookies, or the cache files, you delete *all* of them (unless you preserve the cookies and cache files for your favorites). This is a problem because you often only want to remove the data for a single site or a few sites.

Fortunately, Internet Explorer has a feature that solves these problems: InPrivate browsing. When you activate this feature, Internet Explorer temporarily stops storing browsing history when you visit websites. It no longer saves temporary Internet files, cookies, browsing history, form data, passwords, and so on.

To use InPrivate browsing, select **Tools>Safety>InPrivate Browsing** (or press **Ctrl+Shift+P**). Internet Explorer opens a new browser window as shown in Figure 21.4. The big difference visually is that you see the InPrivate icon in the address bar, which tells you you're traveling incognito.

The InPrivate icon

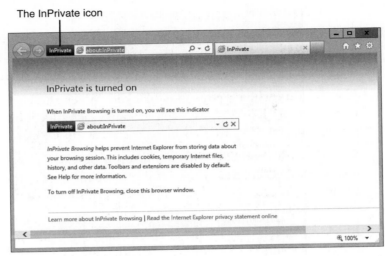

Figure 21.4: *When you activate InPrivate browsing, Internet Explorer opens a new window and displays the InPrivate icon in the address bar.*

Blocking Pop-Up Windows

One of the most annoying things on the web is those ubiquitous pop-up windows that infest your screen with advertisements when you visit certain sites. (A variation on the theme is the "pop under," a window that opens under your current browser window, so you don't know it's there until you close the window.) Pop-up windows can also be dangerous because some unscrupulous software makers have figured out ways to use them to install spyware on your computer without your permission. They're nasty things, any way you look at them.

Fortunately, Microsoft has given us a way to stop pop-ups before they start. It's called the Pop-up Blocker and it looks for pop-ups and prevents them from opening. Follow these steps to use and configure the Pop-up Blocker:

1. In Internet Explorer, select **Tools>Internet options**. The Internet Options dialog box appears.

2. Select the **Privacy** tab.

3. Make sure the **Turn on Pop-up Blocker** check box is activated.

4. Click **Settings** to display the Pop-up Blocker Settings dialog box. You have the following options:

- **Address of website to allow.** Use this option when you have a site that displays pop-ups you want to see. Type the address and then click **Add**.

- **Play a sound when a pop-up is blocked.** When this check box is activated, Internet Explorer plays a brief sound each time it blocks a pop-up. If this gets annoying after a while, deactivate this check box.

- **Show Notification bar when a pop-up is blocked.** When this check box is activated, Internet Explorer displays a message at the bottom of the window each time it blocks a pop-up, just so you know it's working on your behalf.

- **Blocking Level.** Use this list to choose how aggressive you want Internet Explorer to be with pop-ups. Medium should work fine, but if you still get lots of pop-ups, switch to High.

5. Click **Close**.

Pop-up Blocker, now on the case, monitors your surfing and steps in front of any pop-up window that tries to disturb your peace. Figure 21.5 shows the Notification bar that appears to let you know when a pop-up was thwarted. If you want to see the pop-up anyway, click **Allow once**. If you want to see this site's pop-ups full-time, click **Options for this site** and then click **Always allow**.

Internet Explorer blocked a pop-up from **www.popuptest.com**.   Allow once   Options for this site ▼   ✕

Figure 21.5: *When the Pop-up Blocker is active, it displays the Notification bar each time it blocks a pop-up window.*

The Least You Need to Know

- To guard against email–borne viruses, never open attachments that come from strangers, and double-check with friends before opening unexpected attachments they send your way.

- To cut down on the spam you receive, don't use your real address in a newsgroup; use a fake address whenever possible when signing up for things online, and never respond to spam or open suspected spam messages.

- Only submit sensitive data (such as your credit-card number) to a secure site (that is, one that has a lock icon in the status bar).
- To access the security settings in Mail, select **File>Options>Safety options**.
- To access the security settings in Internet Explorer, select **Tools>Safety**.

Troubleshooting and Recovering from Problems

In This Chapter

- Determining the source of a problem
- Using general troubleshooting strategies to solve common problems
- Getting into the Windows 8 recovery environment
- Running the Windows 8 recovery tools

A long time ago, somebody with way too much time on his or her hands proved mathematically that it's impossible to make any reasonably complex software program problem-free. As the number of variables increase, as the interactions of subroutines and objects become more complex, and as the underlying logic of a program grows beyond the ability of a single person to grasp all at once, errors inevitably creep into the code. Given the status of Microsoft Windows 8 as one of the most complex software packages ever created, it's certain that there are problems lurking in the weeds. The good news is that, if Windows 8 is like most of its predecessors, the great majority of these problems will be extremely obscure and will appear only under the rarest of circumstances.

However, this doesn't mean you're guaranteed a glitch-free computing experience. Far from it. Most computer woes are caused by third-party programs and devices, either because they have inherent problems themselves or because they don't get along perfectly with Windows 8. Using software, devices, and device drivers designed for Windows 8 can help tremendously, as can the maintenance program I outlined in Chapter 20. Nonetheless, you need to know how to troubleshoot and resolve the computer problems that invariably will come your way. In this chapter, I help you do just that by showing you my favorite techniques for determining problem sources, and by taking you through all the Windows 8 recovery tools.

Determining the Source of the Problem

One of the ongoing mysteries experienced by all Windows 8 users (at one time or another) is what might be called the now-you-see-it-now-you-don't problem. This is a glitch that plagues you for a while and then mysteriously vanishes without any intervention on your part.

Unfortunately, most computer ills don't get resolved so easily. For these more intractable problems, your first order of business is to track down the source of the snag. This is, at best, a black art, but it can be done if you take a systematic approach. Over the years, I've found that the best method is to ask a series of questions designed to gather the required information and to narrow down clues to the culprit. Here are the questions:

- **Did you get an error message?** Unfortunately, most computer error messages are obscure and do little to help you resolve a problem directly. However, error codes and error text can help you down the road, either by giving you something to search for in an online database (see Troubleshooting Using Online Resources, later in this chapter) or by providing information to a tech support person. Therefore, you should always write down the full text of any error message that appears.

> **WINDOWS WISDOM**
>
> If the error message is lengthy and your computer isn't frozen stiff, don't bother writing down the full message. Instead, while the message is displayed press **Windows+Print Screen** to place an image of the current screen in your Pictures library.
>
> If the error message appears before Windows 8 starts, but you don't have time to write it down, press the **Pause/Break** key to pause the startup. After you record the error, press **Ctrl+Pause/Break** to resume the start-up.

- **Did you recently change any Windows settings?** If the problem started after you changed your Windows configuration, try reversing the change. Even something as seemingly innocent as starting the screen saver can cause problems, so don't rule anything out.

- **Did you recently change any application settings?** If so, try reversing the change to see if it solves the problem. If that doesn't help, check to see if an upgrade or patch is available. Also, some applications come with a Repair option that can fix corrupted files. Otherwise, try reinstalling the program.

- **Did you recently install a new program?** If you suspect a new program is causing system instability, restart Windows 8 and try using the system for a while without running the new program. If the problem doesn't reoccur, then the new program is likely the culprit. Try using the program without any other programs running. You should also examine the program's README file (if it has one) to look for known problems and possible workarounds. It's also a good idea to check for a Windows 8–compatible version of the program. Again, you can also try the program's repair option, or you can uninstall and then reinstall the program.

> **SEE ALSO**
>
> To learn how to uninstall a program, see Chapter 6 in the section titled Giving a Program the Heave-Ho.

- **Did you recently upgrade an existing program?** If so, try uninstalling the upgrade.

- **Did you recently install a device driver that is not Windows 8 compatible?** Windows 8 allows you to install drivers that aren't Windows 8 certified, but it also warns you that this is a bad idea. Incompatible drivers are one of the most common sources of system instability, so whenever possible you should uninstall the driver and install one that is designed for Windows 8. Windows 8 automatically sets a system restore point before it installs the driver, so if you can't uninstall the driver, you should use that to restore the system to its previous state. (See Recovering Using System Restore, later in this chapter.)

- **Did you recently apply an update from Windows Update?** Updates rarely make things worse (thankfully, since they're *supposed* to make things better), but nothing is certain in the Windows world. If your machine has been discombobulated since installing an update, try removing the update. Press **Windows+W** to open the Settings search pane, type **updates**, and then click **View installed updates** to meet up with the Installed Updates window. Select the update that you want to trash and then click **Uninstall**.

General Troubleshooting Tips

Figuring out the cause of a problem is often the hardest part of troubleshooting, but by itself it doesn't do you much good. Once you know the source, you need to parlay that information into a fix for the problem. I discussed a few solutions in the previous section, but here are a few other general fixes you need to keep in mind:

- **Close all programs.** You can often fix flaky behavior by shutting down all your open programs and starting again. This is a particularly useful fix for problems caused by low memory or low system resources.

- **Sign out of Windows 8.** Signing out clears the memory and gives you a slightly cleaner slate than merely closing all your programs. On the Start screen, click your user account tile in the upper right corner and then click **Sign out**.

- **Reboot the computer.** If problems exist with some system files and devices, logging off won't help because these objects remain loaded. By rebooting the system, you reload the entire system, which is often enough to solve many computer problems.

- **Turn off the computer and restart.** You can often solve a hardware problem by first shutting your machine off. Wait for 30 seconds to give all devices time to spin down and then restart.

- **Check connections, power switches, and so on.** Some of the most common (and some of the most embarrassing) causes of hardware problems are the simple physical things: making sure a device is turned on; checking that cable connections are secure; ensuring that insertable devices are properly inserted.

- **Use the troubleshooters.** Windows 8 comes with a few features called *troubleshooters* that are designed to tackle problems using simple, step-by-step procedures. Press **Windows+W** to reawaken the Settings search pane, type **trouble**, and then click **Troubleshooting**. The Troubleshooting window offers up a bunch of problem-solving tools for topics such as programs, hardware, network, and system.

Restoring a Previous Version of a File

When you activate File History on your PC as described in Chapter 20, Windows 8 periodically (once an hour by default) inspects your personal files to see if any have changed since the last check. If it finds a changed file, File History takes a snapshot of that file and saves that version of the file to the external drive you specified when you set up File History.

SEE ALSO

For info on how to activate File History, in Chapter 20, see the section titled Step 6: Back Up Your Files.

This means Windows 8 can reverse the changes you've made to a file by reverting to an earlier state of the file. In Windows 8 lingo, an earlier state of a file is called a *previous version*.

DEFINITION

A **previous version** is a copy of a file taken at an earlier time.

Why on earth would anyone want to revert to a previous version of a file? One reason is you might improperly edit a file by deleting or changing important data. In some cases, you may be able to restore that data by going back to a previous version of the file. Need another reason? Okay, the file might become corrupted if the program or Windows 8 crashes, so you can get a working version of the file back on its feet by restoring a previous version.

Convinced? Good. Here's how you restore a previous version of a file:

1. Press **Windows+W** to get the always-busy Settings search pane onscreen.

2. Type **history** and then click **File History** in the search results. The File History window shows up on the desktop.

3. Click **Restore personal files**. The Home – File History window appears.

4. Double-click the library that contains the file you want to restore and then open the folder that contains the file (see Figure 22.1).

5. Click **Previous Version** (highlighted in Figure 22.1) until you open the version of the folder you want to use.

6. Click the file you want to restore.

7. Click **Restore to Original Location** (also pointed out in Figure 22.1). If the original folder has a file with the same name, File History scratches its digital head and asks what you want to do.

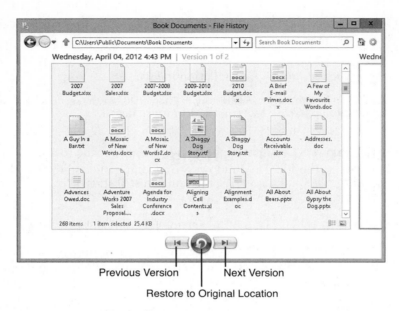

Previous Version   Next Version

Restore to Original Location

Figure 22.1: *Use this window to choose the previous version you want to restore.*

8. Select one of the following:

    - **Replace the file in the destination folder.** Click this to overwrite the existing file with the previous version.

    - **Skip this file.** Click this to do nothing.

    - **Choose the file to keep in the destination folder.** Click this option to decide which file you prefer to keep. This is the way to go if you're not sure whether to replace an existing file with a previous version. In the File Conflict dialog box that appears, activate the check box beside both versions and then click **Continue.** This leaves the existing file as is and restores the previous version with *(2)* tacked on to the name.

Entering the Recovery Environment

Windows 8 offers a Recovery Environment (RE) that gives you a simple, easily navigated set of screens that offer a bunch of troubleshooting tools and utilities. There are many paths you can take to arrive at the RE, but here the three most common:

- Use the PC Settings app from within Windows 8.
- Boot to a recovery drive.
- Boot to your Windows 8 installation media.

The next few sections discuss each method in more detail.

Getting to the RE Using PC Settings

If you're having trouble with your PC, but you can still start Windows 8, then you can use the PC Settings app to access the RE:

1. Press **Windows+W** to open the Settings search pane.

2. Type **advanced** and then click **Advanced startup options** in the search results. Windows 8 opens the PC Settings app and helpfully displays the General tab for you.

3. In the Advanced Startup section, click **Restart now**. The Choose an Option screen appears.

4. Click **Troubleshoot**. The Troubleshoot screen rides in, as shown in Figure 22.2. This is the initial RE screen.

Figure 22.2: *The Troubleshoot screen is your entry point for the Windows 8 Recovery Environment.*

Getting to the RE Using a Recovery Drive

If the problem you're trying to solve is so bad that you can't even start Windows 8, you're toast, right? Nope. If you had the foresight to create a USB recovery drive before the problem reared its head, you can still access a version of the RE using the recovery drive:

> **SEE ALSO**
>
> To learn how to get your very own recovery drive, head for the section in Chapter 20 titled Step 8: Create a Recovery Drive.

1. Insert the recovery drive.

2. Restart your PC and boot to the USB flash drive:

   - If you have a newer PC, Windows 8 should recognize the flash drive automatically and display the Use a Device screen. Click your flash drive in the list that appears.

   - If you have an older PC, you will need to access your PC's settings and configure them to boot to the flash drive. Look for a message right after you turn on the PC that says something like *Press Del to access BIOS/ Start settings*. Press the key and then use the screen that shows up to configure your PC to boot to the USB flash drive.

3. For some reason the first thing the recovery drive does is ask you to select a keyboard layout, so select the layout you want to use. The Choose an Option screen appears.

4. Click **Troubleshoot**. This gets you to the Troubleshoot screen, shown earlier in Figure 22.2.

Getting to the RE Using the Windows 8 Install Media

So you can't start Windows 8 *and* you didn't create a recovery drive. *Now* all is lost, correct? Nope. If you still have your Windows 8 installation media, follow these steps to boot to the RE using the install media:

1. Insert your Windows 8 install media.

2. Restart your PC and boot to the install drive.

WINDOWS WISDOM

You'll likely need to adjust your computer settings to boot to the install media. Restart the computer and look for a start-up message prompting you to press a key or key combination to modify the settings (which might be called *Setup* or something similar). Find the boot options and either enable a media drive-based boot or make sure that the option to boot from the media drive comes before the option to boot from the hard disk.

3. When the Windows Setup dialog box appears, click **Next**.

4. Click **Repair your computer**. The Choose an Option screen appears.

5. Click **Troubleshoot**. This buys you a ticket to the Troubleshoot screen, shown earlier in Figure 22.2.

Recovering from a Problem

Ideally, solving a problem will require a specific tweak to the system: a setting change, a driver upgrade, a program uninstall, etc. But sometimes you need to take a big-picture approach and revert your system to some previous state in the hope that you leap past the problem and get your system working again. The Windows 8 Recovery Environment offers five tools that enable you to try this big-picture approach: Safe Mode, Automatic Repair, System Restore, Refresh Your PC, and System Image Recovery—which should be used in that order. The rest of this chapter takes you through these tools.

Booting Up in Safe Mode

If you can't start Windows 8 normally, or if your system is infected with a virus or other malware, you can use the Safe Mode option. This runs a stripped-down version of Windows 8 that includes only the minimal set of options Windows 8 requires to load. Once you've booted to Safe Mode, you can troubleshoot the problem or run your antimalware program.

To boot to Safe Mode, load the RE as described earlier in Entering the Recovery Environment, click **Advanced Options**, click **Startup Settings**, and then click **Restart**. This eventually gets you face to screen with the Startup Settings screen. Press **4** to select the **Enable Safe Mode** command, and then sign in to your user account. When Windows 8 finally loads, as shown in Figure 22.3, the desktop reminds you that you're in Safe mode by displaying *Safe Mode* in each corner. (Also, Windows Help and Support appears with Safe mode–related information and links.)

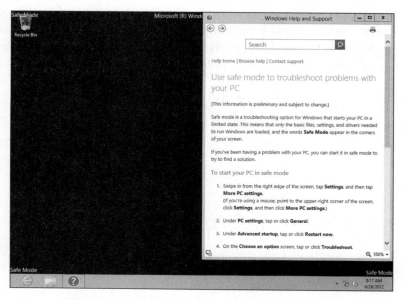

Figure 22.3: *Windows 8 doing the Safe Mode thing.*

Automatically Repairing Your PC

What's a body to do if Windows 8 won't start normally *and* it won't start in Safe Mode? The next item on your recovery agenda should be the RE Automatic Repair option, which attempts various repair strategies that are often useful for getting a PC back on its feet.

To use it, boot to the RE, as described earlier in Entering the Recovery Environment, then click **Advanced Options**. In the Advanced Options screen, click **Automatic Repair**. Windows 8 reboots and Automatic Repair prompts you for your user account. Click your user account, type your account password, and then click **Continue**. Automatic Repair begins the repair process. Fingers should be crossed at this point.

Recovering Using System Restore

If you make software or hardware changes and then find that your system won't start or is just messed up somehow, you can tell Windows 8 to load using the earlier configuration that worked. (That is, a configuration that doesn't include your changes.) The theory is that by using a previously working configuration, your system should return to good working order since it's bypassing the changes that caused the problem.

To revert the system to a previous configuration (one in which Windows 8 started successfully), you need to use the System Restore feature. I showed you how to use System Restore to set restore points in Chapter 20. Remember, too, that Windows 8 creates automatic restore points at regular intervals and when you perform certain actions (such as installing an uncertified device driver). To revert your system to a restore point, close all running programs, and then follow these steps:

1. Bring up the RE, as described earlier in Entering the Recovery Environment, click **Advanced Options**, and then click **System Restore**.

WINDOWS WISDOM

System Restore is available in Safe Mode. So if Windows 8 won't start properly because of some recent change, perform a Safe Mode start-up as described earlier in Booting Up in Safe Mode and run System Restore from there.

2. When prompted by the RE, choose your user account, enter your password, and then click **Continue**.

3. The first dialog box just gives you an overview of System Restore, so click **Next**. System Restore displays a list of restore points.

4. If you don't see the restore point you want to use, activate the **Show more restore points** check box.

5. Click the restore point you want to use and then click **Next**.

6. Click **Finish**. Windows 8 asks you to confirm that you want your system restored.

7. Click **Yes**. System Restore begins reverting to the restore point. When it's done, it restarts your computer and displays a message telling you the results of the restore.

8. Click **Close**.

> **WINDOWS WISDOM**
>
> If restoring your system makes things worse or causes additional problems, you can undo the restore. Follow steps 1 through 4, select the **Restore Operation** restore point, and click **Next**.

Refreshing Your PC

If the Automatic Repair and System Restore features didn't solve your problem, the next recovery step to try is Refresh Your PC. This is a new Windows 8 tool that reinstalls a fresh copy of Windows 8 while keeping your data, settings, and apps intact. When you refresh your PC, the computer boots to the RE, gathers your data, copies it to another part of the hard drive, reinstalls Windows 8, and then restores your data.

Here are the steps to follow to refresh your PC:

1. Boot to the RE, as described earlier in Entering the Recovery Environment, and then click **Refresh Your PC**.

2. Click **Next**. Refresh Your PC prompts you to insert your installation media or a recovery drive.

3. Insert the media. Refresh Your PC validates the media and prompts you to start the process.

4. Click **Refresh**. Refresh Your PC reboots the computer and runs the refresh.

Restoring a System Image

If you can't reset your PC because you don't have your Windows 8 install media or a recovery drive, you can still get your system back on its feet if you created a system image, as I described in Chapter 20.

> **SEE ALSO**
>
> For instruction on how to perform a system image backup, see the section in Chapter 20 titled Step 7: Create a System Image Backup.

Follow these steps to restore a system image:

1. Connect the external drive that you used to save the system image.

2. Boot to the RE, as described earlier in Entering the Recovery Environment, and then click **Advanced Options**. The Advanced Options screen appears.

3. Click **System Image Recovery**. Windows 8 asks you to choose a target operating system.

4. Click **Windows 8**. System Image Recovery prompts you to select a system image backup and offers two options:

   - **Use the Latest Available System Image.** Activate this option to restore Windows 8 using the most recently created system image. This is almost always the best way to go because it means you'll restore the maximum percentage of your data and programs. If you choose this option, click **Next** and skip to step 7.

   - **Select a System Image.** Activate this option to select from a list of system images. This is the way to go if you saved a system image to your network, or if the most recent system image includes some change to your system that you believe is the source of your system problems. Click **Next** and continue with step 5.

5. Click the location of the system image and then click **Next**.

6. Click the system image you want to use for the restore and then click **Next**. If you want to use a system image saved to a shared network folder, click **Advanced** and then click **Search for a System Image on the Network**.

7. If you replaced your hard drive, activate the **Format and Repartition Disks** check box.

8. Click **Next**. System Image Recovery displays a summary of the restore process.

9. Click **Finish**. System Image Recovery asks you to confirm.

10. Click **Yes**. System Image Recovery begins restoring your computer and then reboots to Windows 8 when the restore is complete.

The Least You Need to Know

- If a problem occurs soon after you changed something on your computer—a Windows setting, a program, a device, and so on—try reversing that change to see if this fixes the error.

- You can often recover from problems just by shutting down all running programs, logging off Windows 8, or rebooting the computer.

- To access the Recovery Environment in Windows 8, press **Windows+W**, type **advanced**, click **Advanced startup options**, click **Restart now**, and then click **Troubleshoot**. You can also access a version of the RE using a recovery drive or the Windows 8 install media.

- To recover from a more serious problem, use the following RE tools and techniques, in this order: Safe Mode, Automatic Repair, System Restore, Refresh Your PC, and System Image Recovery.

The Complete Idiot's Keyboard Command Reference

Windows Logo Key Shortcuts

Press	To
Windows	Switch between the Start screen and the most recent Windows 8 app.
Windows+B	Switch to Desktop and activate the taskbar's Show Hidden Icons arrow.
Windows+C	Display the Charms menu.
Windows+D	Switch to the Desktop app.
Windows+E	Run File Explorer.
Windows+F	Display the Files search pane.
Windows+H	Display the Share pane.
Windows+I	Display the Settings pane.
Windows+K	Display the Devices pane.
Windows+L	Lock your computer.
Windows+M	Switch to the desktop and minimize all windows.
Windows+O	Turn the tablet orientation lock on and off.
Windows+P	Switch to a second display.
Windows+Q	Display the Apps search pane.
Windows+R	Open the Run dialog box.
Windows+T	Switch to the desktop and cycle through the taskbar icons.
Windows+U	Open the Ease of Access Center.
Windows+V	Cycle through your current notifications.
Windows+W	Display the Settings search pane.
Windows+X	Display a menu of Windows tools and utilities.
Windows+Z	Display the application bar in a Windows 8 app.
Windows+=	Open Magnifier and zoom in.
Windows+-	Zoom out (if already zoomed in using Magnifier).

continues

Windows Logo Key Shortcuts (continued)

Press	To
Windows+,	Temporarily displays the desktop.
Windows+Enter	Open Narrator.
Windows+PgUp	Move the current Windows 8 app to the left- hand monitor.
Windows+PgDn	Move the current Windows 8 app to the right-hand monitor.
Windows+PrtSc	Capture the current screen and save it to the Pictures folder.
Windows+Tab	Switch between running Windows 8 apps.

Keyboard Shortcuts for Programs

Press	To
Working with Program Windows	
Alt+Esc	Cycle through open Desktop program windows.
Alt+Tab	Cycle through thumbnails of open program windows.
Alt+F4	Close the active program window.
F1	Display context-sensitive Help.
Working with Documents	
Ctrl+N	Create a new document.
Ctrl+O	Display the Open dialog box.
Ctrl+P	Display the Print dialog box.
Ctrl+S	Save the current file. If the file is new, display the Save As dialog box.

Keyboard Shortcuts for Working with Data

Press	To
Backspace	Delete the character to the left of the insertion point.
Delete	Delete the selected data or the character to the right of the insertion point.
Ctrl+A	Select all the data in the current window.
Ctrl+C	Copy the selected data.
Ctrl+X	Cut the selected data.
Ctrl+V	Paste the most recently cut or copied data.
Ctrl+Z	Undo the most recent action.

Keyboard Shortcuts for Dialog Boxes

Hold Down	To
Tab	Move forward through the dialog box controls (check boxes, buttons, etc.).
Shift+Tab	Move backward through the dialog box controls.
Ctrl+Tab	Move forward through the dialog box tabs.
Alt+Down arrow	Display the list in a drop-down list box.
Spacebar	Toggle a check box on and off; select the active option button or command button.
Enter	Select the default command button or the active command button.
Esc	Close the dialog box without making any changes.

Keys to Hold Down While Dragging and Dropping

Hold Down	To
Ctrl	Copy the dragged object.
Ctrl+Shift	Display a shortcut menu after dropping a dragged object.
Esc	Cancel the current drag.
Shift	Move the dragged object.

File Explorer Keyboard Shortcuts

Press	To
Backspace	Navigate to the parent folder of the current folder.
Delete	Delete the selected object.
Ctrl+A	Select all the objects in the current folder.
Delete	Send the currently selected objects to the Recycle Bin.
Shift+Delete	Delete the currently selected objects without sending them to the Recycle Bin.
F2	Rename the selected object.
F3	Display the Search tab.
F4	Open the Address toolbar's drop-down list.

Internet Explorer Keyboard Shortcuts

Press	To
Alt+C	View Favorites, Feeds, and History.
Alt+X	Display the Tools menu.
Alt+Home	Surf to the Internet Explorer home page.
Alt+Left arrow	Navigate backward to a previously displayed web page.
Alt+Right arrow	Navigate forward to a previously displayed web page.
Ctrl+A	Select the entire web page.
Ctrl+B	Display the Organize Favorites dialog box.
Ctrl+D	Add the current page to the Favorites list.
Ctrl+G	Display the Feeds list.
Ctrl+H	Display the History list.
Ctrl+I	Display the Favorites list.
Ctrl+J	Display the Downloads list.
Ctrl++	Zoom in on the page.
Ctrl+-	Zoom out of the page.
Esc	Stop downloading the web page.
F4	Open the Address toolbar drop-down list.
F5	Refresh the web page.
F11	Toggle between full-screen mode and the regular window.

Index